D1204291

The

FRANCIS A. SCHAEFFER

TRILOGY

By *Francis A. Schaeffer*
The God Who Is There
Escape from Reason
He Is There and He Is Not Silent
Death in the City
Pollution and the Death of Man
The Church at the end of the 20th Century
The Mark of the Christian
The Church Before the Watching World
True Spirituality
Basic Bible Studies
Genesis in Space and Time
The New Super-Spirituality
Back to Freedom and Dignity
Art and the Bible
No Little People
Two Contents, Two Realities
Joshua and the Flow of Biblical History
No Final Conflict
How Should We Then Live?
Whatever Happened to the Human Race?
(with *C. Everett Koop*)
A Christian Manifesto
The Great Evangelical Disaster
The Complete Works of Francis Schaeffer
(including all the above titles in five volumes)
Everybody Can Know (with *Edith Schaeffer*)
Letters of Francis A. Schaeffer

The

FRANCIS A. SCHAEFFER

T R I L O G Y

*The Three Essential Books
in One Volume*

Book One:

THE GOD WHO IS THERE

Book Two:

ESCAPE FROM REASON

Book Three:

HE IS THERE AND
HE IS NOT SILENT

⠿ CROSSWAY

WHEATON, ILLINOIS

Francis A. Schaeffer Trilogy

Copyright © 1990 by Crossway

Published by Crossway
        1300 Crescent Street
        Wheaton, Illinois 60187

The God Who Is There: copyright © 1968 by Francis A. Schaeffer.
Published by InterVarsity Press (U.S.A. and Canada).

Escape from Reason: copyright © 1968 by Francis A. Schaeffer.
Published by InterVarsity Press (U.S.A.), and
Hodder and Stoughton (Canada).

He Is There and He Is Not Silent: copyright © 1972 by Francis A. Schaeffer;
published by Tyndale House (U.S.A. and Canada).

Published in this edition with the arrangement of the original
U.S. publishers and Canadian publishers.

Printed in the United States of America

Cover Photo: Sylvester Jacobs

First printing, 1990

Library of Congress Catalog Card Number 89-81267

ISBN 13: 978-0-89107-561-5
ISBN 10: 0-89107-561-5

Crossway is a publishing ministry of Good News Publishers.

TS		20	19	18	17	16	15	14	13	12
29	28	27	26	25	24	23	22	21	20	19

Publisher's Preface

This Trilogy brings together Francis A. Schaeffer's three foundational books into one volume. Schaeffer saw these three books as essential to everything he wrote (twenty-three books in all), and it is here that he lays the foundation for all of his work.

We have decided to reissue these three books in this new edition as a trilogy, because of the continuing significance and relevance of Dr. Schaeffer's thought. In fact much of his writing seems as contemporary today as when his books were first published ten, twenty, and even thirty years ago.

Francis Schaeffer's unique contribution is seen in his ability to understand the desperate need of modern man from truth, beauty, meaning in life. This was especially evident in the work of L'Abri Fellowship in Switzerland, founded by Francis and Edith Schaeffer and centered largely in their home. Thousands came to L'Abri, from all walks of life and from around the world. As Edith Schaeffer wrote in her book *L'Abri*:

> Rather than studying volumes in an ivory tower separated from life, and developing a theory separated from the thinking and struggling of men, [Dr. Schaeffer talked for years] to men and women in

the very midst of their struggles. He has talked to existentialists, logical positivists, Hindus, Buddhists, liberal Protestants, liberal Roman Catholics, Reformed Jews and atheistic Jews, Muslims, members of occult cults, and people of a wide variety of religions and philosophies, as well as atheists of a variety of types. He has talked to brilliant professors, brilliant students, and brilliant drop-outs! He has talked to beatniks, hippies, drug addicts, homosexuals and psychologically disturbed people. He has talked to Africans, Indians, Chinese, Koreans, Japanese, South Americans, people from the islands of the sea, from Australia and New Zealand and from all the European countries as well as from America and Canada. He has talked to people of many different political colors. He has talked to doctors, lawyers, scientists, artists, writers, engineers, research men in many fields, philosophers, businessmen, newspapermen and actors, famous people and peasants. . . .

In it all God has been giving him an education which it is not possible for many people to have. The answers have been given, not out of academic research (although he does volumes of reading constantly to keep up) but out of this arena of live conversation. He answers real questions with carefully thought out answers which are the real answers. He gets excited himself as he comes to me often saying, "It really *is* the answer, Edith; it fits, it really fits. It really *is* truth, and because it is true it fits what is really there."

Out of this encounter with real people and real needs, Dr. Schaeffer wrote the books that make up this trilogy. Briefly these relate to each other as follows:

The God Who is There was written first; it lays the groundwork, establishes the terminology, and sets out the basic thesis. In this book, Dr. Schaeffer shows how modern thought has abandoned the idea of truth with tragic consequences in every area of culture — from philosophy, to art, to music, to theology, and within society as a whole. The only hope, Schaeffer argues, is to confront our culture with the historic, Christian truth — presented with compassion and without compromise, and lived out fully in every area of personal and corporate life.

Escape from Reason complements the first book by working out these principles in the philosophical area of nature and grace. *Escape from Reason*, moreover, makes a significant contribution in showing how modern culture has grown from corrupted roots reaching far back into the late Middle Ages.

The last book in the Trilogy is *He Is There and He Is Not Silent*. As Dr. Schaeffer explains in his own words, "This book deals with one of the most fundamental of all questions: how we know, and how we know we know. Unless our epistemology is right, everything else is going to be wrong." Thus Schaeffer argues that modern thought is fundamentally wrong in its assumptions about how we know and what we know. In contrast to the silence and despair of modern man, Schaeffer shows that we can indeed know "The God Who Is There" because "He Is Not Silent."

It would not be an exaggeration to say that these three books have had a profound impact upon a generation of Christians over the last three decades. In reissuing these now in this new edition, it is our hope that Dr. Schaeffer's timeless insights will continue to reach a new generation in search of truth, beauty and meaning in life.

A note concerning this edition: The text used here is the revised text which Dr. Schaeffer re-edited for the publication of his *Complete Works* in 1982. Dr. Schaeffer's revisions included updating and clarification where needed, and the addition of some new material. (See especially Schaeffer's new appendix on apologetics, pages 175-187.) It should be noted that the revised text is available only in this Trilogy and the five-volume *Complete Works*, and not otherwise available in the one-volume editions of Schaeffer's books.

Finally, we would include the following comments by Dr. Schaeffer. Although these were written in 1982 as part of the *Preface* for the *Complete Works* they express Schaeffer's general concerns about his books, but concerns which also apply specifically to the Trilogy:

[I have written my books] to be read and useful to both Christians and non-Christians. Time has proved this to be the case far beyond our hopes.

They were not written to be only used on the academic scene, though they have been used there, but also for the less academic—though, of course, we realize that they do take care and study and are not popular reading to be pursued while dozing in an armchair. Some have though the terminology difficult, but I have letters from many parts of the world saying that it was the use of this terminology that for them showed that Christianity has something to say to twentieth-century people, and that it was this terminology which has the bridge which caused them to study the books and to be helped by them. We have tried to make the terminology easier where possible.

The Bible translations have been maintained as they were in the original editions: that is, the *King James* in the earlier books, and the *New International Version* in [the later ones].

Another choice to be made was whether to leave the word *man*, as designating men and women, or go to the recent usage of indicating in each case that *she* or *he* is meant. When the earlier books were written, this was not a problem. In my later books the newer way of speaking and writing has been used. However, bringing the earlier books in line in this regard would have been a horrendous task. Please therefore forgive me, anyone who would be disturbed, and please read the usage in the older accepted way. I would be over-whelmingly sorry if anyone would be "put off." Please read it as "man" equaling a human being and all human beings — whoever you are — women and men, children and adults.

The basic trilogy has been : *The God Who Is There, Escape From Reason,* and *He Is There and He Is Not Silent.* All the others fit into these as spokes of the wheel fit into the hub.

The early books broke ground in calling for the Lordship of Christ in the arts — art, literature, cinema, philosophy and so on. [The later books] bring this body of thought forward into the area of a Christian's duty, under the Lordship of Christ, in the whole of life as a citizen, especially in the area of law, government, and standing for a high view of human life.

We have been overwhelmed at the way these books have been used over such a wide spectrum of kinds of people and geographically. I can truly say it has brought us to awe and worship. . . .

What did Francis Schaeffer really have to say? What is the significance of his work? Why did he have such a far-reaching impact in the last half of the twentieth century? The best way to know this is to find out firsthand, by reading his essential works as found in this Trilogy. Few who begin this journey will come to the end without having their life be profoundly changed.

> — Lane T. Dennis, Ph.D.
> President, Crossway Books

Contents

Foreword
Francis A. Schaeffer:
The Man and His Vision

by J. I. Packer

He was physically small, with a bulging forehead, furrowed brow, and goatee beard. Alpine knee-breeches housed his American legs, his head sank into his shoulders, and his face bore a look of bright abstraction. Nothing special there, you would think; a serious, resolute man, no doubt, maybe a bit eccentric, but hardly unique on that account.

Nevertheless, what he said was arresting. It had firmness, arguing vision; gentleness, arguing strength; simple clarity, arguing mental mastery; and compassion, arguing an honest and good heart. There was no guile in it, no party narrowness, no manipulation, only the passionate persuasiveness of the prophet who hurries in to share with others what he himself sees.

Who was Francis Schaeffer? Schaeffer was a reading, listening, thinking man who lived in the present, learned from the past, and looked to the future, and who had an unusual gift for communicating ideas at a nontechnical level. His communicative style was not that of a cautious academic who labors for exhaustive coverage and dispassionate objectivity. It was rather that of an impassioned thinker who paints his vision of eternal truth in bold strokes and stark contrasts.

Academics never tired of censuring Schaeffer for communicating in this way. Yet it is a fact that many young thinkers and artists, in outraged anger at the fashions in their professional fields, have found Schaeffer's analyses a lifeline to sanity without which they literally could not have gone on living. Schaeffer saw himself as an evangelist, called to speak the truth with an uncompromising urgency to real people in real trouble, whose lives have been broken by the relativism, irrationalism, fragmentation and nihilism of our culture today. And thus I think it truest to call him a prophet-pastor, a Bible-based visionary who by the light of his vision sought out a world in need and shepherded the Lord's sheep.

What gave Schaeffer his importance? To understand this, it may be helpful to outline the essential perceptions which shaped his vision and work.

First, Schaeffer vividly perceived the wholeness of created reality, of human life, of each person's thinking, and of God's revealed truth. He had a mind for first principles, for systems, and for totalities, and he would never discuss issues in isolation or let a viewpoint go till he had explored and tested its implications as a total account of reality and life. He saw fundamental analysis of this kind as clarifying, for, as he often pointed out, there are not many basic worldviews, and we all need to realize how much our haphazard, surface-level thoughts are actually taking for granted. Exposure of presuppositions was thus central to Schaeffer's method of encounter with all opinions on any subject. He always presented Christianity in terms of its own presuppositions and in theologically systematic form, as the revealed good news of our rational and holy Creator who became our gracious and merciful Redeemer in space and time.

Second, Schaeffer perceived the primacy of reason in each individual's makeup and the potency of ideas in the human mind. He saw that "ideas have legs," so that how we think determines what we are. So the first task in evangelism, in the modern West or anywhere else, is to persuade the other person that he ought to embrace the Christian view of reality. And the first step in doing this would be to convince him of the *nonviability* of *all* other views, including whatever form of non-Christianity is implicit in his own thinking. This is to treat him, not as an "intellectual," but as the human being that he undoubtedly is. To address his mind in this way is to show respect for him as a human being, made for truth because he is made in God's image.

Third, Schaeffer perceived the Western mind as adrift on a trackless sea of relativism and irrationalism. He saw that the notion of truth as involving exclusion of untruth, and of value as involving exclusion of dysvalue, had perished in both sophisticated and popular thinking. Into its place had crept the idea of ongoing synthesis — the idea that eventually there is no real distinction between right and wrong or truth and untruth, and that antithesis will eventually be swallowed up in a category-less "pan-everythingism."

To make people realize how this viewpoint has victimized them across the board, Schaeffer regularly introduced his topics with an historical analysis showing how Western thought about them had reached its current state of delirium. The aim of these analyses was to reestablish the notion that there is an absolute antithesis between truth and error, good and evil, beauty and the obscenely ugly, and so to refurnish our ravaged and pillaged minds in a way that makes significant thinking about life, death, personhood, and God possible for us once more.

Fourth, Schaeffer perceived the importance of identifying — in all apologetic and evangelistic discussion, and all teaching on what being a Christian involves — that which he called the antithesis and the point of tension. The antithesis is between truth and untruth, right and wrong, good and evil, the meaningful and the meaningless, Christian and non-Christian value systems, secular relativism and Christian absolutism. He made it his business on every topic he handled to cover the "either-or" choices that have to be made at the level of first principles and to show that the biblical-Christian options for personal and community life are the only ones that are consistently rational and satisfyingly human. In this way he sought to remake disordered and disorderly minds, with regard both to ontological options facing the individual and to ethical options facing the contemporary West.

Fifth, Schaeffer perceived the need to live truth as well as think it — to demonstrate to the world through the transformed lifestyle of believing groups that the "the Personal-Infinite God is *really there* in our generation." Out of this conviction was born L'Abri in Huémoz, Switzerland, and the satellite L'Abris around the Western world. Each L'Abri is study center, rescue mission, extended family, clinic, spiritual convalescent home, monastery, and local church rolled into one: a milieu where visitors learn to be both Christian and human through being part of a community that trusts God the Creator and worships him through Christ the Redeemer.

Christian credibility, Schaeffer saw, requires that truth be not merely defended, but practiced; not just debated, but done. The knowledge that God's truth was being done at L'Abri sustained his boldness as he called for that same truth to be done elsewhere.

What long-term significance has Schaeffer for the Christian cause? We wait to see. The law of human fame will no doubt treat Schaeffer as it has treated others, eclipsing him temporarily now that he is dead and only allowing us to see his real stature ten or twenty years down the road. My guess is that his verbal and visual sketches, simple but brilliant as they appear to me to be, will outlive everything else, but I may be wrong. I am sure, however, that I shall not be at all wrong when I hail Francis Schaeffer, the little Presbyterian pastor who saw so much more of what he was looking at and agonized over it so much more tenderly than the rest of us do, as one of the truly great Christians of my time.

— J. I. Packer
February 1990

BOOK ONE

THE GOD WHO
IS THERE

Preface to
The God Who Is There
and Escape from Reason

With the republishing of *The God Who Is There* and *Escape from Reason* in one volume, we faced a dilemma. I wrote *The God Who Is There* first. Then, before it was published, I gave a series of lectures at Swanwick, England which I called "Escape from Reason." I had no idea these lectures would be published, and thus used some of the same material as in *The God Who Is There*. At the conclusion of the lectures, the British Inter-Varsity asked me to allow them to publish the lectures as a book. I did this and have been glad for its wide use. Though written later, *Escape from Reason* was released before *The God Who Is There*.

As we came to putting these together in one volume [*The Complete Works of Francis A. Schaeffer*], we were torn in two directions. To put them both in, one after the other, meant some duplication. If we left out *Escape from Reason* as an entity, many might feel they had lost an old friend which had helped them.

At first I tried to combine them, but it became clear this would not do. The problem was not in joining them in outline; that was fairly easy. The problem was that in the content itself there were different facts and nuances which would be lost in the subjects which were treated in both books. Both books are equally needed

1

in order to understand how we have gotten to where we are today.

Escape from Reason was originally given as lectures. Because of the group to which I was speaking, in each lecture I stressed the meaning of modern thinking to Christian thinking. Thus I returned to this subject at various points rather than in one section as in *The God Who Is There*, which was planned and written as a book.

If I were giving the lectures again now I would do the same, for much Christian thinking today is still ignorant of its own infiltration by the present prevalent surrounding thought-forms. When the lectures were first given, the problem and confusion often came from people working in the sciences. Today it comes from the theological side, but it is the same problem and confusion and more destructive. Thus it continues to be as important today as it was in the 1960's to stress our urgent need to understand the modern system as a whole, and to appreciate the dichotomy and desparate "leap of faith" in modern thinking. In order to confront modern man truly you must not have this dichotomy; you must have instead the Scriptures speaking truth both about God Himself, and about the real world of history and the cosmos.

> — Francis A. Schaeffer, 1982
> [From the *Preface* to the
> *Complete Works*]

The Intellectual and Cultural Climate of the Second Half of the Twentieth Century

. . . Lord . . .
thou didst create all things,
and by thy will they existed and were created.
(Revelation 4:11)

So God created man in his own image, in the image of God
he created him; male and female he created them.
(Genesis 1:27)

But now thus says the LORD,
he who created you, O Jacob,
he who formed you, O Israel:
"Fear not, for I have redeemed you;
I have called you by name, you are mine;
When you pass through the waters I will be with you;
and through the rivers, they shall not overwhelm you;
when you walk through fire you shall not be burned,
and the flame shall not consume you.
For I am the LORD your God,
the Holy One of Israel, your Saviour."
(Isaiah 43:1-3)

The universe was not pregnant with life nor the biosphere with man.
Our number came up in a Monte Carlo game. (Jacques Monod)

To man qua man we readily say good riddance. (B. F. Skinner)

CHAPTER ONE

The Gulf Is Fixed

Before the Chasm

The present chasm between the generations has been brought about almost entirely by a change in the concept of truth.

Wherever you look today, the new concept holds the field. The consensus about us is almost monolithic, whether you review the arts, literature or simply read the newspapers and magazines such as *Time, Life, Newsweek, The Listener* or *The Observer*. On every side you can feel the stranglehold of this new methodology — and by "methodology" we mean the way we approach truth and knowing. It is like suffocating in a particularly bad London fog. And just as fog cannot be kept out by walls or doors, so this consensus comes in around us, until the room we live in is no longer unpolluted, and yet we hardly realize what has happened.

The tragedy of our situation today is that men and women are being fundamentally affected by the new way of looking at truth, and yet they have never even analyzed the drift which has taken place. Young people from Christian homes are brought up in the old framework of truth. Then they are subjected to the modern framework. In time they become confused because they do not understand the alternatives with which they are being presented.

Confusion becomes bewilderment, and before long they are over-whelmed. This is unhappily true not only of young people, but of many pastors, Christian educators, evangelists and missionaries as well.

So this change in the concept of the way we come to knowledge and truth is the most crucial problem, as I understand it, facing Christianity today.

If you had lived in Europe, let us say prior to about 1890, or in the United States before about 1935, you would not have had to spend much time, in practice, in thinking about your presupposi-tions. (These dates are arbitrary as the change came, in Europe at least, fairly gradually. In America the crucial years of change were from 1913 to 1940, and during these relatively few years the whole way of thinking underwent a revolution; 1913 was a most important year in the United States, not because it was the year before the First World War, but for another highly significant reason, as we shall see later.)

Before these dates everyone would have been working on much the same presuppositions, which in practice seemed to accord with the Christian's own presuppositions. This was true both in the area of epistemology and methodology. Epistemology is the theory of how we know, or how we can be sure that what we think we know of the world about us is correct. Methodology is how we approach the question of truth and knowing.

Now it may be argued that the non-Christians had no right to act on the presuppositions they acted on. That is true. They were being romantic in accepting optimistic answers without a suffi-cient base. Nevertheless they went on thinking and acting as if these presuppositions were true.

What were these presuppositions? The basic one was that there really are such things as absolutes. They accepted the possibility of an absolute in the area of Being (or *knowledge*), and in the area of *morals*. Therefore, because they accepted the possibility of absolutes, though people might have disagreed as to what these were, nevertheless they could reason together on the classical basis of antithesis. They took it for granted that if anything was true, the opposite was false. In morality, if one thing was right, its opposite was wrong. This little formula, "A is A" and "If you have A it is not non-A," is the first move in classical logic. If you understand the extent to which this no longer holds sway, you will understand our present situation.

Absolutes imply antithesis. The non-Christian went on romantically operating on this basis without a sufficient cause, an adequate base, for doing so. Thus it was still possible to discuss what was right and wrong, what was true and false. One could tell a non-Christian to "be a good girl" and, while she might not have followed your advice, at least she would have understood what you were talking about. To say the same thing to a truly modern girl today would be to make a "nonsense" statement. The blank look you might receive would not mean that your standards had been rejected, but that your message was meaningless.

The shift has been tremendous. Thirty or more years ago you could have said such things as "This is true" or "This is right," and you would have been on everybody's wavelength. People may or may not have thought out their beliefs consistently, but everyone would have been talking to each other as though the idea of antithesis was correct. Thus in evangelism, in spiritual matters and in Christian education, you could have begun with the certainty that your audience understood you.

Presuppositional Apologetics Would Have Stopped the Decay[1]
It was indeed unfortunate that our Christian "thinkers," in the time before the shift took place and the chasm was fixed, did not teach and preach with a clear grasp of presuppositions. Had they done this, they would not have been taken by surprise, and they could have helped young people to face their difficulties. The really foolish thing is that even now, years after the shift is complete, many Christians still do not know what is happening. And this is because they are still not being taught the importance of thinking in terms of presuppositions, especially concerning truth.

The floodwaters of secular thought and liberal theology overwhelmed the Church because the leaders did not understand the importance of combating a false set of presuppositions. They largely fought the battle on the wrong ground and so, instead of being ahead in both defense and communication, they lagged woefully behind. This was a real weakness which it is hard, even today, to rectify among evangelicals.

The use of classical apologetics before this shift took place was effective only because non-Christians were functioning, on the surface, on the same presuppositions, even if they had an inadequate base for them. In classical apologetics though, presuppositions were rarely analyzed, discussed or taken into account.

So, if a man got up to preach the gospel and said, "Believe this, it is true," those who heard would have said, "Well, if that is so, then its opposite is false." The presupposition of antithesis pervaded men's entire mental outlook. We must not forget that historic Christianity stands on a basis of antithesis. Without it, historic Christianity is meaningless. The basic antithesis is that God objectively exists in contrast (in antithesis) to His not existing. Which of these two are the reality, changes everything in the area of knowledge and morals and in the whole of life.

The Line of Despair
Thus we have a date line like this:

EUROPE BEFORE 1800 AND THE
U.S. BEFORE 1935

THE LINE OF DESPAIR ———————————————————

EUROPE AFTER 1890
THE U.S. AFTER 1935

Notice that I call the line, the line of despair. Above this line we find men living with their romantic notions of absolutes (though with no sufficient logical basis). This side of the line, all is changed. Man thinks differently concerning truth.

In order to understand this line of despair more clearly, think of it not as a simple horizontal line but as a staircase:

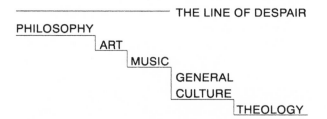

Each of the steps represents a certain stage in time. The higher is earlier, the lower later. It was in this order that the shift in truth affected men's lives.

The shift spread gradually, and in three different ways. People did not suddenly wake up one morning and find that it had permeated everywhere at once.

First of all it spread geographically. The ideas began in Germany and spread outward. They affected the Continent first, then crossed the Channel to England, and then the Atlantic to America. Secondly, it spread through society, from the real intellectual to the more educated, down to the workers, reaching the middle class last of all. Thirdly, it spread as represented in the diagram, from one discipline to another, beginning with the philosophers and ending with the theologians. Theology has been last for a long time. It is curious to me, in studying this whole cultural drift, that so many pick up the latest theological fashion and hail it as something new. *But in fact, what the new theology is now saying has already been said previously in each of the other disciplines.*

It is important to grasp the fundamental nature of this line. If Christians try to talk to people as though they were above the line when in reality they are this side of it, we will only beat the air. This goes as much for dockers as for intellectuals. The same holds true for the concept of spirituality. This side of the line, "spirituality" becomes exactly opposite to Christian spirituality.

Unity and Disunity in Rationalism

There is a real unity in non-Christian thought, as well as differences within that unity. The shift to moving below the line of despair is one of the differences within the unity of non-Christian thought. The unifying factor can be called rationalism, or if you prefer, humanism — though if we use the latter term, we must be careful to distinguish its meaning in this context from the more limited sense of the word *humanism* in such a book as *The Humanist Frame*,[2] edited by Sir Julian Huxley. This latter kind of humanism has become a technical term within the larger meaning of the word. Humanism in the larger, more inclusive sense is the system whereby men and women, beginning absolutely by themselves, try rationally to build out from themselves, having only Man as their integration point, to find all knowledge, meaning and value. We must also ensure that the word *rationalism*, which means the same thing as humanism in the wider sense, is not confused with the word *rational*. *Rational* means that the things which are about us are not contrary to reason; or, to put it another way, man's aspiration of reason is valid. And so the Judeo-Christian position is rational, but it is the very antithesis of rationalism.

So rationalism or humanism is the unity within non-Christian thought. Yet if Christians are going to be able to understand and talk to people in their generation, they must take account of the form rationalism is currently taking. In one way it is always the same — people trying to build from themselves alone. In another sense it is constantly shifting, with different emphases with which a Christian must be acquainted if he is not equipping himself to work in a period which no longer exists.

The line of despair indicates a titanic shift at this present time within the unity of rationalism. Above the line, people were rationalistic optimists. They believed they could begin with themselves and draw a circle which would encompass all thoughts of life and life itself without having to depart from the logic of antithesis. They thought that on their own, rationalistically, finite people could find a unity within the total diversity — an adequate explanation for the whole of reality. This is where philosophy stood prior to our own era. The only real argument between these rationalistic optimists concerned what circle should be drawn. One person would draw a circle and say, "You can live within this circle." The next person would cross it out and would draw a different circle. The next person would come along and, crossing out the previous circle, draw his own — *ad infinitum.* So if you start to study philosophy by pursuing the *history* of philosophy, by the time you are through with all these circles, each one of which has been destroyed by the next, you may feel like jumping off London Bridge!

But at a certain point this attempt to spin out a *unified* optimistic humanism came to an end. The philosophers came to the conclusion that they were not going to find a unified rationalistic circle that would contain all thought, and in which they could live. It was as though the rationalist suddenly realized that he was trapped in a large round room with no doors and no windows, nothing but complete darkness. From the middle of the room he would feel his way to the walls and begin to look for an exit. He would go round the circumference, and then the terrifying truth would dawn on him that there was no exit, no exit at all! *In the end the philosophers came to the realization that they could not find this unified rationalistic circle and so, departing from the classical methodology of antithesis, they shifted the concept of truth, and modern man was born.*

In this way modern man moved under the line of despair. He was driven to it against his desire. He remained a rationalist, but he had changed. Do we Christians understand this shift in the contemporary world? If we do not understand it, then we are largely talking to ourselves.

Tendency Towards a Uniform Culture
The importance of understanding the chasm to which man's thinking has brought him is not of intellectual value alone, but of spiritual value as well. The Christian is to resist the spirit of the world. But when we say this, we must understand that the world-spirit does not always take the same form. So the Christian must resist the spirit of the world *in the form it takes in his own generation.* If he does not do this, he is not resisting the spirit of the world at all. This is especially so for our generation, as the forces at work against us are of such a total nature. It is our generation of Christians more than any other who need to heed these words attributed to Martin Luther:

> If I profess with the loudest voice and clearest exposition every portion of the truth of God except precisely that little point which the world and the devil are at that moment attacking, I am not confessing Christ, however boldly I may be professing Christ. Where the battle rages, there the loyalty of the soldier is proved, and to be steady on all the battlefield besides, is mere flight and disgrace if he flinches at that point.

It would be false to say that there is a totally uniform culture. This is not so. And yet, as we study the art and literature of the past, and those things which help us to understand a culture, we find that there tends to be a drift towards a monolithic and uniform whole.

Through a study of archaeology it is possible to show how a certain idea developed in one place and then over a period of several hundred years spread over wide areas. One could give as an example the Indo-European culture, whose spread can be traced through the flow of certain words.

In the distant past, it took so long for cultural concepts to spread that by the time they had reached other areas they had sometimes already changed at their place of origin. But today the world is small, and it is very possible to have a monolithic culture spreading rapidly and influencing great sections of mankind. No artificial barriers, such as the Iron Curtain, can keep out the flow of these ideas. As the world has shrunk, and as it has largely become post-Christian, both sides of the Iron Curtain have followed the same methodology and the same basic monolithic thought-form — namely, the lack of absolutes and antithesis, leading to pragmatic relativism.

In our modern forms of specialized education there is a tendency to lose the whole in the parts, and in this sense we can say that our generation produces few truly educated people. True education means thinking by associating across the various disciplines, and not just being highly qualified in one field, as a technician might be. I suppose no discipline has tended to think more in fragmented fashion than the orthodox or evangelical theology of today.

Those standing in the stream of historic Christianity have been especially slow to understand the relationships between various areas of thought. When the apostle warned us to "keep [ourselves] unspotted from the world,"[3] he was not talking of some abstraction. If the Christian is to apply this injunction to himself he must understand what confronts him antagonistically in his own moment of history. Otherwise he simply becomes a useless museum piece and not a living warrior for Jesus Christ.

The orthodox Christian has paid a very heavy price, both in the defense and communication of the gospel, for his failure to think and act as an educated person understanding and at war with the uniformity of our modern culture.

CHAPTER TWO

The First Step in the Line of Despair: Philosophy

Hegel, the Doorway

It was the German philosopher Hegel (1770-1831) who became the man to open the door into the line of despair. Before his time truth was conceived on the basis of antithesis, not for any adequate reason but because man romantically acted upon it.

This book is not intended to be exhaustive in its treatment of the developments from the time of the Renaissance leading up to Hegel. *Escape from Reason* gives a more complete resumé of the developments from Aquinas, through the Renaissance, the birth of modern science, and including the place of Immanuel Kant. Kant is most important, and to omit him would leave out one of the key pieces in the development of modern thought.

Truth, in the sense of antithesis, is related to the idea of cause and effect. Cause and effect produces a chain reaction which goes straight on in a horizontal line. With the coming of Hegel this changed.

We must understand the importance of timing. What Hegel taught arrived at just the right moment of history for his thinking to have its maximum effect.

Imagine that Hegel was sitting one day in the local tavern, surrounded by his friends, conversing on the philosophical issues of the day. Suddenly he put down his mug of beer on the table and said, "I have a new idea. From now on let us think in this way: instead of thinking in terms of cause and effect, what we really have is a thesis, and opposite it an antithesis, with the answer to their relationship not a horizontal movement of cause and effect, but a synthesis." Now suppose also that a hard-headed German businessman had been standing by and had overheard his remark. He might have thought, "How abstruse and impractical!" But he could not have been further from the truth. Because whether Hegel himself or those listening understood it to be the case, when Hegel propounded this idea he changed the world.

It has never been the same since. Among other things, the concept of dialectical thinking was based on this idea, and it was, and is, crucial to Marxism. By our era, Hegelian synthesis dominates on both sides of the Iron Curtain.

If one understands the development of philosophy, or morals, or political thought from that day to this, one knows that Hegel and synthesis have won. In other words, Hegel has removed the straight line of previous thought, and in its place he has substituted a triangle. Instead of antithesis we have, as modern man's approach to truth, synthesis. Hegel did not put it this simply. His thinking and writing are complicated, but the conclusion is that all possible positions are relativized, and leads to the concept that truth is to be sought in synthesis rather than antithesis.

But notice, Hegel was only a door to the line of despair. He himself never went below it. A good case can be made from his writings for classifying him as an idealist in that he tried to solve the problem of unity with his religious language. He thought that in practice synthesis could be arrived at by reason. But this did not prove possible, and so the next man we have to consider went below the line.

Kierkegaard, the First Man Below

It is often said that Soren Kierkegaard, the Dane (1813-1855), is the father of all modern thinking. And so he is. He is the father of modern existential thinking, both secular and theological thinking. Our diagram now looks like this:

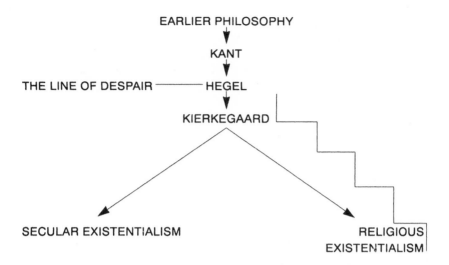

Why is it that Kierkegaard can so aptly be thought of as the father of both? What proposition did he add to the flow of thought that made the difference? Kierkegaard led to the conclusion that you could not arrive at synthesis by reason. Instead, you achieve everything of real importance by a leap of faith.

Kierkegaard was a complex man, and his writings, especially his devotional writings, are often very helpful. For example, the Bible-believing Christians in Denmark still use these devotional writings. We can also be totally sympathetic to his outcry about the deadness of much of the Church in his day. However, in his more philosophical writings he did become the father of modern thought. This turns upon his writing of Abraham and the "sacrifice" of Isaac. Kierkegaard said this was an act of faith with nothing rational to base it upon or to which to relate it. Out of this came the modern concept of a "leap of faith" and the total separation of the rational and faith.

In this thinking concerning Abraham, Kierkegaard had not read the Bible carefully enough. Before Abraham was asked to move toward the sacrifice of Isaac (which, of course, God did not allow to be consummated), he had much propositional revelation from God, he had seen God, God had fulfilled promises to him. In short, God's words at this time were in the context of Abraham's strong reason for knowing that God both existed and was totally trustworthy.

This does not minimize Abraham's faith shown in the long march to Mt. Moriah and all the rest, but it certainly was not a "leap of faith" separated from rationality.

I do not think that Kierkegaard would be happy, or would agree, with that which has developed from his thinking in either secular or religious existentialism. But what he wrote gradually led to the absolute separation of the rational and logical from faith.

The reasonable and faith bear no relationship to each other, like this:

FAITH (NONREASON—OPTIMISM)

THE RATIONAL (PESSIMISM)

It is not our purpose here to discuss all that Kierkegaard taught. There was much more than this. *But the important thing about him is that when he put forth the concept of a leap of faith, he became in a real way the father of all modern existential thought, both secular and theological.*

As a result of this, from that time on, if rationalistic man wants to deal with the really important things of human life (such as purpose, significance, the validity of love), he must discard rational thought about them and make a gigantic, nonrational leap of faith. The rationalistic framework had failed to produce an answer on the basis of reason, and so all hope of a uniform field of knowledge had to be abandoned. We get the resulting dichotomy like this:

THE NONRATIONAL AND NONLOGICAL	Existential experience; the final experience; the first-order experience.
THE RATIONAL AND LOGICAL	Only particulars, no purpose, no meaning. Man is a machine.

Once we appreciate the development of modern philosophy in this way, we may note that though there appear to be many forms of philosophy today, in reality there are very few. They have a uniform cast about them. For example, if you listened to the defining philosophy as taught in Cambridge, and then turn to the existentialism of say, Karl Jaspers, you might think there was no unity between them. But this is not so. There is one basic agreement in almost all of the chairs of philosophy today, and that is a radical denial of the possibility of drawing a circle which will encompass all. In this sense, the philosophies of today can be called in all seriousness antiphilosophies.

The Existentialism of Jaspers, Sartre and Heidegger

In the two halves of existential thinking which we said flowed from Kierkegaard, we will pick up first that of the secular. Later we will pick up the theological existentialism in considering Karl Barth.

There are three main schools of secular existentialist thinking: the Swiss, the French and the German. Most people do not know the work of Karl Jaspers (1883-1969) in Switzerland as well as that of his French or German contemporaries, but he is an exceedingly important man. He is German, but taught at the University of Basel. He placed a great deal of emphasis on the need to wait for a nonrational "final experience," which, he said, would give meaning to life. People who follow Jaspers have come to me and said, "I have had a final experience." They never expect me to ask them what it was. The simple fact is that if I asked such a thing, it would prove that I was among the uninitiated.

To describe it as an *existential* experience means that it cannot be communicated. It is not possible to communicate content with regard to the experience which they have had. Some of these men have sat down with me and said, "It is obvious from looking at you and talking to you, from noticing your sensitivity and sympathy to others, and the openness of your approach to men, that you too are a man who knows the reality of final experience." They mean this as a supreme compliment, and I always say, "Thank you very much indeed." And I mean it, because it is quite remarkable to have one of these men say to an orthodox Christian that they think he understands. But then I go on to say to them, "Yes, I have had a final experience, but it can be verbalized, and it is of a nature that can be rationally discussed." Then I talk of my personal relationship with the personal God who is there. I try to make them understand that this relationship is based on God's written, propositional communication to men, and on the finished work of Jesus Christ in space-time history. They reply that this is impossible, that I am trying to do something that cannot be done. The discussion goes on from there.

Try to put yourself for a moment in such a man's place. He has a deep problem, for he hangs everything to do with his certainty of being and the hope of significance upon some titanic experience he has had at a specific point in the past.

It would be wrong to imagine that these men are not serious. I wish many evangelicals had the integrity these men show in their struggles. I have been told that when Karl Jaspers began his lectures to his best students he warned them that they must not commit suicide, because it cannot be certain that one has a final experience by taking one's own life. Perhaps we might wish that many Christians who say they believe in Christ had such intensity of commitment.

But in their struggles there is a horror of great darkness. Though they may be people of great sincerity, this does not of itself make them able to communicate to others their experience. Nor can the individual verbalize to himself what has happened. Tomorrow morning they may say, "Yesterday I had an experience." The day after they still say, "I had an experience." A month and a year later they are hanging on grimly to their only hope of significance and certainty of being by repeating, "I know I had an experience." The horror of this situation is due to their putting their hope in a nonrational, nonlogical, noncommunicable experience.

If we move from Switzerland and to French existentialism, we come to Jean-Paul Sartre (1905-1980) and Albert Camus (1913-1960). They differ from one another and yet share the same basic concepts. Sartre, perhaps, speaks the more consistently of the two. He says that we live in an absurd universe. The total, he says, is ridiculous. Nevertheless, you try to authenticate yourself by an act of the will. It does not really matter in which direction you act as long as you act.

Let us take the field of morals as a good example of the direction of his thought. You see an old lady, and if you help her safely across the road you have "authenticated yourself." But if instead you choose to beat her over the head and snatch her handbag, you would equally have "authenticated yourself." The content is unimportant; you just choose and act. That is it; you have authenticated yourself. This is existentialism in its French form. As I shall show later, neither Sartre nor Camus were able to live this out in practice, but it was their theoretical position.

How is it that these men get to such a strange and desperate position? It is because they have gone below the line of despair.

They have given up the hope of a rational circle to give an answer to life, and are left with only the antirational.

Finally we have the German form of existentialism, as it was propounded by Martin Heidegger (1889-1976). The fascinating thing about Heidegger is that there are two distinct periods in his life. The first period takes him up to the age of about seventy, and the second from then on. Some of my students have joked about this and made up a song about how "The old Heidegger is the new Heidegger!" The change came because he could no longer live on the basis of his system. Before the change, which we will consider more closely later, Heidegger was a true existentialist. He came to the same need for authentication as Sartre. How was this to be achieved? Not by an act of the *will*, but by a vague *feeling* of dread. Dread is not to be confused with fear. To him fear had an object; dread had not. Authentication comes through feeling the dread, *Angst*, of something that is beyond your comprehension — a foreboding, and that is all.

The Antiphilosophy of the Anglo-Saxon World

Two main types of philosophy have recently held the field in the Anglo-Saxon world. They are logical positivism and defining philosophy. Neither of these are rooted in existentialism; indeed both would claim to differ sharply from existentialism. They would strongly insist that they are logical and rational. While we would concede that they are not related in origin to existentialism, nevertheless they have this in common: in their different ways they are all antiphilosophies.

Logical positivism claims to lay the foundation for each step as it goes along, in a rational way. Yet in reality it puts forth no theoretical universal to validate its very first step. Positivists accept (though they present no logical reason why this should be so) that what reaches them from the "outside" may be called "data"; i.e., it has objective validity.

This dilemma was well illustrated by a young man who had been studying logical positivism at Oxford. He was with us in Switzerland as a student in Farel House, and he said one day, "I'm confused about some of these things. I would like to lead a seminar and see how this whole matter stands." So he did. When he began he said, "Well, when this data reaches you . . ."

At once I said, "How do you know, on the basis of logical positivism, that it is data?"

He started again, and went on for another sentence or two, and then said a second time, "When this data reaches you . . ."

I felt very much that I was slapping a child's hands when it reaches over into the box of chocolates; but I had to say, "No, you must not use the word data. It is loaded with all kinds of meaning; it assumes there is objectivity, and your system has never proved it."

"What do I say then?" he replied.

So I said, "Just say blip. You don't know what you mean by data, so substitute blip."

He began once more, "When blip reaches you . . ." and the discussion was over. On the basis of their form of rationalism, there is just as much logic in calling something "blip" as "data."

Thus, in its own way, though it uses the title of positivism and operates using reason, it is just as much a leap of faith as existentialism—since it has no postulated circle within which to act which validates reason nor gives a certainty that what we think is data is indeed data.

Michael Polanyi's (1891-1976) work showed the weakness of all forms of "positivism," and today positivism in theory is dead. However, it must be said that the materialistic, rationalistic scientists have shut their eyes to its demise and continue to build their work upon it as though it were alive and well. They are doing their materialistic science with no epistemological base. In the crucial area of knowing, they are not operating on facts but faith.

However, the defining philosophy is more important in England and the United States today.

The starting-point of those who subscribe to this philosophy is, as the title suggests, definition. They say they will on no account take any first step without rationally and logically defining the terms they use. And they will go no further than can be accurately defined.

This is all very well, but even if we overlook the differences in their own ranks as to whether their categories are accurate or not, they still have other problems. Many of them would agree that all their work is no more than *prologomena*—that is, preparation for philosophy. They start off by defining terms in the hope that one day some of the random pieces may be fitted together. Now this is helpful insofar as they have demonstrated that some problems cease to exist when they have carefully defined the terms involved. In providing a tool for careful thinking, their work has also been most helpful. But they are carefully defining terms without dealing with meaning and purpose. Classical philosophy up through Kant consisted of two parts. It dealt, certainly, with details. But the details were to be set within a circle which, it was claimed, could contain all knowledge and life. But defining philosophy deals with the details only. It would not claim to be a system. In this sense, as a contrast to classical philosophy, it is an antiphilosophy. In it, language leads to neither values nor facts, but only to language.

Then secondly, many of these men also have their own personal leap of faith. As defining philosophers, they have a prestige in their own field. At the same time many of them take a strong position for optimistic humanism.[1] That is, many of them would make the same optimistic statements as a man like Sir Julian Huxley. But what they are doing is this: they are using their prestige as instructors in the art of defining philosophy in order to enhance the strength of their humanistic view regarding man. But it should be observed that weight of scholarship in defining words does not make up for weakness of argument in the larger questions. In fact, there is no bridge at all between their limited philosophy, which says nothing about meaning or purpose, and their optimistic statements. They have leapt over the gap between the two by faith. However careful and rational their definitions of words may be, their observation of man, in that it is optimistic humanism, is unadulterated faith.

And the evolutionary humanism as a whole, which is current today, is in the same plight. Anyone can assert with all the persuasion at his command that mankind can expect a rosy future. But this again is a leap of faith, if there is no point of observation, either clinically or sociologically, to demonstrate that man will be better tomorrow than he was yesterday or is today.

Sir Julian Huxley has taken such a purely optimistic answer one step further by stating that man will only be improved by accepting a new mystique. Thus he suggests that society will function better if it has a religion, even though no god really exists.[2] For example, he says:

> From the specifically religious point of view, the desirable direction of evolution might be defined as the divinisation of existence—but for this to have operative significance we must frame

a new definition of 'the divine' free from all connotations of external supernatural beings.

Religion today is imprisoned in a theistic frame of ideas, compelled to operate in the unrealities of the dualistic world. In the unitary humanist frame it acquires a new look and new freedom. With the aid of our new vision it has the opportunity of escaping from the theistic impasse and of playing its proper role in the real world of unitary existence.

Now it may be true that it can be shown by observation that society copes better with life through believing that there is a god. But in that case, surely optimistic humanism is essentially unreasonable (and, like the others we have discussed, shows exactly the same irrational leap of faith) if in order to be optimistic, its optimism rests upon the necessity of mankind believing and functioning upon a lie.

The Use of Drugs

It is not only the existentialist who has talked about an experience as a means of validating oneself. Right up to the time of his death Aldous Huxley suggested that a way of achieving what he described as a "first-order experience" would be through drugs.[3] This experience would, like the final experience advocated by the existentialists, be above the line of rational validation, in this way:

THE NONRATIONAL AND NONLOGICAL	A first-order experience by the use of drugs.
THE RATIONAL AND LOGICAL	No purpose or meaning found.

This overwhelming desire for some nonrational experience was responsible for most of the serious use of the drugs LSD and STP in the 1960s. For the sensitive person, drugs were then not usually used for escape. On the contrary, he hoped that by taking them he would experience the reality of something which would give his life some meaning. Intriguingly enough, Professor Timothy Leary, formerly of Harvard University, linked up the LSD experience with that described in the *Tibetan Book of the Dead*.[4] Thus he shows that the desire for, and the form of, this experience changes very little from West to East. Whether it is the existentialist speaking, or Aldous Huxley, or Eastern mysticism, we find a uniform need for an irrational experience to make some sense of life. Their views have brought them to a wall, and by an unrelated leap of faith they hope to clear the wall. Each of their views may be distinguished in detailed description, but they have come to the same wall and are making the same attempt to clear it. Each case involves a nonrational leap of faith.

The chairs of philosophy in most universities have come under the line of despair. The living philosophical discussions have tended to move into unusual settings — such as philosophic astronomy, modern jazz, or among the counterculture. It is in such fields that philosophy is being hammered out. Academic philosophy as such, including Anglo-Saxon philosophy, has tended to be antiphilosophy.

In concluding this section, let us note that when we speak of being under the line of despair, we do not mean that these people necessarily sit down and weep, but that they have given up all hope of achieving a rational, unified answer to knowledge and life.

What Does and Does Not Happen in These Experiences

It is obvious that often when a man claims to have had an experience, whether under drugs or not, something has certainly happened to him. When he experiences, for example, the "redness" of a red rose, he has really touched something. But what?

Usually only two live options are presented as to what happens in an Eastern religious experience, an existential experience, or a drug experience. One is told either that they have stumbled on "nothing" in their experience, or else that they have met "the reality of god." This latter is especially true when the Eastern religious experience is under consideration. The *guru* says, "I have met something." Usually people describe it as nonsense or say that he has "met God."

The built-in trouble with all these existential experiences is that the content of such an experience is not open to communication. Only the unknowing would demand, "Please describe to me in normal categories what you have experienced."

But I believe that there is a third live option when we ask our-

selves what these people have touched. It is an alternative explanation Christians are able to give because we see these people *as
they really are* in God's universe.

God has created a real, external world. It is not an extension of
His essence. That real, external world exists. God has also created man as a real, personal being, and he possesses a "mannishness" from which he can never escape. On the basis of their own
worldview often these experience-seekers are neither sure the
external world is there, nor that man as man is there. But I have
come to the conclusion that despite their intellectual doubts,
many of them *have had* a true experience of the reality of the
external world that exists, and/or the "mannishness" that exists.
They can do this precisely because this is how God has made
man, in His own image, able to experience the real world and
man's "mannishness." Thus they have hit upon something which
exists, and it is neither nothing, nor is it God. We might sum up
this third alternative by saying that when they experience the
"redness" of the rose, they are having the experience of the
external world, as is the farmer who plows his field. They are
both touching the world that is.

In the same way, lovers on the left bank of the Seine in Paris
experience the "mannishness" of man when they fall in love and
yet cry because they do not believe love exists. If I met any of
these, I would put my hand gently on their shoulders and say,
"You are separated from God if you do not accept Christ as your
Savior, but at this moment you understand something real about
the universe. Though your system may say love does not exist,
your own experience shows that it does." They have not touched
the personal God who exists, but for a fleeting moment they have
touched the existence of true personality in their love. This is
indeed an objective reality, because God has made their personalities in this way. It is true that in these experiences man has
touched something, not nothing; but what he has touched is not
God, but the objective reality of the external world and the "mannishness" of man that God has created.

Some have wondered why Christians should not use drugs
since drugs are said to sharpen perception. But the price paid for
increased perception is much too great. A while ago an anonymous poem was published in *The Listener* based on the 23rd
Psalm. It began:

King Heroin is my shepherd, I shall always want,
He maketh me to lie down in the gutters.
He leadeth me beside the troubled waters.
He destroyeth my soul.

With the exception of their use for medical purposes, and therefore under careful control, drugs are destructive. Playing with drugs is foolish, as well as wrong.

CHAPTER THREE

The Second Step: Art

If it is true that philosophy, the first step in the line of despair, touched only a few people, art, the second step, influenced very many more.

As in philosophy, so in art there is a doorway into the line, and this is provided by the Impressionists. When they began they did not see themselves as rebelling against classic concepts. They were interested in a study of light, as was the Englishman Turner who had preceded them. But later their work changed and expressed the new mentality.

Van Gogh and Gauguin

There are three men who stand out above all. They are Van Gogh (a Dutchman), Gauguin and Cezanne (Frenchmen). Each was a genius; they were very real human men, and each produced pictures which show their genius as artists. However, as we enjoy these pictures as art, appreciating their composition, their use of color and all the other things to admire, we must also see their place in the second step in the "line of despair." They are the three pillars of modern art. In each case they tried to find a universal in their art as Leonardo da Vinci[1] had tried many centuries

27

before them. What the philosopher was trying to do within the scope of the whole universe, they now tried to do on a limited scale on their canvases. As they crossed the threshold of the line of despair, they began a desperate search to find a universal that would give them back reality, something more than just particulars. They were seeking to express a form and a freedom which would be valid in the scope of their discipline, art.

Van Gogh (1853-1890) can be thought of first. Very often people say he committed suicide because he was mentally ill or because Gauguin stole a woman he was interested in. These may have been contributing factors, but the suicide was due to a much more basic problem. There may have been psychological problems, but the final explosion came as a result of disillusionment on a much more fundamental issue. Van Gogh thought to make a new religion in which the sensitive people, the artists, would blaze the trail. For this purpose, he dreamt of starting an artistic community in Arles where he was living. He was joined by Gauguin, but after a few months they began to quarrel violently. Van Gogh's hope of his new religion was gone and soon after, he committed suicide. The death of hope in man had taken place in Van Gogh. He died in despair.

Gauguin (1846-1903) did the same thing. He too was seeking for a universal. He went to Tahiti and there he, following the concepts of Jean-Jacques Rousseau (1712-1778), championed the idea of the noble savage. The savage was to be the return to the primitive, the child of the race, and it was here, going back in time, that he hoped to find the universal. So Gauguin began to paint the beauty of the women he found there. For a time he felt that he had successfully removed himself from the loss of innocence in civilization, and that this was enough. But his last great painting tells the conclusion he came to eventually.

This painting is called *What? Whence? Whither?*,[2] and it now hangs in the Boston Museum of Art. The title is painted on a yellow corner on the upper left of the picture, thus making quite sure that anyone who looks at the work will understand its meaning. Elsewhere[3] in discussing the painting, he tells us that we are to look at it the opposite way to normal — namely, from the right to the left. So at the right, where we look first, we see the same kind of beauty as in his other paintings. There is the same exotic symbolism, the same appeal to the sensuous in the concept of the noble savage. But by the time our eye has moved across the canvas to the far left, we see a very different end to the story. He began the painting in 1897 and finished it in 1898. This is what he says about it: "I have finished a philosophical work on this theme, comparable to the gospel. A figure lifts up its arms into the air and, astonished, looks at these two personages who dare to think of their destination." A little farther on he continues:

"Whither? Close to the death of an old woman, a strange, stupid bird concludes: What? The eternal problem that punishes our pride. O Sorrow, thou art my master. Fate, how cruel thou art, and always vanquished, I revolt."[4] When you look at the left-hand side of the picture you see three figures. The first is a young Tahitian woman in all her beauty. Beside her is a poor old woman dying, watched only by a monstrous bird, which has no counterpart in nature. When Gauguin finished this painting he too tried to commit suicide, though in fact he did not succeed.

Both of these men were attempting to find a humanistic universal. They failed dismally and remained below the line of despair.

Cezanne and Picasso

It was in the basic geometrical form that Cezanne (1839-1906) attempted to discover his universal. Many of his landscape paintings look like a taut diaphragm, a diaphragm pulled over geometric forms. Later he painted people as geometric forms — for example, *The Bathers*, now hung in the National Gallery in London. As far as we know, tragedy never caught up with him. He died, as far as I have been able to discover, without ever coming to the conclusion of despair.

But someone else carried on from where he left off. This was Picasso (1881-1973). Again we must stress, as we have concerning the others before him, that he was a genius of the first rank, he was overwhelmingly productive, an amazing man as a man, and all of us will find parts of his body of work which will move us, and perhaps will move us deeply.

Picasso saw the work of Cezanne at the large exhibitions of his work in Paris in 1905 and 1907, and discussed the problems involved in Paris in Gertrude Stein's home where many painters used to gather.

Picasso brought together the noble savage of Gauguin, the geometric form of Cezanne, and also incorporated something from the African masks that had just become known in Paris, developing between 1906 and 1911 what was to be called Cubism. The great picture of 1906-1907, *Les Demoiselles d'Avignon* (now in the Museum of Modern Art, New York), shows this development. The women on the left are much like those he painted before, but already showing Cezanne's influence in an exaggerated form. In Picasso's private collection which was broken up at his death, there was a small copy of Cezanne's *The Bathers*, made just before Picasso painted *Les Demoiselles d'Avignon*. When one turns to the women on the right, one finds that instead of their being women, they have become demonic beings and symbols as in the African masks. Their humanity has been lost.

Picasso then pushed further. Unlike, say, Renoir, who painted his wife in such a way that she could be recognized (that is, the subject was a particular), Picasso was seeking for a universal. As he abstracted further, one cannot tell whether his women are blondes or brunettes. This is a move towards the universal and away from the particular. But if you go far enough, your abstracted women can become "all women" or even everything. But the difficulty is that when you get to that point the viewer has no clue what he is looking at. You have succeeded in making your own world on your canvas, and in this sense you have become god. But at the same time you have lost contact with the person who views your painting. We have come to the position where we cannot communicate. The problem of modern man's loss of communication and his alienation did not have to wait for the computers and cybernetics. Picasso, the modern man, exhibited this far earlier in his art.

Picasso "solved" his problem with a romantic leap. One day he fell in love, and because he felt the force of love he wrote on the canvases, "*J'aime Eva*" (I love Eva).[5] The painting could have been of anything, a chair or something else abstracted. But suddenly, with the words sprawled across the picture, he was in touch again with the man who looked on. But the communication has no logical relationship to the subject of his canvas. Picasso has failed; his abstraction carried to its logical conclusion has left him with no communication. What remains to him is that which, in his worldview, is a leap.

It is interesting that with the two women he married, Olga and Jacqueline, he painted them at times in the style closer to his earlier pink and blue periods, when as a younger man he was showing his great dexterity in the use of the classical style. But in the ongoing flow of his work, Picasso was the modern man with the brokenness which is involved in it.

This is modern man. This is the concept of truth by which we are surrounded. This is the spirit of the world to which we must say "No," no matter what face it puts on, including a theological one. This is what makes the chasm between the last generation and our generation, a break of more than 400 years, a greater break than that between the Renaissance and the generation before ours. The tragedy is not only that these talented men have reached the point of despair, but that so many who look on and admire really do not understand. They are influenced by the concepts, and yet they have never analyzed what it all means.

Mondrian

Mondrian (1872-1944) picked up Picasso's position in art and developed Picasso's style to an extreme conclusion. Mondrian's horizontals and verticals are lovely and magnificent. In architecture they have been used as a practical model. However, for him they were not just horizontals and verticals, for he too was fighting for a universal.

One day I went to the museum in Zurich. They have a big collection of modern paintings there. I went into one of the rooms, and I was aghast. There was a Mondrian with a frame on it. Mondrian did not put frames on his pictures. So I went to the office and asked the man in charge if the Mondrian had a frame on it when he received it. He replied, "No, we put it on." So I said, "Don't you understand? If Mondrian came in here, he would just smash the picture against the wall." As far as I could tell, this was a new idea to him. Really this man did not seem to understand the picture in his museum, because Mondrian's whole concept was the building of a universal.

Mondrian painted his pictures and hung them on the wall. They were frameless so that they would not look like holes in the wall. As the pictures conflicted with the room, he had to make a new room. So Mondrian had furniture made for him, particularly by Rietveld, a member of the De Stijl group, and Van der Leck. There was an exhibition in the Stedelijk Museum in Amsterdam in July-September 1951, called "De Stijl," where this could be seen. As you looked, you were led to admire the balance between room and furniture, in just the same way as there is such a good balance in his individual pictures. But if a man came into that room, there would be no place for him. It is a room for abstract balance, but not for man. This is the conclusion modern man has reached, below the line of despair. He has tried to build a system out from himself, but this system has come to the place where there is not room in the universe for man.

Mondrian himself seemed to have come to understand that what he had tried had come to a dead end. He made a big shift in his painting, as shown by the painting *Broadway Boogie Woogie*, which now hangs in the Metropolitan Gallery of Art in New York.

Dada, Marcel Duchamp, the Happenings and the Environments
I have a poem that appeared on page 1 of the last issue of the magazine called *De Stijl*,[6] which was published by the De Stijl school of painting with which Mondrian was connected. It is written by Hans Arp (1887-1966), one of the members of the original Dada group. This is a translation from the German:

> the head downward
> the legs upward
> he tumbles into the bottomless
> from whence he came.
>
> he has no more honour in his body
> he bites no more bite of any short meal
> he answers no greeting
> and is not proud when being adored
>
> the head downward
> the legs upward
> he tumbles into the bottomless
> from whence he came
>
> like a dish covered with hair
> like a four-legged sucking chair
> like a deaf echotrunk
> half full half empty
>
> the head downward
> the legs upward
> he tumbles into the bottomless
> from whence he came.

On the basis of modern man's methodology, whether expressed in philosophy, art, literature or theology, there can be no other ending than this — man tumbling into the bottomless.

Dada is a chance concept. The very word was chosen by chance. One day some people flipped through a French dictionary in Zurich in the Café Voltaire. They put a finger down at random and found it rested on the word *dada*. It means "a rocking horse." And so it was by blind chance that they conceived the name for their school of art.

In the same way they composed their poems. They cut printed words out of the newspaper, threw them in a hat, and picked them out by chance. But these men were deadly serious; it really was no game they were playing.

One such man was Marcel Duchamp (1887-1968), whom every Christian ought to know about. He could be called the high priest of destruction. He is best known by many for his picture *Nude descending a stairway*, which is now in the Philadelphia Museum of Art. He was brilliant and destructive — and he meant to destroy. He sought to destroy you from within yourself. The best collection of his work in the world is at the Philadelphia Museum of Art. There is a picture in the Museum of Modern Art in New York, *Le passage de la vierge a la mariee* (the words are written on the canvas and mean, "The passage of the virgin to the married state"). Naturally every man or woman who goes to look at the picture tries to find in the picture something which relates to its title. But no matter how long one looks, one finds no picture of a virgin, nor of a virgin becoming a married woman. Thus he causes the viewer to make himself dirty.

His last work, which no one knew existed, came to light at his death. It is now in the Duchamp collection in the Philadelphia Museum of Art. One must look through a small peephole in an old Spanish door to see it. And it is indeed both pornographic and totally absurd. Why is this placed in the staid Philadelphia Museum of Art by the staid directors? Because it is "Art," and so the message is passed on to the population!

He was the man who, about 1950, gave birth to the *happenings*, and then beyond this the *environments*. The happenings began in New York. We might say that though America was behind at the time of the Armory Show in New York in 1913, today, in modern art and in many other areas under the line of despair, she leads the world.

In the happenings you are put as it were within the picture. You look at people acting; and, as the observer, you are forced to participate. There is always a nonsense element, and there is usually a dirty action as well. Always the observer is involved and is deliberately destroyed.

What are they saying? Everything is chance. Chance, the nothingness, is not just shut up in a framed picture, but it is the entire structure of life. You are in the chance, in the nothingness. You are the destroyed ones.

A good example of the environments was some of the rooms in the art show "Art Zero, Art Nul," held in the Stedelijk Museum, Amsterdam, in the summer of 1965. It was the most important show held on the Continent at the time. One entered the rooms in the gallery and looked at objects. But there was something more than mere looking at individual objects; rather you felt permeated by a total context which was almost subliminal. Almost against your wish you got drawn into the mood of the room. I watched young couples going through these rooms in Amsterdam. I knew that most of them did not understand what they saw. But I was certain that by the time they came out, the atmosphere would have had its effect and their moral defenses would have been weakened. They were touched at a deeper level than only the mind, and though the girl could not perhaps analyze what she saw, yet surely she would be more ready to say "Yes" by the time she came out.

In this connection it is important to note that the leaders of the Provos, an anarchist movement in Amsterdam which had been much in the international news through 1966 and 1967, and which has an influence in The Netherlands into the 1980s, said that this movement was the logical result of the exposition program at the Stedelijk Museum in Amsterdam through the previous fifteen years. It is also interesting to note that the Provos called their public demonstrations "Happenings."

These paintings, these poems, and these demonstrations which we have been talking about are the expression of men who are struggling with their appalling lostness. Dare we laugh at such things? Dare we feel superior when we view their tortured expressions in their art? Christians should stop laughing and take such men seriously. Then we shall have the right to speak again to our generation. These men are dying while they live; yet where is our compassion for them? There is nothing more ugly than a Christian orthodoxy without understanding or without compassion.

CHAPTER FOUR

The Third and Fourth Steps:
Music and the General Culture

Just as in philosophy and art, there is a doorway into the line of despair in music as well. Debussy (1862-1918) is the doorway into the field of modern music. It is not as easy to trace the steps in music as it is in visual art; yet the parallels are there. It is not as easy because, inevitably, music has a more subjective element in it. Nevertheless, the general trend from Debussy until now is clear enough.

An exhaustive study, which we cannot undertake here, would involve considering jazz as well as classical music. Such a consideration would involve discussing the shift in form and content in the twenties and thirties when jazz was introduced into the white man's culture, and how the jazz of the forties was the doorway to the despair of a section of modern jazz.[1]

But we will turn our attention to music more in line with the classical tradition. A few illustrations must suffice for the whole. There could be much discussion of detail in this, and yet the total direction of movement is clear. In a later chapter I will deal with the music of John Cage. Here I want to look at *musique concrète.*

Musique Concrète
This was developed by Pierre Schaeffer (1910-) in Paris. *Musique concrète* is not electronic music — that is, music made electronically and therefore consisting of sounds one does not normally hear. *Musique concrète* is real sound, but seriously distorted. In the beginning it was created by jumping grooves on a phonographic record. Later Pierre Schaeffer invented a machine by which the distortions can be carefully controlled. With his machine he can lift out the source of the sound, split it up, reverse it, slow it down or speed it up — in fact, do just about anything to alter it. To hear the result is to begin to distrust your ears, just as in Op Art you begin to distrust your eyes. The effect is overwhelming. The message which comes across from the distortion is the same as in modern painting. All is relative, nothing is sure, nothing is fixed, all is in flux. *Musique concrète* is just one more way of presenting the uniform message of modern man.

UNESCO has put out a record, entitled *Premiere Panorama de Musique concrète*.[2] In it is a clear example of what these men are doing, including a selection by one of Schaeffer's friends, Pierre Henry.

He used the human voice speaking Greek. Greek, of course, is exactly the right language to speak in such a setting, for it is the language representative of our Western culture. The voice is first built up out of chance sounds, reflecting modern man's view that man who verbalizes arose by chance in a chance universe with only a future of chance ahead of him. Henry portrays this remorselessly in sound. Suddenly something else begins to happen; the voice begins to degenerate and to fall apart. It is as though one is watching a beautiful woman die and totally decompose before one's eyes. But in this case it is not just the physical body, but the whole person who rots away. It begins to shiver, to shake, to be corrupted. It begins with chance sounds, goes on to the Greek, and ends in chaos. *There can be no other terminus when antithesis dies, when relativism is born and when the possibility of finding any universal which would make sense of the particulars is denied.* This is the consensus of the cultural environment, and this is that world-spirit which we must reject and into which we must speak.

Henry Miller
With this American novelist (1891-1980), we begin our consideration of the fourth step in the line of despair, which I have named

general culture. This could be divided into a number of steps, but I have placed these subjects together under this heading for convenience.

Young people often said that the writing of Henry Miller was not just pornographic, but was a philosophical statement. Parents of these young people ask me whether I agree. I reply, "Yes, your child is right. They are certainly dirty books and because of this will soil you. However, they were not intended to be mere pornography. Miller was an antilaw writer. He smashed everything to pieces so that there is nothing left. Even sex is smashed. This is especially devastating because it is often in the sexual area of life that men hope to find some kind of meaning when they have abandoned the search elsewhere."

Not only with Miller, but also with other modern writers we can appreciate the result of this as we notice how they use the girl in their books. The playmate becomes the plaything, and we are right back with the Marquis de Sade. (I want to talk about the later changed Henry Miller a little farther on.)

Philosophic Homosexuality

Some forms of homosexuality today are of a similar nature, in that they are not just homosexuality but a philosophic expression. One must have understanding for the real homophile's problem. But much modern homosexuality is an expression of the current denial of antithesis. It has led in this case to an obliteration of the distinction between man and woman. So the male and the female as complementary partners are finished. This is a form of homosexuality which is a part of the movement below the line of despair. In much of modern thinking, all antithesis and all the order of God's creation is to be fought against — including the male-female distinctions. The pressure toward unisex is largely rooted here. But this is not an isolated problem; it is a part of the world-spirit of the generation which surrounds us. It is imperative that Christians realize the conclusions which are being drawn as a result of the death of absolutes.

John Osborne

In the area of drama, another aspect of general culture, it is important to consider John Osborne (1929-1980), one of the Angry Young Men. In many ways he is a great playwright, but he has been accurately described as an idealist who has not been able to find an ideal. This is a magnificent description. Osborne is a man of temperament, courage and sensitivity; a man to ride on a charger with his lance at the ready into the great battles of life. He is an idealist by choice, but without an ideal: a man who cares and yet has found nothing worth caring about. His whole approach is summed up with magnificent clarity in his play *Martin Luther*. As history it has weaknesses, but in general it portrays the early part of Luther's life with considerable accuracy. But the moment of truth comes with great force at the very end. Luther is standing with one of his babies in his arms. The elderly head of Luther's old monastery comes to visit him. They face each other. The old man says, "Martin, do you know you are right?" And against all history Osborne makes him reply, "Let's hope so." The lights come on, the curtain is down, and the play is finished. The drama critic of *The* (London) *Times* understood. He said, "Isn't it interesting that he had to put in that last line to make it a twentieth-century play!"

Dylan Thomas
When we review modern poetry as part of our own general culture, we find the same tendency to despair. Near the time of his death, Dylan Thomas (1914-1953) wrote a poem called *Elegy*.[3] He did not actually put it together himself, so we cannot be too sure of the exact order of the stanzas. But the way it is given below is probably the right order. This poem is by a fellow human being of our generation. He is not an insect on the head of a pin, but shares the same flesh and blood as we do, a man in real despair:

> Too proud to die, broken and blind he died
> The darkest way, and did not turn away,
> A cold kind man brave in his narrow pride
>
> On the darkest day, Oh, forever may
> He lie lightly, at last, on the last, crossed
> Hill, under the grass, in love, and there grow
>
> Young among the long flocks, and never lie lost
> Or still all the numberless days of his death, though
> Above all he longed for his mother's breast.
>
> Which was rest and dust, and in the kind ground
> The darkest justice of death, blind and unblessed.
> Let him find no rest but be fathered and found.

I prayed in the crouching room, by his blind bed,
In the muted house, one minute before
Moon, and night, and light. The rivers of the dead

Veined his poor hand I held, and I saw
Through his unseeing eyes to the roots of the sea.
(An old tormented man three-quarters blind),

I am not too proud to cry that He and he
will never never go out of my mind.
All his bones crying, and poor in all but pain.

Being innocent, he dreaded that he died
Hating his God, but what he was was plain:
An old kind man brave in his burning pride.

The sticks of the house were his; his books he owned.
Even as a baby he had never cried;
Nor did he now, save to his secret wound.

Out of his eyes I saw the last light glide.
Here among the light of the lording sky
An old blind man is with me where I go

Walking in the meadow of his son's eye
On whom a world of ills came down like snow.
He cried as he died, fearing at last the spheres

Last sound, the world going out without a breath:
To proud to cry, too frail to check the tears,
And caught between two nights, blindness and death.

O deepest wound of all that he should die
On that darkest day. Oh, he could hide
The tears out of his eyes, too proud to cry.

Until I die he will not leave my side.

In the Festival Hall in London, in one of the higher galleries in the rear corridor, there is a bronze of Dylan Thomas. Anyone who can look at it without compassion is dead. There he faces you with a cigarette at the side of his mouth, the very cigarette hung in despair. It is not good enough to take a man like this or any of the others and smash them as though we have no responsibility for them. This is sensitivity crying out in darkness. But it is not mere emotion; the problem is not on this level at all. These men were not producing art for art's sake, or emotion for emotion's sake. These things are a strong message coming out of their own world-view.

There are many means for killing men, as men, today. They all operate in the same direction: no truth, no morality. You do not have to go to art galleries or listen to the more sophisticated music to be influenced by their message. The common media of cinema and television will do it effectively for you.

Modern Cinema, the Mass Media and the Beatles

We usually divide cinema and television programs into two classes — good and bad. The term "good" as used here means "technically good" and does not refer to morals. The "good" pictures are the serious ones, the artistic ones, the ones with good shots. The "bad" are simply escapist, romantic, only for entertainment. But if we examine them with care, we notice that the "good" pictures are actually the worst pictures. The escapist film may be horrible in its own way, but the so-called "good" pictures have almost all been developed by men holding the modern philosophy of no certain truth and no certain distinction between right and wrong. This does not imply they have ceased to be men of integrity, but it does mean that the films they produce are tools for teaching their beliefs. Three outstanding modern film producers are Fellini and Antonioni of Italy, and Bergman of Sweden. Of these three producers, Bergman has given the clearest expression perhaps of the contemporary despair. He has said that he deliberately developed the flow of his pictures — that is, the whole body of his movies rather than just individual films — in order to teach existentialism.

His existentialist films led up to but do not include the film *The Silence*. This film was a statement of utter nihilism. Man, in this picture, did not even have the hope of authenticating himself by an act of the will. *The Silence* was a series of snapshots with immoral and pornographic themes. The camera just took them without any comment. "Click, click, click, cut!" That is all there is. Life is like that: unrelated, having no meaning as well as no morals.

In passing, it should be noted that Bergman's presentation in *The Silence* was related to the American "Black Writers" (nihilistic writers), the antistatement novel which was best shown perhaps in Capote's *In Cold Blood*. These, too, were just a series of snapshots without any comment as to meaning or morals.

Such writers and directors have had a large impact upon the mass media, and so the force of the monolithic worldview of our age presses in on every side.

The 1960s was the time of many powerful, philosophic films. The posters advertising Antonioni's *Blow-Up* in the London Underground were inescapable as they told the message of that film: "Murder without guilt; love without meaning." The mass of people may not enter an art museum, may never read a serious book. If you were to explain the drift of modern thought to them, they might not be able to understand it; but this does not mean that they are not influenced by the things they see and hear — including the cinema and what is considered "good," nonescapist television.

No greater illustration could be found of the way these concepts were carried to the masses than "pop" music and especially the work of the Beatles. The Beatles moved through several stages, including the concept of the drug and psychedelic approach. The psychedelic began with their records *Revolver,*[4] *Strawberry Fields Forever*, and *Penny Lane.*[5] This was developed with great expertness in their record *Sergeant Pepper's Lonely Hearts Club Band*[6] in which psychedelic music, with open statements concerning drug-taking, was knowingly presented as a religious answer. The religious form was the same vague pantheism which predominates much of the new mystical thought today. One indeed does not have to understand in a clear way the modern monolithic thought in order to be infiltrated by it. *Sergeant Pepper's Lonely Hearts Club Band* was an ideal example of the manipulating power of the new forms of "total art." This concept of total art increases the infiltrating power of the message by carefully conforming the technical form used to the message involved. This is used in the Theatre of the Absurd, the Marshall McLuhan type of television program, the new cinema and the new dance with someone like Merce Cunningham. The Beatles used this in *Sergeant Pepper's Lonely Hearts Club Band* by making the whole record one unit so the whole is to be listened to as a unit and makes one thrust, rather than the songs being only something individually. In this record the words, the syntax, the music, and the unity of the way the individual songs were arranged form a unity of infiltration.

Those were the days of the ferment of the 1960s. Two things must be said about their results in the 1980s. First, we do not understand the 1980s if we do not understand that our culture went through these *conscious* wrestlings and expressions of the 1960s. Second, most people do not understandably think of all this now, but the results are very much still at work in our culture.

Our culture is largely marked by relativism and ultimate mean-inglessness, and when many in the 1980s "join the system" they do so because they have nothing worth fighting for. For most, that was ended by the 1970s. It is significant that when *Sergeant Pepper's Lonely Hearts Club Band* was made a Broadway play (1974, Beacon Theater) it no longer had the ferment; it was "camp" and nostalgia — a museum piece of a bygone time.

CHAPTER FIVE

The Unifying Factor in the Steps of Despair

The line of despair is a unit, and the steps in the line have a distinguishing and unifying mark. With Hegel and Kierkegaard, people gave up the concept of a rational, unified field of knowledge and accepted instead the idea of a leap of faith in those areas which make people distinctive as people — purpose, love, morals and so on. It was this leap of faith that originally produced the line of despair.

The various steps on the line — philosophy, art, music, theatre and so on — differ in details, and these details are interesting and important, but in a way they are only incidental. The distinctive mark of the twentieth-century intellectual and cultural climate does not lie in the differences, but in the unifying concept. The unifying concept is the concept of a divided field of knowledge.

Whether the symbols to express this are those of painting, poetry or theology is incidental. The vital question is not the symbols used to express these ideas (for example, the words of the existential philosophers or the sounds of *musique concrète*), but the concept of truth and the method of attaining truth. *The watershed is the new way of talking about and arriving at truth, not the terms the individual disciplines use to express these ideas.*

Leopold Sedar Senghor (1906-), president of Senegal, is probably the only real intellectual who is head of a government today anywhere in the world. He studied in France. Senghor has written a book which consists of three political speeches given to groups in his own country. The book is called *On African Socialism.*[1] Some years ago he very kindly sent me an autographed copy of this book. As well as this, he has written some magnificent poetry which has, fortunately, been well translated into English.[2]

As I read his speeches I was very moved. If a man stood up in any of the Western countries and delivered these as political speeches, very few Christians would understand their real significance. The fact that Senghor is an African underlines the need to train our overseas missionaries in a new way, for the problem of communication in our day extends beyond the Sorbonne, Oxford, Cambridge, Harvard or the Massachusetts Institute of Technology to those places which we have traditionally thought of as "the mission-field." The problem of communication does not end at our own shores. Among educated men the new way of thinking is everywhere.

Senghor showed in these speeches on African socialism that he understands the modern issues exceedingly well. He points out that the methodology affecting thought today is the same on both sides of the Iron Curtain. In his book he develops in detail the change from the classical concept of logic (A is not non-A) to the general acceptance today of Hegel's methodology of synthesis.

He points out correctly that originally the Marx and Engels form of communism had an interest in man, which gave it much of its drive. We shall note, of course, that later, as it developed naturally from its presuppositions, man became devalued in the communist state. (The Marx-Engels form of communism should properly be regarded as a Christian heresy. Only Christianity, of all the world's religions, has produced a real interest in man. Buddhism, Hinduism and Islam could never have produced *idealistic* communism because they do not have sufficient interest in the individual.) The one thing about communism which really caught the fancy of idealistic communists was this concern for man. But, as I have said, the source of a real care for people *as individuals* comes from biblical Christianity. Are we losing our impact? It may be due largely to a failure to communicate that we believe that man, in the presence of the God who is there, is truly wonderful. But let us return to Senghor.

He argues that one must not think of Marxism as being primarily an economic theory. Nor must one think that its atheism is central. Atheistic it most certainly is, but that is not the crux of the system. If you want to understand what Marxism really is, says Senghor, you must remember that it rests upon the dialectical methodology.

Senghor goes on to say that he and Senegal cannot accept Marxism's economic theory completely. Neither will they accept its atheism. But they will hold fast to its method of dialectic. In doing this, they will follow Teilhard de Chardin.[3] In other words, Senghor realizes that there is no basic difference between the dialectical approach of Marx and that of Teilhard de Chardin.[4] He appreciates that in methodology, they are both on the same side. The fact that the Jesuit priest uses the word *god* and Marx does not makes no difference, for the word by itself is meaningless until given content. The really important thing is that they both use the dialectical methodology.

If you want to understand the century you live in, you must realize that it is not the outward form which the dialectic takes which is the real enemy. This may be expressed in theistic or atheistic forms. The real enemy is not the form it takes, but the dialectical methodology itself.

Romanticism Is Dead:
Christianity's Opportunity If Antithesis Is Maintained
In one way, a Christian ought to be glad that so many live under the line of despair and are fully aware of their position. The Christian should be thankful that when he talks to these people, he does not have to remove page after page of optimistic answers which are against all the evidence and without any base. For Christianity is not romantic; it is realistic.

Christianity is realistic because it says that if there is no truth, there is also no hope; and there can be no truth if there is no adequate base. It is prepared to face the consequences of being proved false and say with Paul: If you find the body of Christ, the discussion is finished; let us eat and drink, for tomorrow we die.[5] It leaves absolutely no room for a romantic answer. For example, in the realm of morals, Christianity does not look over this tired and burdened world and say that it is slightly flawed, a little chipped, but easily mended. Christianity is realistic and says the world is marked with evil and man is truly guilty all along the line. Christianity refuses to say that you can be hopeful for the future if you are basing your hope on evidence of change for the better in mankind. The Christian agrees with the people in genuine despair that the world must be looked at realistically, whether in the area of Being or in morals.

Christianity is poles apart from any form of optimistic humanism. But it also differs from nihilism, for nihilism, though it is correctly realistic, nevertheless can give neither a proper diagnosis nor the proper treatment for its own ills. Christianity has a diagnosis and then a solid foundation for an answer. The difference between Christian realism and nihilism is not that the Christian worldview is romantic. We should be pleased that the romanticism of yesterday has been destroyed. In many ways this makes our task of presenting Christianity to modern man easier than it was for our forefathers.

But to rejoice that romantic answers will no longer do, and to be glad in one sense that men like Dylan Thomas have ended by weeping, does not mean that we should not be filled with compassion for our fellowmen. To live below the line of despair is not to live in paradise, whether that of a fool or any other kind. It is in a real sense to have a foretaste of Hell now, as well as the reality in the life to come. Many of our most sensitive people have been left absolutely naked by the destruction. Should we not grieve and cry before God for such people?

In this situation which so desperately cries out for the remedy which only biblical Christianity can give we seem to be failing. This cannot be due to lack of opportunity; already men are partway to the gospel, for they too believe that man is *dead*, dead in the sense of being meaningless. Christianity alone gives the reason for this meaninglessness, that their revolt has separated them from God who exists, and thus gives them the true explanation of the position to which they have come. But we cannot take advantage of our opportunity, *if we let go* in either thought or practice the methodology of antithesis (that is, that A is A and A is not non-A). If a thing is true, the opposite is not true; if a thing is right, the opposite is wrong.

If our own young people within the churches and those of the world outside see us playing with the methodology of synthesis, in our teaching and evangelism, in our policies and institutions, we can never expect to take advantage of this unique moment of opportunity presented by the death of romanticism. If we let go of our sense of antithesis, we will have nothing left to say.

Moreover, not only will we have nothing to say, we become nothing. Christianity ceases to exist, though it may still keep its outward institutional form. Christianity demands antithesis, not as some abstract concept of truth, but in the fact that God exists, and in personal justification. The biblical concept of justification is a total, personal antithesis. Before justification, we were dead in the kingdom of darkness. The Bible says that in the moment that we accept Christ we pass from death to life. This is total antithesis at the level of the individual man. Once we begin to slip over into the other methodology — a failure to hold on to an absolute which can be known by the whole man, including what is logical and rational in him — historic Christianity is destroyed, even if it seems to keep going for a time. We may not know it, but when this occurs, the marks of death are upon it, and it will soon be one more museum piece.

To the extent that anyone gives up the mentality of antithesis, he has moved over to the other side, even if he still tries to defend orthodoxy or evangelicalism. If Christians are to take advantage of the death of romanticism, we must consciously build back the mentality and practice of antithesis among Christians in doctrine and life. We must do it by our teaching and by example in our attitude toward compromise, both ecclesiastically and in evangelism. To fail to exhibit that we take truth seriously at those points where there is a cost in our doing so, is to push the next generation into the relative, dialectical millstream that surrounds us.

Finally, and with due reverence, may I emphasize that not only should we have genuine compassion for the lost among whom we live, but also concern for our God. We are His people, and if we get caught up in the other methodology, we have really blasphemed, discredited and dishonored Him — for the greatest antithesis of all is that God exists as opposed to His not existing; He is the God who is there.

The Relationship of the New Theology to the Intellectual Climate

CHAPTER ONE

The Fifth Step: Theology

Departure from Biblical Christianity
Modern existential theology finds its origin in Kierkegaard, as
does secular existentialism. They are related together at the very
heart of their systems — that is, "the leap of faith." Theology
comes as the last step, but it is by no means isolated from the rest
of the cultural consensus we have been reviewing.

There is diversity within the unity of the new theology. There is
a difference, for example, between neo-orthodoxy and the new
liberalism following the new Heidegger. Careful scholarship
demands that we appreciate such differences. But if we miss the
unity which binds together all expressions of modern theology,
we have missed the essential point.

At the time of the Reformation, the reformers were confronted
with a total system. They did not say that there were no Christians
within the Roman Catholic Church, nor did they say that there
were no differences in the teaching and emphases of the various
Roman Catholic Orders. But they understood that there was one
underlying system which bound every part of the Church
together, and it was this system *as a system* that they said was
wrong and in opposition to the teaching of the Bible.

Today evangelicals are again confronted with an overwhelming consensus, a methodology accepted by theologians on every side. Thus, while one can get some insights (for example, Bultmann has some good exegesis in some details), yet this is not the place for ambivalent judgment — nor mere disagreement concerning details — we must realize that their system *as a system* is wrong.

As Senghor pointed out that the basic factor of Marxism was neither its economic theory nor its atheism but its dialectical methodology, so the unifying factor of the new theology is its wrong methodology. Since its concept of truth is wrong, what sounds right often means something entirely different from that which historic Christianity means by the same phrase. It is naive to discuss the theological questions as theological questions until one has considered what truth means to the one who is making the theological statements.

Theology has been through the same process as philosophy, though several decades later. Prior to Hegel, rationalistic man was still trying to draw his circles to encompass the whole of life. Then came the line of despair. Naturalistic theology has followed this very closely. The old liberal theologians in Germany began by accepting the presupposition of the uniformity of natural causes as a closed system. Thus they rejected everything miraculous and supernatural, including the supernatural in the life of Jesus Christ. Having done that, they still hoped to find an historical Jesus in a rational, objective, scholarly way by separating the supernatural aspect of Jesus' life from the "true history."

But they failed in the same way that the rationalistic philosophers had failed. They too were caught in the round room without an exit. Their search for the historical Jesus was doomed to failure. The supernatural was so intertwined with the rest that if they ripped out all the supernatural, there was no Jesus left! If they removed all the supernatural, no historical Jesus remained; if they kept the historical Jesus, the supernatural remained as well.

After their failure, they could have done two things in order to continue in a rational and logical framework. They could have left their rationalism and returned to the biblical theology of the Reformation (which they had rejected on the basis of naturalistic presuppositions); or they could have become nihilistic concerning thought and life. But instead of choosing either of these two rational alternatives, they chose a third way, just as the philosophers had already done — a way which had been unthinkable to educated man before this, and which involved the division of the concept of truth.

Why did theology follow philosophy in this tremendously important step? For two reasons: firstly, their old optimistic rationalism had failed to produce an historically credible Jesus, once the miraculous had been rejected; secondly, since the surrounding consensus of thought which they were carefully following was normative to them, when philosophy developed in this direction, they eventually followed.

So it was not so much neo-orthodoxy which destroyed the older form of liberalism, even though Karl Barth's teaching might have been the final earthquake which shook down the tottering edifice; rather, it had already been destroyed from within. To say it in another way — if Barth had spoken fifty years before, it is doubtful if any would have listened.

Neo-orthodoxy gave no new answer. What existential philosophy had already said in secular language was now expressed in theological language. We can represent it like this:

THE NONRATIONAL AND NONLOGICAL	A crisis first-order experience. Faith as an optimistic leap without verification or communicable content.
THE RATIONAL AND LOGICAL	The Scripture full of mistakes — pessimism.

Neo-orthodoxy leaped to what I call the "upper story" in order to try to find something which would give hope and meaning to life. The "lower story" is the position to which their presuppositions would have rationally and logically brought them.

So theology too has gone below the line of despair:

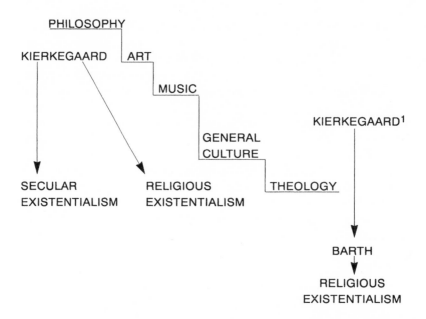

The new theology has given up hope of finding a unified field of knowledge. Hence, in contrast to biblical and Reformation theology, it is antitheology.

Seen in this way, it is naive to study the new theology as if it were a subject on its own. Some years ago I was speaking at one of the most solidly biblical seminaries in the world. I began by saying that if our American theologians had understood the Armory Show of 1913 in New York, when modern art was first shown in the United States, perhaps the big denominations in American would not have been captured by the liberals in the thirties. By that time, the trends which would come much later in theology were being foreshadowed in art. This is why, earlier in this book, I gave 1913 as such an important date. Had the Christians understood the message of this art at the Armory Show, it would have been a tremendous opportunity to have been ahead rather than to have lagged behind. Conservative theology has not yet caught up. It has been far too provincial, isolated from general cultural thinking.

Karl Barth was the doorway in theology into the line of despair. He continued to hold to the day of his death the higher (negative) critical theories which the liberals held and yet, by a leap, sought to bypass the two rational alternatives — a return to the historic view of Scripture or an acceptance of pessimism. After the first edition of his *Commentary on the Epistle to the Romans*, he no longer acknowledged his debt to Kierkegaard. However, still believing the higher critical theories, his "leap" continued to be the base of his optimistic answers. In later years, as his followers have carried his views forward he drew back from their consistent extensions. But as Kierkegaard, with his leap, opened the door to existentialism in general, so Karl Barth opened the door to the existentialistic leap in theology. As in other disciplines, the basic issue is the shift in epistemology.

He has been followed by many more, men like Reinhold Niebuhr and Paul Tillich. They may differ in details, but their struggle is the same — it is the struggle of modern man who has given up a unified field of knowledge. As far as the theologians are concerned, they have separated religious truth from contact with science on the one hand and history on the other. Their new system is not open to verification; it must simply be believed.

Thus, though their position rests on a "liberal" view of Scripture, yet in the new theology the real issue is now not only their view of Scripture but their divided view of truth.

CHAPTER TWO

Modern Mysticism: Despair Beyond Despair

The despair of modern man takes many forms. It is despair in depth in that it tends to use formulations and forms which seem to give hope and yet in the nature of the case lead to more profound depths of despair.

Modern nihilism is the simplest form of despair. For example, it is transparently clear in Gauguin's painting *What? Whence? Whither?* and in *musique concrète.* Nihilism accepts the conclusion that everything is meaningless and chaotic.

The second level of despair is the acceptance of the dichotomy we have been talking about:

A BLIND OPTIMISTIC HOPE OF MEANING,
BASED ON A NONRATIONAL LEAP OF FAITH

THE RATIONAL AND THE LOGICAL WHICH GIVES NO MEANING

To feel the force of this deeper form of despair, we must keep in mind that the "upstairs" and the "downstairs" of this dichotomy are in two totally watertight compartments. There is *no* interchange between them. *The downstairs has no relationship to*

57

meaning; the upstairs no relationship to reason. Rationalistic man, having given up the methodology of antithesis (if a thing is true, the opposite is not true), has been forced to a nonunified concept of knowledge, and consequently to a resultant monstrous total antithesis between rationality and meaning.

In the rational downstairs, man is only a machine. In the nonrational upstairs, he is less than a Greek "shade." The films *Last Year in Marienbad, Juliet of the Spirits,* and *Blow-Up* put this latter point with force, showing man as he is upstairs without categories.

The dichotomy was presented as an answer to the despair of simple nihilism; but this dichotomy is really a more profound form of despair. It means that man has both divided any unified concept of knowing and also — and this is worse — divided the unity of himself, because rationality is a part of every man. The individual man cannot even communicate to himself in his own thinking except on the basis of antithesis. So he thinks, "I love her," or "The blossom on that tree is beautiful," but these are a quite meaningless jumble of words unless they stand in antithesis to the possibilities that he dislikes her or that the blossom is ugly. This means in practice that a man cannot totally reject the methodology of antithesis, however much his system leads him to it, unless he experiences the total alienation from himself brought about by some form of mental breakdown.

Therefore, those who have sponsored the modern dichotomy of reason and meaning have not been able to live with it. Jean-Paul Sartre quarreled with Camus because he felt Camus was not being consistent to their basic presuppositions. This was true, but then neither was Sartre consistent when he signed the Algerian Manifesto. When he did this, it was not simply in order to authenticate his being by a neutral act of the will (as in the illustration of the old lady we gave concerning Sartre in Chapter Two of Section One), because then it would have made no difference if he had done the opposite. Rather, it was because he took up a deliberately moral attitude and said it was an unjust and dirty war. His left-wing political position which he took as a moral issue is another illustration of the same inconsistency.

As far as many secular existentialists have been concerned, from the moment Sartre signed the Algerian Manifesto he was regarded as an apostate from his own position and toppled from his place of leadership of the avant-garde.

What was true of Camus and Sartre — that they could not live with the conclusions of their system — has been true for men on every step of the line of despair, whether in philosophy, art, music or literature. The result of not being able to stand in the honest integrity of their despair on either level (that of nihilism or that of a total dichotomy between reason and meaninglessness) has led to modern thought being shifted yet one stage further into a *third* level of despair, a level of mysticism with nothing there.

Theology and Semantic Mysticism

Neo-orthodoxy at first glance seems to have an advantage over secular existentialism. It appears to have more substance in its optimistic expressions than its secular counterpart. As we have seen, one difficulty of the final experience is that no one has found a way to communicate this experience — not even to himself. But in the new theology, use is made of certain religious words which have a connotation of personality and meaning to those who hear them. Real communication is not in fact established, but an *illusion* of communication is given by employing words rich in connotations. Expressing the inexpressible existential experience in religious connotation words gives an illusion of communication.

Carl Gustav Jung (1875-1961) speaks of the collective unconscious which emerges from the race as a whole. I think he is mistaken in his thinking, especially in the evolutionary origin which he gives it. And yet there is a certain memory in a culture that is carried on in *its language*. Such a language-related memory, I suggest, is a better explanation for what Jung calls the collective unconscious.[1]

The Use of Words and Symbols

Every word has two parts. There is the dictionary definition, and there is the connotation. Words may be synonymous by definition, but have completely different connotations. Therefore we find that when such a symbol as *the cross* is used, whether in writing or painting, a certain connotation stirs the mind of people brought up in a Christian culture, even if they have rejected Christianity. (Of course, the use of words in this way does not only apply to the symbols of Christianity, but to those of other religions as well.) So when the new theology uses such words, without definition, an illusion of meaning is given which is pragmatically useful in arousing deep motivations.

This is something beyond emotion. An *illusion of communication and content* is given so that when a word is used in this deliberately undefined way, the hearer "thinks" he knows what it means. The use of the word *pantheism* is a good example. Though it really speaks of something absolutely and finally impersonal, yet the *theism* part of the word causes a reaction of acceptance, since *theism* carries overtones of personality. Now suppose you were to substitute the word *pan-everythingism* (which is what it really means). The whole reaction would be different.

It is also important to notice that the new theology has tried to draw on the prestige surrounding the use of the word *symbol* in the scientific world, but with a totally changed concept of symbol. In science the use of symbol is valuable in that it is *well-defined*, at least for two people, the person who uses it and at least one other. It is said that when Einstein first propounded his theory of relativity, perhaps only three or four men in the world understood it at first sight. But he would never have written it in the form he did if at least these three or four had not been able to understand it as a well-defined communication of content. So the scientific symbol has become an important tool for writing increasingly lengthy formulae with greater accuracy. In other words, it has value according to the sharpness of its definition.

But the new theology uses the concept of symbol in exactly the opposite way. The only thing the theological and scientific uses have in common is the *word* symbol. *To the new theology, the usefulness of a symbol is in direct proportion to its obscurity.* There is connotation, as in the word *god*, but there is no defini-tion. The secret of the strength of neo-orthodoxy is that these reli-gious symbols with a connotation of personality give an illusion of meaning, and as a consequence it appears to be more optimistic than secular existentialism. One could not find a clearer example of this than Tillich's phrase "God behind God."

At first acquaintance this concept gives the feeling of spiritu-ality. "I do not ask for answers, I just believe." This sounds spir-itual, and it deceives many fine people. These are often young men and women who are not content only to repeat the phrases of the intellectual or spiritual *status quo.* They have become rightly dissatisfied with a dull, dusty, introverted orthodoxy given only to pounding out the well-known clichés. The new theology sounds spiritual and vibrant, and they are trapped. But the price they pay for what seems to be spiritual is high, for to operate in the upper story using undefined religious terms is to fail to know and func-tion on the level of the whole man. The answer is not to ask these people to return to the poorness of the *status quo*, but to a living orthodoxy which is concerned with the whole man, including the rational and the intellectual, in his relationship to God.

Whenever men say they are looking for greater reality, we must show them at once the reality of *true* Christianity. This is real because it is concerned with the God who is there and who has spoken to us about Himself, not just the use of the symbol *god* or *christ* which sounds spiritual but is not. The men who merely use the symbol ought to be pessimists, for the mere *word* god or the *idea* god is not a sufficient base for the optimism they display.

Speaking rationally, the new theologians are in the same position as Pierre Schaeffer with his *musique concrète*. But it is as though they were asking us by a leap of faith to hear *musique concrète* as if it were the same as the unity and diversity of J. S. Bach. This is the kind of "believism" which is demanded by this theology. *The optimistic jump is a necessity because man is still created in the image of God, whatever he may say about himself, and as such he cannot go on living in meaninglessness.* The jump of the new theology is upon the basis of religious and therefore personal terms which give the connotation of personality, meaning and communication. It is no more than a jump into an undefinable, irrational, semantic mysticism.

Even here the new theology is not unique. There are many secular parallels for this use of the stratagem of connotation words to try to alleviate the despair caused by the loss of a rational meaning and purpose. We will now look at some examples in the different disciplines.

The Origins of Semantic Mysticism — Leonardo da Vinci

The best way to understand how modern man has been forced, often against his natural inclination, into these various levels of despair, which he has tried to alleviate by the use of loaded connotation words in the upper story, is by looking at one of the most brilliant men of the Renaissance, Leonardo da Vinci (1452-1519).

Leonardo died as the Reformation was beginning. Francis I, king of France, who took him to France where he died, was the king to whom John Calvin addressed his *Institutes*. As a Renaissance humanist, Leonardo gave an answer to life which was a complete contrast to what the reformers were giving.

The Reformation gave rise to a definite culture, particularly in Northern Europe, and the humanistic elements of the Renaissance (of which Leonardo was a spokesman) ultimately gave rise to the despair of modern man which is now destroying that culture. Listen to what Giovanni Gentile, known, until his death, as Italy's greatest modern philosopher, has to say about Leonardo:

> The unity of the inward illuminates the fantasy; and the intellect comes to break up this unity into the endless multiplicity of sensible appearances. Hence the anguish and the innermost tragedy of this universal man, divided between his irreconcilable worlds, leaves in the mind an infinite longing, made up as it were of regret and sadness. It is the longing for a Leonardo different from the Leonardo that he was, one who could have gathered himself up at each phase and remained, closed himself off either altogether in his fantasy or altogether in his intelligence.[2]

What Gentile is saying is this — that Leonardo as the first real mathematician in the modern sense really understood the problem with which modern man is now grappling. He understood that if man starts with himself alone and logically and rationally moves through mathematics, he never comes to a universal, only to particulars and mechanics. The problem can be formulated thus: how can finite man produce a unity which will cover these particulars? And if he cannot, how can these particulars have unity and meaning for him?

Leonardo was a Neoplatonist who followed Ficino, and he tried to resolve the dilemma on his canvas by painting the soul. The use of the word *soul* here does not mean the Christian idea of soul, but the universal. Thus, for example, he thought he could, as a painter, sketch the universal baby which would cover the particulars for all babies. But he never achieved it, any more than Picasso did in painting his abstractions. But there is a strong difference between these two. Leonardo was not a modern man and therefore could not accept modern man's irrational solution. So Leonardo died in despondency, for he would never let go of his hope of finding a unified field of knowledge which included both the universal and the particular, both mathematics and meaning. Had he been willing to accept an irrational dichotomy, as those who have extended the thinking of Kierkegaard have, he could have been at ease. But for him this would have been an impossible answer; men of his day, humanists though they may have been, would never have accepted such an irrational solution.

So there is an unbroken line from the humanism of the Renaissance to the modern philosophy, but in the process modern man accepted the "leap" which philosophers of the past would never have accepted, and have moved into three areas of despair: (1) simple nihilism; (2) the acceptance of the absolute dichotomy; (3) a semantic mysticism based on connotation words.

This new mysticism does not expect to find a unified field of knowledge. It has firmly concluded that the awful contradictory situation whereby meaning and true rationality (the upper and lower story) are irrevocably separated is intrinsic to the nature of the universe. On the other hand, the old romanticism never gave up the search to find a rational unity between the upper and lower story. This is the fundamental difference between them.

Nature and Grace

This difference exists between the new mysticism and the old formulation of nature and grace.

After Thomas Aquinas (1227-1274), men spent much time in seeking the relationship and possible unity of nature and grace. Before him, the emphasis of the Byzantine thinkers was all on heavenly things, while after him, as a result of Aquinas's emphasis on Aristotle, nature also became important. This was given expression in the painting of Cimabue (1240-1302) and Giotto (1267-1337) and in the poetry of Dante (1265-1321), Boccaccio (1313-1375) and Petrarch (1304-1374). By the time the full Renaissance had flooded Europe, nature had all but overwhelmed grace. We can represent their thought in this way:

GRACE, the higher:	God the Creator; Heaven and heavenly things, the unseen and its influence on the earth; man's soul; unity.
NATURE, the lower:	The created; earth and earthly things; the visible and what it (nature + man) does on earth; man's body; diversity.

At first glance this might seem to be the same as the modern dichotomy:

THE NONRATIONAL AND NONLOGICAL

THE RATIONAL AND LOGICAL

But the difference between these two concepts is so fundamental as to be qualitative rather than quantitative.

The struggle concerning *nature and grace* was the struggle to
find a meaning for these together, and philosophers always hoped
for a unity between the two on the basis of reason. (In passing,
one must add that this question of nature and grace can only be
solved by the full biblical system, and it was because these men
tried to find a rationalistic or humanistic answer that they failed.)
But modern man has given up all hope of finding a unified
answer to the question of nature and grace. Therefore he
describes it differently, and the difference in his formulation indicates his despair.[3] Modern man now formulates it like this:

CONTENTLESS FAITH (NO RATIONALITY)

RATIONALITY (NO MEANING)

To understand this at a profound level is to comprehend how
completely modern man's despair *is* despair. All the new theology
and mysticism is nothing more than a faith contrary to rationality,
deprived of content and incapable of contentful communication.
You can bear "witness" to it, but you cannot discuss it. Rationality and faith are out of contact with each other.

Let us now change the horizontal line a bit and see it as a line
of *anthropology*. Below this line is the area of man. All that the
new theology has above this line is the "philosophic other," a
metaphysical infinite, which is unknown and unknowable. Like
this:

GOD EQUALS THE PHILOSOPHIC OTHER, UNKNOWN AND UNKNOWABLE

THE WORD GOD UNDEFINED

The new theology is totally below the line of anthropology. It
knows nothing of man being created in the image of God, nor of
God revealing Himself truly in the Scriptures.

*The important thing to note is that while for them nothing can
be known above the line, yet nevertheless they go on using the
word god.*

Probably the best way to describe this concept of modern theology is to say that it is faith in faith, rather than faith directed to an object which is actually there. Some years ago at a number of universities I spoke on the topic, "Faith v. faith," speaking on the contrast between Christian faith and modern faith. The same word, *faith*, is used, but has an opposite meaning. Modern man cannot talk about the object of his faith, only about the faith itself. So he can discuss the existence of his faith and its "size" as it exists against all reason, but that is all. Modern man's faith turns inward.

In Christianity the value of faith depends upon the object towards which the faith is directed. So it looks outward to the God who is there, and to the Christ who in history died upon the cross once for all, finished the work of atonement, and on the third day rose again in space and in time. This makes Christian faith open to discussion and verification.

On the other hand, the new theology is in a position where faith is introverted because it has no certain object, and where the preaching of the *kerygma* is infallible since it is not open to rational discussion. This position, I would suggest, is actually a greater despair and darkness than the position of those modern men who commit suicide.

CHAPTER THREE

Modern Mysticism in Action: Art and Language

The Tension of Being Man

There is a real tension in being a modern man because no one can live at ease in the area of despair. A Christian knows that this is because man has been made in the image of God and though man is fallen, separated from God by his true guilt, yet nevertheless he has not become a machine. The fallenness of man does not lead to *machineness*, but to *fallen-manness*. Therefore, when people feel this utter despair, there is a titanic pressure, like being extruded against all the long history of reasoned thinking to accept a dichotomy, and then later to accept some mysticism which gives an illusion of unity to the whole.

I remember sitting in a Lyons' Corner House near Marble Arch in London some years ago, talking to a brilliant young physicist. I asked him about the latest work he was doing, and he told me about a new idea that he thought might solve Einstein's problem concerning electromagnetism and gravity. He became very enthusiastic about this, because I knew enough about the subject to stimulate him, and he was far away in his thought. Then I brought him back by saying, "This is fine for the Christian, who really knows who he is, to say that the material universe may finally be reduced to energy particles moving in opposite directions in a vortex, but what about your naturalistic colleagues? What happens to them when they go home to their wives and families at night?"

He paused for a moment and then said, "Oh, Dr. Schaeffer, they just have to live in a dichotomy."

The very "mannishness" of man refuses to live in the logic of the position to which his humanism and rationalism have brought him. To say that I am only a machine is one thing; to live consistently as if this were true is quite another.

Again I remember one night crossing the Mediterranean on the way from Lisbon to Genoa. It was a beautiful night. On board the boat I encountered a young man who was building radio stations in North Africa and Europe for a big American company. He was an atheist, and when he found out I was a pastor he anticipated an evening's entertainment, so he started in. But it did not go quite that way. Our conversation showed me that he understood the implications of his position and tried to be consistent concerning them. After about an hour I saw that he wanted to draw the discussion to a close, so I made one last point which I hoped he would never forget, not because I hated him, but because I cared for him as a fellow human being. He was accompanied by his lovely little Jewish wife. She was very beautiful and full of life, and it was easy to see, by the attention he paid her, that he really loved her.

Just as they were about to go to their cabin, in the romantic setting of the boat sailing across the Mediterranean and a beautiful full moon shining outside, I finally said to him, "When you take your wife into your arms at night, can you be sure she is there?"

I hated to do it to him, but I did it knowing that he was a man who would really understand the implications of the question and not forget. His eyes turned, like a fox caught in a trap, and he shouted at me, "No, I am not always sure she is there," and walked into his cabin. I am sure I spoiled his last night on the Mediterranean, and I was sorry to do so. But I pray that as long as he lives he will never forget that when his system was placed against biblical Christianity, it could not stand, not on some abstract point, but at the central point of *his own humanity*, in the reality of love.

In a different but related way this is also true of a man like Bernard Berenson (1865-1959). He was the world's greatest expert on Renaissance art during his lifetime. He graduated from Harvard, and lived most of his later life in Florence. He was such an authority on his subject that when he dated and priced a picture, it was generally accepted as decisive. He was a truly "modern" man and accepted sexual amorality. Therefore, when he took Mary Costelloe (sister of the American essayist Logan Pearsall Smith) away from her husband, he lived with her for a number of years until her husband died and then married her (the Costelloes' marriage was Roman Catholic, and so a divorce could not be arranged). When Berenson eventually married her, they had an agreement that they would both be free to engage in extramarital affairs, and both took advantage of the agreement many times. They lived this way for forty-five years. When anyone chided Berenson he would simply say, "You are forgetting the animal basis of our nature." Thus he was perfectly willing in his private life to accept a completely animal situation.

But in contrast to this, he expressed a completely different view where his real love and true integration point — Renaissance art — was concerned. "Bernard Berenson found that modern figure painting in general was not based on seeing, on observing, but on exasperation and on the preconceived assumption that the squalid, the sordid, the violent, the bestial, the misshapen, in short . . . low life was the only reality!"[1] In the area of sexual morals, he was perfectly willing to live consistently to his view of life as an animal. But in the area which had become his attempt to find an integration point, that of art, he was prepared to say that he disliked modern art *because it is bestial!* No man like Berenson can live with his system. Every truly modern man is forced to accept some sort of leap in theory or practice, because the pressure of his own humanity demands it. He can say what he will concerning what he himself is; but no matter what he says he is, he still is man.

These kinds of leaps, produced in desperation as an act of blind faith, are totally different from the faith of historic Christianity. On the basis of biblical Christianity a rational discussion and consideration can take place, because it is fixed in the stuff of history. When Paul was asked whether Jesus was raised from the dead, he gave a completely nonreligious answer, in the twentieth-century sense. He said: "There are almost 500 living witnesses; go and ask them!"[2] This is the faith that involves the whole man, including his reason; it does not ask for a belief into the void. As the twentieth-century mentality would understand the concept of religion, the Bible is a nonreligious book.

Mysticism in Art — Paul Klee and Salvador Dali

In one of his writings, Paul Klee (1879-1940) speaks of some of his paintings as though they were a kind of artistic Ouija board. (A Ouija board is a little board used by spiritists upon which participants place their hands and then ask questions. The spirits are supposed to move the board and spell out the answers.)

Paul Klee and men like him use art like a Ouija board; not because they believe there are any spirits there to speak, but because they hope that the universe will push through and cause a kind of automatic writing, this time in painting. It is an automatic writing with no one there, as far as anyone knows, but the hope is that the "universe" will speak.

Klee not only painted and drew, but also wrote about his work to explain what he was doing. In his essay "Creative Confession"[3] he has this to say: "People used to reproduce things seen on earth — things which had been or would be seen with pleasure. Today the reality of visible objects has been revealed and the belief has been expressed that, in relation to the universe, the visible is only an isolated case and that other truths exist latently and are in the majority." He goes on to employ a phrase, "plastic polyphony," which means "elements and their regrouping." To Klee the word *elements* is a technical term. He defined this term in his essay as "points, the energy of the line, surface and space." He is referring to these as he continues: "But that [the elements] is not art in its most exalted form. In its most exalted form there is behind the ambiguity a last mystery and at that point the light of the intellect dies away miserably." So he too allows himself to be placed in the dichotomy. He hopes that somehow art will find a meaning, not because there is a spirit there to guide the hand, but because through it the universe will speak even though it is impersonal in its basic structure.

I would add that in almost all forms of the new mysticism there is a growing acceptance of the ideas of pantheism. The West and the East are coming together, and these pantheistic concepts are one of the strongest elements in the semantic mysticism of which we are speaking.

In his earlier days Salvador Dali (1901-) was a surrealist. As such he united the teaching of Dada with the concept of the

Freudian unconscious, because this is what surrealism is. But at a certain point he could stand this no longer, and so he changed.

One day he painted his wife and called the picture, *The Basket of Bread*. It is obvious from looking at the picture that on that day he really loved her. It is the same kind of situation as when Picasso wrote on his canvas, "I love Eva." Before I had heard of any change in Dali, I saw a reproduction of this picture, and it was obvious that there was something different being produced. It is significant that his wife has kept this painting in her private collection.[4]

So on this particular day Dali gave up his surrealism and began his new series of mystical paintings. He had, in fact, already painted two other pictures with the title *A Basket of Bread*, one in 1926 and one in 1945. These just showed baskets of coarse Spanish bread. But this third picture, also painted in 1945, was of his wife Galarina, and shows her with one breast exposed. Her name is written on the picture, and the wedding ring is prominent on her finger.

The second painting in his new style was called *Christ of Saint John of the Cross*, painted in 1951, which now hangs in the Glasgow Art Gallery. Salvador Dali has written about this painting in a little folder on sale in the museum: "In artistic texture and technique I painted the *Christ of Saint John of the Cross* in the manner in which I had already painted my *Basket of Bread*, which even then, more or less unconsciously, represented the Eucharist to me."

What does he mean? He means that when he looks at his wife one day, really loving her, and paints her with one breast exposed, this is equated by him to the Eucharist; not in the sense that anything really happens, either in the Roman Catholic Mass, or that anything really happened back there in Palestine 2,000 years ago, but his love jarred him into a modern type of mysticism.[5]

In this painting he differed from Picasso's *J'aime Eva*. As far as we know, Picasso never really went beyond the problems of his individual loves; but to Dali it became the key to a mysticism. In order to express the leap that he felt forced to take, he picked up Christian symbols, not to express Christian concepts, but a nonrational mysticism.

After these two paintings he painted his next Crucifixion, called *Corpus Hyperoubus*, now in the Metropolitan Museum of Art in New York, and then later *The Sacrament of the Last*

Supper, which is in the National Gallery of Art in Washington. This latter painting expresses his thought vividly. As the viewer looks at Jesus he can see the background showing through him; he is a mist. This is no Christ of history. Above him stands a great human figure with arms outspread, its head cut off by the top edge of the picture. No one is sure what this figure is. However, it is strongly reminiscent of the "Yakso" which in Hindu art and architecture often stands behind the "saviors" ("savior" here bearing no relation to the Christian idea). Yaksa and Yaksi connect vegetable life with man on one side and the complete concept of pantheism on the other. I *think* this is what Dali is also saying by this cut-off figure in the painting. Whether this is so or not, the symbolism of the form of the "room" is clear because it is constructed by means of the ancient Greek symbol of the universe.

In an interview Dali connects this religious interest of his later life with science's reduction of matter to energy: ". . . the discoveries in quantum physics of the nature of energy, that matter becomes energy, a state of dematerialization. I realized that science is moving toward a spiritual state. It is absolutely astonishing, the mystical approach of the most eminent scientists: the declaration of Max Planck and the views of Pierre Teilhard de Chardin, a great Jesuit scientist: that man in his constant evolution is coming closer and closer to a oneness with God."

Here he relates his own mysticism and the religious mysticism of Teilhard de Chardin to impersonal dematerialization rather than to anything personal. He is quite correct and need not have confined himself to modern liberal Roman Catholicism, but could also have included the Protestant forms of the new theology as well.

It is perfectly possible to pick up nondefined Christian symbols or words and use them in this new mysticism, while giving them opposite meanings. Their use does not necessarily imply that they have Christian meanings. Dali's secular mysticism, like the new theology, gives the philosophic other or impersonal "everything" a personal name in order to get relief by connotation from meaninglessness.

Mysticism in Language — Heidegger
Because he could not live with his existentialism, Heidegger as an older man moved his position. His new position rests on these

points: (1) Something, *Being*, is there; (2) This something makes itself known; (3) Language is one with Being and makes Being known. We can never know rationally about what is there (brute fact), but language does reveal that something is there. Thus language is already itself an interpretation (a hermeneutic).

He postulates that there was long ago an era, before Aristotle (and before the entrance of rationality), when men spoke in Greek in such a way that the universe was speaking ideally. He then tries to transfer this to all of man's language — not the content of what is spoken, but simply the existence of language. In this way, the existence of language becomes for Heidegger the mysticism by which he tries to find relief from his previous existential dichotomy. It is semantic mysticism because it does not deal with content in language but simply language as such. Man speaking becomes the mouthpiece of the impersonal "What is" (Being). The impersonal and unknown Being speaks through the being who speaks (verbalizes) — that is, man.

This could be a quite correct view if there were any personality behind man to speak meaningfully to and through man. But because Heidegger is a rationalist and begins absolutely from himself, he cannot accept that a person behind man has spoken. So he is shut up to his particular form of semantic mysticism. The word *language* is a connotation word which seems to involve personality. The whole solution hangs on the connotation inherent in the one word *language*.

At the end of his book *What Is Philosophy?*[6] he says that in our modern day this use of language is found particularly in the poet. So the conclusion of this view is that we are to listen to the poet. This does not mean we are to listen to the *content* of what the poet says, but to listen to the fact that *there is a speaking which exists*. That is all.

There is a strong parallel between Klee and Heidegger here. Both speak of their hope that somehow the universe will speak either through art or language. However, Heidegger has much more importance in the flow of modern thought because by using connotation words he has become the father of a new form of the new theology — the new liberalism. There is no real difference between Heidegger's secular mysticism and the mysticism of the new theology.

CHAPTER FOUR

Modern Mysticism in Action: Music and Literature

Mysticism in Music—Leonard Bernstein and John Cage
Leonard Bernstein's *Third Symphony*, which he has recorded with the New York Philharmonic Orchestra, gives an example of the same kind of mysticism in music. It is called the *Kaddish Symphony* (1963).[1] The Kaddish is a Jewish form of music, a Hebrew paean to God. This form Bernstein (1918-) has absorbed into his modern unbelief. Now in contrast to the original Kaddish, this one indicates that we can know nothing of what is there, but can only listen to the musician, for he will make something of god for us. In this modern Kaddish, the concert hall is "the sacred house," and in it the artist will "continue to create you, Father, and you, me." Art is seen as the one surviving miracle god has left.

The reviewer Leonard Marcus, in an early 1965 issue of *High Fidelity Magazine*, rightly concludes his review in this way: "Theologians have always had artists to bridge the gap to their flock. Now, for better or worse, the antitheologian has a powerful, artistic statement." Marcus correctly brings together the new secular mysticism and the new theology. There is no certainty that a god is there, but the poet, musician, or art as art is the prophet where there is no certainty about anything.

We should love good art. But art as art does not have the right to speak *ex cathedra* regardless of content.

There was a very interesting Profile of John Cage (1912-) in *The New Yorker*,[2] part of which we shall quote in considering his music. The Profile says: ". . . what he is proposing is, essentially, the complete overthrow of the most basic assumptions of Western art since the Renaissance." We have already seen that the young person caught in the modern generation is 400 years away from the previous generation. So Cage is seeking to overthrow a total concept stretching right back at least through those 400 years to the Renaissance. The article goes on to say what it is he is smashing:

> The power of art to communicate ideas and emotions, to organize life into meaningful patterns, and to realize universal truths through the self-expressed individuality of the artist are only three of the assumptions that Cage challenges. In place of a self-expressive art created by the imagination, tastes, and desires of the artist, Cage proposes art born of chance and indeterminacy.

If God exists and we are made in His image we can have real meaning, and we can have real knowledge through what He has communicated to us. If this is taken away, we are left only with man and his finite self-expression. At this point all one has is the expression of the individual man. But Cage quite logically sees that this will not do, and so he carries man's dilemma further, smashes self-expression, and leaves chance speaking. This is the basis of his music. The article continues:

> A number of painters, writers, and composers in various countries have been moving in roughly the same direction in recent years, and many of them have used chance methods as a means to that end.

It names the Frenchman Pierre Boulez, and the American Jackson Pollock. In the last stage of his painting Jackson Pollock (1912-1956) put his canvases horizontally on the floor and dripped paint on them by chance. After doing this for some time he felt he had exhausted the chance method. This left him no way to go on further, so he committed suicide. The article continues:

> Painters like the late Jackson Pollock in America and Georges Mathieu, in France, whose goal was and is certainly not anonymity, have nevertheless sought in the accidents of throwing or dripping paint a key to creation beyond the reach of the artist's conscious mind and will.

In other words, this is not merely self-expression; it is in the same direction as Paul Klee's art — the hope that through the art form the impersonal universe will somehow speak as the artist works. *The New Yorker* Profile continued:

> Then just as he was beginning to feel ready to stop what he called "window-shopping" among the world's philosophies and religions, he discovered Zen-Buddhism. Dr. Daisetz T. Susiki, the first important spokesman for Zen in the West, had recently come to America and was giving weekly lectures at Columbia University that were attended by psychoanalysts, scientists, painters, sculptors, and philosophy students. They were also attended by Cage. . . . By a rare coincidence, Cage found this Oriental idea perfectly summed up in the words of seventh-century English music commentator Thomas Mace, who once wrote that the function of music was "to sober and quiet the mind, thus rendering it susceptible to divine influences."

However, it is important to note that when Mace wrote this in the seventeenth century he had the idea not only that music would quieten the mind, but that afterwards the personal God could speak to it. God was really speaking. Cage, on the other hand, had come to the point where there is nobody there to speak to him. This is the fundamental distinction. Notice how clearly this comes across in a later section of the article:

> One day, young Wolff brought a copy of an ancient Chinese book — the "I Ching" or "Book of Changes," which Pantheon had just published in an English translation. "The moment I opened the book and saw the charts and the hexagrams that were used for obtaining oracles according to the tossing of coins or yarrow sticks, I saw a connection with the charts I had been using," Cage says. "It was immediately apparent to me that I could derive a means of composing from these operations, and right then and there I sketched out the whole procedure for my 'Music of Changes,' which took its title from the book. I ran over to show the plan to Morty Feldman, who had rented a studio in the same building, and I can still remember him saying, 'You've hit it.'"

Back in the Chinese culture long ago the Chinese had worked out a system of tossing coins or yarrow sticks by means of which the spirits would speak. The complicated method which they developed made sure that the person doing the tossing could not allow his own personality to intervene. Self-expression was eliminated so that the spirits could speak.

Cage picks up this same system and uses it. He too seeks to get rid of any individual expression in his music. But there is a very great difference. As far as Cage is concerned, there is nobody there to speak. There is only an impersonal universe speaking through blind chance.

Cage began to compose his music through the tossing of coins. It is said that for some of his pieces, lasting only twenty minutes, he tossed the coin thousands of times. This is pure chance, but apparently not pure enough; he wanted still more chance. So he devised a mechanical conductor. It was a machine working on cams, the motion of which could not be determined ahead of time, and the musicians followed that. Or as an alternative to this, sometimes he employed two conductors who could not see each other, both conducting simultaneously; anything, in fact, to produce pure chance. But in Cage's universe nothing comes through in the music except noise and confusion or total silence. All this is below the line of anthropology. Above the line there is nothing personal, only the philosophic other, or the impersonal everything.

There is a story that once, after the musicians had played Cage's total chance music, as he was bowing to acknowledge the applause, there was a noise behind him. He thought it sounded like steam escaping from somewhere, but then to his dismay realized it was the musicians behind him who were hissing. Often his works have been booed. However, when the audience boo at him they are, if they are modern men, in reality booing the logical conclusion of their own position as it strikes their ears in music.

Cage himself, however, is another example of a man who cannot live with his own conclusions. He says that the truth about the universe is a totally chance situation. You must just live with it and listen to it; cry if you must, swear if you must, but listen and go on listening.

Towards the end of *The New Yorker* Profile we read this:

In 1954 . . . the sculptor David Weinrib and his wife moved into an old farmhouse on a tract of land in Stony Point, Rockland County, forty miles from New York, which the Williamses had bought. Cage lived and worked in an attic room that he shared with a colony of wasps, and often took long, solitary walks in the woods. His eye was caught right away by the mushrooms that grew so abundantly in Rockland County, in all shapes, and sizes and brilliant colors. He started to collect books on mushrooms and to learn everything he could about them, and he has been doing so ever since. After all, mushroom hunting is a decidedly chancy, or indeterminate pastime.

No matter how much mycology one knows — and Cage is now one of the best amateur mycologists in the country, with one of the most extensive private libraries ever compiled on the subject — there is always the possibility of a mistake in identification. "I became aware that if I approached mushrooms in the spirit of my chance operations, I would die shortly," Cage said not long ago. "So I decided that I would not approach them in this way!"

In other words, here is a man who is trying to teach the world what the universe intrinsically is and what the real philosophy of life is, and yet he cannot even apply it to picking mushrooms. If he were to go out into the woods and begin picking mushrooms by chance, within a couple of days there would be no Cage!

We have said before that the ideas of modern people are destroying what "man" is in himself. But not only that, their views cut right across what the existence of the form and structure of the external universe indicates as well. As we see in the dilemma of Cage and his mushrooms, they cannot live on the basis of a consistent application of their views in regard to the universe, any more than they can in regard to man.

However, while Cage is forced into a hopeless dichotomy with his mushrooms, with his music he has continued to live consistently with his position, even though his music is nothing more than noise or silence. He has resisted the pressure to dress up impersonal Being in connotation words or sounds. Most modern men have not had this much courage.[3]

Mysticism in Literature — Henry Miller

In the writing of his earlier books, Miller (1891-1980) had not just set forth something which is dirty in a trivial sense, but he had succeeded in murdering everything which is meaningful, including sexual things. In these books he expressed his antilaw position, in every sense. However, Miller is another man who could not stand by his own position. Many others have been destroyed in their inner lives by his books, but he was not able to be so tough-fibered. So he joins the growing list of modern men who have accepted the new mysticism. In his later life Miller held to a pantheistic view of the world.

His later views are very cogently and consistently expressed in the Preface which he wrote to the French edition of Elie Favre's *History of Art*. He calls his preface, "A Sense of Wonder."[4] This is an important title, for it implies that he is going to contrast the "sense of wonder" with the intellect. And this in fact is what he does. For example, he says, "Above all, he [Elie Favre] was a devout worshipper of the creative spirit in man. His approach, like our own Walt Whitman's, was nothing less than cosmic." This already has a pantheistic ring about it. Later on he continues, "What impact his work may have today, particularly on the young who are almost immune to wonder and mystery because of all the knowledge which has been crammed into their heads, I do not know." This is a significant sentence because he has set the intellect and knowledge against the sense of wonder. One's intellect would lead one only to the lower story of rationality and logic where there is no meaning in life, only machines. But in contrast to this one has a sense of wonder which bypasses the rational, and this sense is very much related to the use of the word *awe* that is so much in vogue today. The intellect is divorced and rejected.

A swift glance at Miller's introduction might lead the reader to think that he had suddenly become a Christian. He uses words and phrases which sound so correct. Thus, "In investing himself (man) with the powers of a god, man has divorced himself from God — and from the universe as well. That which was his inheritance, his gift and salvation, he has vitiated through pride and arrogance of intellect. He has not only turned his back on the source, he is no longer aware that there is a source, the source from which, as the Good Book says, all blessings flow."

It sounds most credible, and there is more to come: "The spirit which first breathed upon the waters will create anew. . . . There is no last word, unless it be the Word itself: 'In the beginning was the Word, and the Word was with God, and the Word was God.'" We are forced on the basis of this to ask, "Is Henry Miller one of us?" But the answer, which is negative, can be gleaned from a full reading of what he has said in this Preface.

He says, "It forces me, the knowledge of this truth, to observe as I have again and again that behind all creation, whether human or divine, lies an impenetrable mystery. All those epoch-making names which he [Favre] reels off in his works, devastating forces when one thinks on it, because forces for good and evil simultaneously, all bear witness to the inexhaustible energy which invests even the tiniest particle of matter and demonstrate in miraculous everyday fashion that what is called matter or substance is but the adumbration of a luminous reality too powerful for our feeble senses to apprehend." There is a strong connection here with what Salvador Dali says concerning the dematerializing of the universe.

A little further on he writes, "It is only embryonic man to be sure who is staging this drama of annihilation." (The preceding context shows that what he is speaking of is the dropping of the atomic bomb.) "The true self is indestructible." You may think that he is referring to the individual soul here, but it is not so. He continues, "Art more than religion offers us the clue to life," and at the beginning of the Preface, "Did he [Walt Whitman] not say somewhere that religions are born from art and not vice-versa?" We can link this statement with what Heidegger says about the poet: *just listen* to the poet. Miller tells us to look at art and not to worry about the content; art as art is the new prophet. "Art more than religion offers us the clue to life, but only to those who practice it, those who dedicate themselves, and who come ultimately to realize that they are but the humble instruments whose privilege it is to unveil the glory and the splendor of life." Rationality brings one to the content of Miller's books, *The Tropic of Cancer* and *The Tropic of Capricorn* and the rest. Therefore the intellect and knowledge must be put aside, and a leap made into contentless mysticism and awe.

But the man who has arrived at this point does not really matter anyway. "What matters, in the ultimate, if for a few aeons of time this creature called man remains in abeyance, absent from the scene?" In other words, go ahead and drop the bomb, what does it matter?

The usual way of thinking, as exhibited by the shock shown following the publication of Nevil Shute's book, *On the Beach*, would be: if everybody is going to be annihilated tomorrow, what is the use of writing a poem or making a painting today? But Henry Miller and his new pantheistic mysticism would claim that it would not matter if tomorrow the oceans were calm and there were no man on the shore. *Individual* man does not matter.

However, he goes on to say, "This is an end, one of many — not *the* end. What man is in essence can never be destroyed. The spirit which first breathed upon the waters will create anew." He is not speaking of a personal God. He is using these connotation words to speak of pantheistic cycles. Everything, including human history, is being viewed as a series of cycles. What happens to the individuals does not matter, the cycles roll on! This is a thoroughgoing pantheistic idea. The man who can never be destroyed is not individual man, but just Man springing from the universe of what is. "Man, this embryonic form of a being which has neither beginning nor end, will give way to man again. Present-day man, the man of history, need not and will not be the last word. There is no last word, unless it is the Word itself. 'In the beginning was the Word, and the Word was with God, and the Word was God.'"

To Miller, the world can only be conceived of in pantheistic terms, in endless cycles which repeat themselves. But in order to give it a personal sound, he uses biblical terms and phrases. In this way he utilizes the connotation attached to these forms, which comes out of the history of our race, to heighten the feeling of the semantic mysticism he has accepted.

The Preface is concluded with these words: "Let us therefore, in reviewing this vast panorama of human achievement, think less of what was accomplished by the giants who parade throughout these volumes and more of the imperishable energy of which they were the fiery sparks. All may be lost, all forgotten, if only we remember that nothing is lost, nothing ever forgotten. 'As it was in the beginning, is now, and ever shall be: world without end.'" And with this devastating blow at the individual, who counts as nothing except as a part of the energy of the universe to which he is united as a spark to the fire, Miller finishes his Preface.

It must be plain that the later Henry Miller cannot in any sense be called a Christian. He is doing the same as Salvador Dali and the new theologians are doing — namely, using Christian symbols to give an illusion of meaning to an impersonal world which has no real place for man.

This is Henry Miller, the writer of *The Tropics*, who in this Preface takes up basically the same position as the new theologians. We have ample warning not to accept the "god words" of many modern theologians without being certain that they, like Henry Miller, are not using these words to give an *illusion* of meaning.

CHAPTER FIVE

The Next Phase of Modern Theology

God Is Dead — Or Almost So!

It should be quite clear by this time that the mysticism of the new theology does not separate it from the intellectual climate of the second half of the twentieth century. Rather, it once more relates the new theology to the surrounding secular climate and consensus, because, as we have seen, the parallel secular semantic mysticisms are found in every one of the steps in the line of despair — philosophy, art, music, and the general culture.

The new theology itself has an internal problem through separating the "upstairs" and "downstairs" into such watertight compartments. It came to this position:

FAITH = NO RATIONALITY; I.E., NO CONTACT WITH THE COSMOS
(SCIENCE) OR HISTORY

ALL RATIONALITY—INCLUDING SCIENTIFIC EVIDENCE AND HISTORY

The tension is very strong because such a total antithesis between rationality and "religious values" destroys the unity of the individual man, and he becomes divided within himself. This gave rise to a deep-seated restlessness amongst many of the modern theologians. A new attempt was made to breach the dichotomy. This attempt took two forms: one form is to try to find a unity of the whole on the level of the lower story, the other on the level of the upper.

The first form was widely publicized as the "God is dead" theology. Its adherents chose the downstairs as a place to find a unity, and they have dispensed with God altogether, including the term *God*. When the real God-is-dead men say God is dead, they do not merely mean that God is being listened to very little in our modern secular world, *but that He never existed*. They put their emphasis on the lower story and seem to deny the validity of the upper story altogether. This leaves only the word *Jesus* downstairs. But we must be careful not to get caught out, for if we turn our backs for a moment these men use the word *Jesus* as a banner with *upper-story* overtones. We will represent it like this:

GOD IS DEAD

GOD IS DEAD   JESUS . . . . . .

These men chose to call themselves "Christian atheists." They are atheists in the classical sense of that word; and they are Christians only in the sense that they have adopted for themselves Bonhoeffer's definition of Christ, "The man for others." They really differ little from today's optimistic humanists.

This is fairly straightforward; in one sense these men are no longer "having their cake and eating it too." They lost all connotation words except the term *Jesus Christ*, and even this, to the extent to which they defined it, they have ruined as a connotation word. But they were not being left quiet in their atheism. The upper-story men who still want to keep the use of the connotation words fought back.

In actual fact this theology has a dead god in both the upper and lower stories:

THE NEW MYSTICISM—ALL KNOWLEDGE CONCERNING GOD IS DEAD, ANY CONCEPT OF A PERSONAL GOD IS DEAD—THEREFORE GOD IS DEAD

ON THE BASIS OF RATIONALITY GOD IS DEAD

A typical exponent of the upper-story mentality was Paul Tillich (1886-1965). When asked at Santa Barbara, shortly before he died, if he ever prayed, he said, "No, but I meditate."

Thus in the upper story it is not only that *man* becomes a "shade," but the god of the new mysticism is no more than a mist which becomes only Being or Pan-everything. If we look at the theologians operating in this upper story we may say that they are either atheists in the classical sense, or pantheists — depending on how one looks at it. Thus their god is also dead.

This vague pantheism, which we have noted in secular thinking also, creates problems for those brought up within the Christian faith. Thus for example, Bishop Robinson, a British theologian, in his writing insisted that God is actually transcendental after all. He spoiled it, however, when he went on to say that man is transcendental too (which, fascinatingly enough, is the exact word Sir Julian Huxley used about man), for this therefore means that "transcendental" really equals "nontranscendental," and we are back at square one.

When the theologians and the secular men use this word *transcendental*, I would suggest that they mean by it the things that surprise them when they examine man, things they could not expect to find on the basis of what they believe about man's origin. Or again, it means little more than Henry Miller's "sense of wonder." So when they use this word without definition, it does not thereby mean that they have escaped from the charge of pantheism.

As far as God and man are concerned, modern theology then is like this:

NONRATIONAL, NONLOGICAL = FAITH	No categories for God, all knowledge concerning God is dead. The personal God is dead. No faith categories for man or his meaning.

ALL RATIONALITY; I.E.,	ALL CONTACTS WITH THE COSMOS (SCIENCE), = ALL CONTACTS WITH HISTORY	God is dead and man is a machine

A Quest by the Upper-Story Men

This position is a high price to pay for rejecting historic Christianity, the Christianity of the Scripture and the Creeds. But instead of returning to the biblical position, they are making a further attempt to solve their difficulties apart from it. The next move was an attempt by the upper-story men to put a toe back into history.

Karl Barth, who can be said to be the inaugurator of all this, felt the need to try to hold back from the logical extension of his position developed by his followers. In his last years he spoke of an historic resurrection of Christ. It is not quite as simple as that, however; for on the presuppositions of these theologians, the Bible contains historical and scientific errors. Thus dichotomy, a divided concept of truth, is necessarily central in their concept of "religious truth."

They cannot go back to the old liberalism — there can be no going back to the old quest for the historical Jesus, for it failed. However, if they give up the division of truth (*which has been their answer to the old liberalism when it failed*), then they have to face again what the older liberalism faced: on the one side nihilism (God is dead, man is dead, and meaning is dead); on the other side, the answer of the historic and Reformation Christian position which states that there is a personal God, that man is made in His image, that He has communicated to His creature by a propositional, verbalized revelation of content, and thus this is able to be considered by the whole man. Or to put it very briefly, the only way out of their dilemma is to move back to the methodology of antithesis. Until they do this, no amount of talk about a physical resurrection of Christ will touch the heart of the discussion.[1]

This need to get a toe back into history by the upper-story men was ably dealt with in an article in *The Listener*, April 12, 1962, by Dr. John Macquarrie, then lecturer in Systematic Theology at Glasgow University, later at Union Theological Seminary, New York. We quote a relevant part of it. The article is called, "History and the Christ of Faith":

A NEW QUEST

It should not surprise anybody that some of Bultmann's disciples, afraid of losing themselves in a world of myth and make-believe, have turned again to the question of the historical Jesus. Gunther Bornkamm, for instance, says that "we must look for the history in the Kerygma" and that we should not be resigned or skeptical about the historical Jesus. Does this mean that we must reopen the interminable arguments as to whether this incident or that saying took place as recorded? It cannot mean this, for the earlier quest of the historical Jesus showed that no clear answers are to be had. The new quest is intended to be different; but unfortunately there is a good deal of confusion among those who have embarked on it as to what is intended, and Bultmann himself has been severely critical of some of them. He is content to hold that our knowledge is confined to the bare fact that there was a Jesus who was crucified, and does not extend to the manner of his life or personality.

My own view is that the Christian theologian needs to assert a minimal core of factual history if the Kerygma is to present us with a way of life that is realistic and not culled from a dream world. This minimal core is not a short list of essential incidents or sayings, but simply the *assertion*[2] that at the source of the Christian religion there was an actual historical instance of the pattern of life proclaimed in the Kerygma.

Here Dr. John Macquarrie acknowledges that the theologians cannot go back to the old liberal exhaustive search for the historical Jesus, for that ended in total failure. His own solution is the *assertion* that Jesus lived such and such a life. In other words, just say it is so.

There are two main attempts by the upper-story theologians to get a toe back into history in order not to lose themselves and God "in a world of myth and make-believe."

Firstly, there is the use of the phrase "God's saving acts in history." This sounds very fine. But they do not mean by this that God has literally entered our space-time world at a particular point in order to begin and complete man's salvation. They mean that God is in some way saving or redeeming *all* history, including the most grizzly acts of sin and cruelty which have been committed by individuals or groups.

Secondly, they just use the *word* "history" — this can take several forms. Macquarrie says that we must assert that certain events are history. The events are chosen arbitrarily and, of course, are not open to real historical enquiry. Or else they use the Bible as a vehicle for continuous existential experiences. They say such experiences did happen back in Bible times, but the way they are expressed in the Bible has no necessary relationship to the way the experience occurred. The biblical accounts are just the faulty cultural expression of that day. This way of looking at history is closely related to what the new Heidegger said about the mystique of language. These new theologians, both Protestants and some in the Roman Catholic Church, attempt therefore to manipulate biblical language as a help towards present existential experience.[3]

To these men language is always an interpretation, and therefore the words of the Bible are already an interpretation of the unknowable thing which occurred. The upper-story men are left with a flood of words.

Thus neither the lower-story men nor the upper-story men did very well in trying to ease the tension. But we can be sure the hopeless attempts will continue, for on one hand their dichotomy is uncomfortable in the extreme; and on the other hand, they must keep it because this division of truth is the essence of the new theology.

Today's Opportunity for the New Theology

In spite of the confusion among the new theologians and in spite of the fact that they are not really saying anything unique among the secular mysticisms which surround us, yet there are reasons why this is a moment of opportunity for the new theology to take a privileged place in our culture, a place theology has not enjoyed for a long time. It could become a leader in tomorrow's affairs.

For some time society has been in danger of losing all sociological form. Men are facing a society without structure, and they want to fill the void that has appeared. For a long time Reformation ideas formed the basis of North European culture, and this extended to include that of the United States and English-speaking Canada, etc. But today that has been destroyed by the relativism both inside and outside the churches. Hence historic Christianity is now a minority group. Even the memory of past cultural forms is becoming weak. Moreover, the structural form of Northern Europe is not the only one which is being battered to pieces. For example, one can see that Marxist Russia is moving in the same direction though at a slower rate because of its totalitarian controls. That is why modern Russian artists are being prevented from speaking freely, for they are carrying the modern thinking into Russian life.

Society cannot function without form and motivation. As the old sociological forms have been swept away, new ones must be found or society breaks down altogether. Sir Julian Huxley stepped in at this point with his suggestion that religion has a real place in modern society. But, he contended, it must be understood that religion is always evolving and that it needs to come under the control of society.

This suggestion is not as ridiculous as it sounds, even coming from a convinced humanist, if one understands the mentality of our age. The prevailing dialectical methodology fits itself easily into religious forms. After all, Senghor has said that on the basis of dialectical thinking his country would follow Teilhard de Chardin. It is well to remember that now men think dialectically on *both* sides of the Iron Curtain.

Teilhard de Chardin, incidentally, illustrates that "the progressive" Roman Catholic theologians are further away from historic Reformation Christianity than classical Roman Catholicism, because they are also dialectical thinkers.

The orthodox Roman Catholic would have told me that I was bound for Hell because I rejected the true Church. He was dealing with a concept of absolute truth. But the new Roman Catholic who sits at my fireside says, "You are all right, Dr. Schaeffer, because you are so sincere." In the new Roman Catholicism such a statement often means that the dialectical method has taken over.

Therefore we are not surprised to find that the new Heidegger has followers, such as Karl Rahner, among some of the leading progressive Roman Catholic thinkers; and others such as Hans Kung have been strongly influenced by neo-orthodoxy. It is important to note that the position on Scripture by the Vatican Council shifted in the same direction, and men such as Raymond Panikkar,[4] Dom Bede Griffiths, O.S.C.[5] and Anthony de Mello, S.J.[6] are proclaiming a synthesis between Roman Catholicism and Hinduism. Truly these men have come a long way, but it is not in the direction of biblical Christianity. Neal Ascherson, under the dateline April 29, 1967, reported in a London newspaper the conversations at Marienbad between the Paulus Society, which follows Karl Rahner, and Roger Garaudy, who was chief theoretician of the French Communist Party. He showed a streak of genius when he used the heading: "This Year in Marienbad — Where Marxist and Catholic Meet," thus relating this dialogue to the loss of categories as it was stressed by the film *The Last Year at Marienbad.*

The time, therefore, does seem right for this new theology to give the needed sociological forms and motivations. Of course, society could look elsewhere amongst the secular mysticisms for a new evolving religion, but the new theology has some strong advantages.

Firstly, the undefined connotation words that the new theology uses are deeply rooted in our Western culture. This is much easier and more powerful than using new and untraditional words.

Secondly, these men control many of the large denominations of Protestantism, and if the progressives in the Roman Catholic Church consolidate their position, that Church as well. The liberal Roman Catholic theologians already have great influence in the Roman Catholic Church, and they use it widely. This gives the liberal theologians the advantage of functioning within the organizational stream of the Church, and thus both its organization and linguistic continuity is at their disposal.

Thirdly, people in our culture in general are already in process of being accustomed to accept nondefined, contentless religious words and symbols, without any rational or historical control. Such words and symbols can be filled with the content of the moment. The words *Jesus* or *Christ* are the most ready for the manipulator. The phrase *Jesus Christ* has become a contentless banner which can be carried in any direction for sociological purposes. In other words, because the phrase *Jesus Christ* has been separated from true history and the content of Scripture, it can be used to trigger religiously motivated sociological actions directly contrary to the teaching of Christ. This is already in evidence, as for example in the "new" morality being advocated by many within the Church today.

So there is open to the new theology the possibility of supplying society with an endless series of religiously motivated arbitrary absolutes. It is against such manipulated semantic mysticism that we do well to prepare ourselves, our children and our spiritual children.

How Historic Christianity Differs from the New Theology

CHAPTER ONE

Personality or a Devilish Din

Our forefathers used the term *systematic theology* to express their view that Christianity is not a series of isolated religious statements, but that it has a beginning and flows on to an end. Each part relates to each other part and to the whole, and to what stands first in the system. It is perfectly possible that such a systematic understanding of Christianity can become a dead thing, but let us not despise the word *systematic* as if it were automatically a corpse.

Rightly understood, Christianity as a system has the answers to the basic needs of modern man. In this it differs from the new theology, which has no adequate basis upon which to give answers which will stand up to the test of rationality and the whole of life as we must live it.

The first basic need is caused by the lack of certainty regarding the reality of individual personality. Every man is in tension until he finds a satisfactory answer to the problem of who he himself is.

The biblical Christian answer takes us back first to the very beginning of everything and states that personality is intrinsic in what is; not in the pantheistic sense of the universe being the extension of the essence of God (or what is), but that a God who is personal on the high order of Trinity created all else. Within the Trinity, before the creation of anything, there was real love and real communication.[1] Following on from this statement, the Bible states that this God who is personal created man in His own image. A personal God created all things freely in a nondeterminate fashion, and man is created in a special situation — what I would call a special circle of creation. He is the image of this kind of God, and so personality is intrinsic to his makeup. God is personal, and man is also personal.

It might be helpful to illustrate the situation in this way. Imagine you are in the Alps, and from a high vantage point you can see three parallel ranges of mountains with two valleys in between. In one valley there is a lake, but the other is dry. Suddenly you begin to witness what sometimes happens in the Alps — a lake forming in the second valley where there was none before. As you see the water rising, you may wonder what its source is. If it stops at the same level as the lake in the neighboring valley, you may, after careful measurements, conclude that there is a possibility that the water has come from the first valley. But if your measurement shows that the level of the second lake is twenty feet higher than the first, then you can no longer consider that its source may be from the neighboring valley and you would have to seek another explanation. Personality is like that; no one has ever thought of a way of deriving personality from nonpersonal sources.

Therefore, biblical Christianity has an adequate and reasonable explanation for the source and meaning of human personality. Its source is sufficient — the personal God on the high order of Trinity. Without such a source men are left with personality coming from the impersonal (plus time, plus chance).

The two alternatives are very clear-cut. Either there is a personal beginning to everything, or one has what the impersonal throws up by chance out of the time sequence. The fact that the second alternative may be veiled by connotation words makes no difference. The words used by Eastern pantheism; the theological words such as Tillich's "Ground of Being"; the secular shift from mass to energy or motion — all eventually come back to the impersonal, plus time, plus chance. If *this* is really the only answer to man's personality, then personality is no more than an illusion, a kind of sick joke which no amount of semantic juggling will alter. Only some form of mystical jump will allow us to accept that personality comes from impersonality. This was the position into which Teilhard de Chardin was forced. His answer is only a mystical answer of words.

Because these men will not accept the only explanation which can fit the facts of their own experience, they have become metaphysical magicians. No one has presented an idea, let alone demonstrated it to be feasible, to explain how the impersonal beginning, plus time, plus chance, can give personality. We are distracted by a flourish of endless words, and lo, personality has appeared out of the hat! This is the water rising above its source. No one in all the history of humanistic, rationalistic thought has found a solution. As a result, either the thinker must say man is dead, because personality is a mirage; or else he must hang his reason on a hook outside the door and cross the threshold into the leap of faith which is the new level of despair.

A man like Sir Julian Huxley has clarified the dilemma by acknowledging, though he is an atheist, that somehow or other, against all that one might expect, man functions better if he acts as though God is there. This sounds like a feasible solution for a moment, the kind of answer a computer might give if you fed the sociological data into it. God is dead, but act as if He were alive. However, a moment's reflection will show what a terrible solution this is. Ibsen, the Norwegian, put it like this: if you take away a man's lie, you take away his hope.[2] These thinkers are saying in effect that man can only function as man for an extended period of time if he acts on the assumption that a lie (that the personal God of Christianity is there) is true. You cannot find any deeper despair than this for a sensitive person. This is not an optimistic, happy, reasonable or brilliant answer. It is darkness and death.

Imagine that a universe existed which was made up only of liquids and solids, and no free gases. A fish was swimming in this universe. This fish, quite naturally, was conformed to its environment, so that it was able to go on living. But let us suppose that by blind chance, as the evolutionists would have us believe, this fish developed lungs as it continued swimming in this universe without any gases. Now this fish would no longer be able to function and fulfill its position as a fish. Would it then be higher or lower in its new state with lungs? It would be lower, for it would drown. In the same way, if man has been kicked up by chance out of what is only impersonal, then those things that make him man—hope of purpose and significance, love, motions of morality and rationality, beauty and verbal communication—are ultimately unfulfillable and are thus meaningless. In such a situation, is man higher or lower? He would then be the lowest creature on the scale. The green moss on the rock is higher than he, for it can be fulfilled in the universe which exists. But if the world is what these men say it is, then man (not only individually but as a race), being unfulfillable, is dead. In this situation man should not walk on the grass, but respect it—for it is higher than he!

The Logical End of Denying Personality

In the 1960s while I was giving a series of lectures at an American college, I received an anonymous note from one of the students. This note read: "A question I would like you to answer on one of your broadcast talks if you could: with reference to what you have said about some artists destroying man, what should I do? I *want* to destroy too." Many of the students of the 1960s sought to destroy (as the Punks do in the 1980s). And if the smashing of things stops, and people come to the conclusion that there are no better answers than they have been given, the general apathy of the later 1970s and the early 1980s dominates.

In face of this modern nihilism, smashing, or the apathy, Christians are often lacking in courage. We tend to give the impression that we will hold on to the outward forms whatever happens, even if God really is not there. But the opposite ought to be true of us, so that people can see that we demand the truth of what is there and that we are not dealing merely with platitudes. In other words, it should be understood that we take this question of truth and personality so seriously that if God were not there, we would be among the first to have the courage to step out of the queue. Insofar as we show this to be our attitude, maybe the far-out ones will begin to take us seriously and listen to what we have to say. If they do not see that in our integrity we would join with them in destruction, "dropping out," or apathy, except that we know we have an adequate basis for personality and the reality of morals, then they will not and should not listen to us.

According to the tape recording of my lecture that night in the 1960s, my answer to the student who said that he or she wanted to destroy was: "I would say to you tonight that if we live in this intrinsically impersonal world, dress it up if you will with the word *pantheism*, either in the Eastern thought or in the new theology, or if I speak of it in secular terms, if this is what I am, and all men are, with their aspirations, if this is all they are, unfulfillable products of chance, a sterile sport, then come beside me, because I wish to destroy too. If indeed these ideas are your ideas, you should stand beside such a man to destroy. If I am an artist, I should wish to destroy. I should say with the Dutch artist, Karel Appel, 'I do not paint, I hit.' I should say with John Cage, 'It is only chance,' with a resultant noise and a devilish din. But further, let us understand, in such a case, what love will mean. Love will mean facing the problem of pushing the button that destroys the human race. This is the distinction between there being a real meaning of personality that makes it reasonable to love and have compassion, a real reason to keep humanity alive; and no real meaning, and therefore a love resulting in that which should destroy. This then would be nearer to the truth of what is, and what will eventually happen, not only to the individual, but to the human race.

"This person who wrote this note understands something. In such a case I would ask him to come to my side and destroy, but I would ask him also to be honest in considering the other possibility, that all this is not so, but rather that we started with a personal beginning and therefore there is intrinsic meaning to personality, my personality, and other men's personality in this universe. This is the distinction between the two positions. The things we have considered are not only theoretical things — they are things that cut down into the warp and woof of the understanding of life. We would say indeed to the man who would destroy a romantic concept which has no base, destroy it indeed. Demand a realistic answer. Here we stand face to face with the real issue of the new theology and the whole new thought."

This is the crux of the matter; either an intrinsically personal "what is," in the sense of a creation by the personal God, or John Cage's devilish din!

CHAPTER TWO

Verifiable Facts and Knowing

In historic Christianity a personal God creates man in His own image, and in such a case there is nothing that would make it nonsense to consider that He would communicate to man in verbalized form. Why should He not communicate in verbalized form when He has made man a verbalizing being, in his thoughts as well as in communication with other men? Having created man in His own image, why should He fail to communicate to that verbalizing being in such terms? The communication would then be three ways: God to man, and vice versa; man to man; and man to himself. Someone may raise queries as to whether in fact such communication has taken place, but, in this field of reference, it is neither a contradictory nor a nonsense statement. Such a concept would be nonsense if one had the presupposition of a totally closed field of cause and effect. But if you are a person who holds that cause and effect has been and is totally closed, then you need to ask if such a view as yours really stands up to all we know, and specifically whether your worldview explains why people verbalize to each other.

Why should God not communicate *propositionally* to the man, the verbalizing being, whom He made in such a way that we communicate propositionally to each other? Therefore, in the biblical position there is the possibility of verifiable facts involved: a personal God communicating in verbalized form propositionally to man — not only concerning those things man would call in our generation "religious truths," but also down into the areas of history and science.

God has set the revelation of the Bible in history; He did not give it (as He could have done) in the form of a theological textbook. Having set the revelation in history, what sense then would it make for God to give us a revelation in which the *history* was wrong? God has also set man in the *universe*, which the Scriptures themselves say speaks of this God. What sense then would it make for God to give His revelation in a book that was wrong concerning the universe? The answer to both questions must be, "No sense at all!"

It is plain, therefore, that from the viewpoint of the Scriptures themselves there is a unity over the whole field of knowledge. God has spoken, in a linguistic propositional form, truth concerning Himself and truth concerning man, history and the universe.

Here is an adequate basis for the unity of knowledge. The unity encompasses both the upstairs and the downstairs. This is the answer to the discussion of the unity between nature and grace and modern man's question of knowledge above and below the line of anthropology. The unity is there because God has spoken truth into all areas of our knowledge.

At the same time, one must avoid the opposite mistake of saying that because God has communicated truly concerning science, all scientific study is wasted. This is a false deduction. To say that God communicates *truly* does not mean that God communicates *exhaustively*. Even in our human relationships we never have exhaustive communication, though what we do have may be true. Thus, as far as our position in the universe is concerned, though the infinite God has said true things concerning the whole of what He has made, our knowledge is not thereby meant to be static. Created in His image, we are rational and, as such, we are able to, and intended to, explore and discover further truth concerning creation.

God says, in effect, "Learn of the truth that I have made in the external world." Finite man in the external universe, being finite, has no sufficient reference point if he begins absolutely and autonomously from himself; thus, he needs *certain knowledge*. God gives us this in the Scriptures. With this in mind the scientist can understand, in their ultimate relationships, the truths that he is looking at. Thus scientific study in itself can be to the glory of God, for here man is functioning properly in the universe in which God has placed him. He is telling us what is truly there, and he is adding to the store of knowledge of his fellowmen.

The new theology cannot give an adequate framework for ascertaining facts and knowledge. It cannot because it removes the possibility of communication at the only two points that can be discussed and verified, namely history and the universe. Religious truths cannot be discussed once they are divorced from the other two. Bezzant, in the book *Objections to Christian Belief*,[1] well illustrates how crucial this matter of truth is. Though Bezzant is an older type of liberal, and though the book is destructive in many ways, nevertheless he has seen this point very clearly. Having attacked the historic Christian position, he then suddenly swings around and trains all his guns on neo-orthodoxy: "When I am told that it is precisely its immunity from proof which secures the Christian proclamation from the charge of being mythological, I reply that immunity from proof can 'secure' nothing whatever except immunity from proof and call nonsense by its name." This is a tremendous sentence. At this point he has truly understood the fatal flaw of modern theology. It may dress up its position with all kinds of clothes, but it remains irrational and what it is talking about can never really be discussed, because it is no longer open to verification.

I remember hearing a speaker in England say at a conference at which we were both speaking, "Bultmann is infallible for twenty minutes each Sunday." That is, all the new theology can do is preach and ask the people to believe or not to believe, without the exercise of reason. In this way, man becomes *less than* the fallen man of the biblical Christian position.

The historic Christian answer concerning verifiable facts and knowing depends on who God is, on who is there. The God who is there according to the Scriptures is the personal-infinite God. There is no other god like this God. It is ridiculous to say that all religions teach the same things when they disagree at the fundamental point as to what God is like. The gods of the East are infinite by definition — the definition being "god is all that is." This is the pan-everythingism god. The gods of the West have tended to be personal but limited; such were the gods of the Greeks, Romans and Germans. But the God of the Bible, Old and New Testaments alike, is the infinite-personal God.

It is this God who has created various orders of creation, like this:

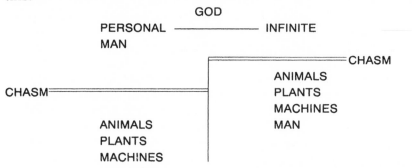

How then is God's creation related to Himself and to itself? On the side of God's infinity there is a break between God and the whole of His creation. I am as separated from God in the area of His being the Creator and infinite, I being the creature and finite, as is the atom or energy particle. I am no closer to God on this side than the machine.

However, on the side of God's *personality*, the break comes between man and the rest of creation. In terms of modern thought this is a dynamic concept, of which modern man and modern theology know nothing. So Albert Schweitzer identified himself with the hippopotamus, for he did not understand that man's relationship is upward; and therefore he looked downward to a creature which does many of the same things as himself. But on the *side of personality*, if our relationship is upward, then everything concerning man's "mannishness" is in place.

The biblical Christian says that, on the side of personality, man can know God truly, though he cannot know God exhaustively. Unlike the new theology, he is not trapped by the two alternatives of knowing God completely or not knowing Him at all. We are not shut up to a total comprehension of the infinite.

Modern man and the new theology have only this:

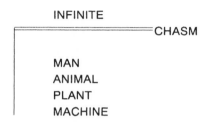

Modern man has driven a wedge between the personal and the infinite and says that personality equals finiteness. He has equated personality with limitedness. But the Christian says that the only *limitation* which personality intrinsically must have is that it cannot be impersonal at the same time. To say that personality must always be limited in other ways is to try to make an absolute which one cannot make. Indeed, human personalities are limited in other ways, but this is because they are created and finite, not because they are personal.

Personality As Such Cannot Necessarily Imply Limitedness
A man from Israel who was an atheist wrote and asked me, "What sense does it make for a man to give his son to the ants, to be killed by ants, in order to save the ants?" I replied that it makes no sense at all for a man to give his son to the ants, to be killed by the ants, in order to save the ants, because man *as a personality* is totally separated from the ants. Man's only relation to the ants is in the areas of Being and creaturehood. However, in the area of personality man's relationship is upward to God, and therefore the incarnation and death of the Son of God for the sake of man's salvation are sensible.

The reasonableness of the incarnation, and the reasonableness of communication between God and man, turn on this point — that man, as man, is created in the image of God.

Divine and Human Communication
The communication which God has made to man is true, but that does not mean it is exhaustive. This is an important distinction which we must always bear in mind. To know anything exhaustively we would need to be infinite, as God is. Even in Heaven we shall not be this.

God has communicated to man, not only about the cosmos and history, but also about Himself. And God's attributes so communicated are meaningful to God, the author of the communication, as well as to man, the recipient of the communication. What God has revealed concerning His attributes is not only meaningful below the line of anthropology. The line of anthropology is not a brazen heaven over our heads which cannot be penetrated. The God who has spoken is not the unknowable infinite above the line. The God who has created man in His own image communicates true truth about Himself. Therefore, this need not be thought of as only an existential experience or contentless "religious ideas." We have true knowledge, for as the Scriptures say so simply and overwhelmingly, when God wrote the Ten Commandments on stone,[2] or when Jesus spoke to Paul on the Damascus road in the Hebrew language,[3] a real language was used subject to grammars and lexicons, a language to be understood.

When we talk to each other, there are three theoretical possibilities in our exchange of words. The first is that we fail to communicate at all, probably because our backgrounds are too far apart. The second possibility is the very opposite of this: that when we use terms we all give to them exactly the same meaning, so that we understand each other exhaustively. Neither of these concepts stands careful analysis.

The weakness of saying that one is not able to communicate at all was shown up in a conversation I once had with an undergraduate at St. Andrews University in Scotland. Other students had said they found him difficult to talk to, that what he said did not seem to make sense, and they were at a loss to know where to start. I had half an hour to spend with him. After only two minutes of talking in his room, he said, "Sir, I don't think we are communicating." I started again. About two minutes later he repeated himself, "Sir, I don't think we are communicating." I began to think that the half-hour would be spent in a nonsense session! I looked down and noticed that he had very thoughtfully prepared a lovely tea. There it all was, pot of tea, cups and so on. So I said rather gruffly to him, "Give me some tea!" He was taken aback, but he passed me a cup, full of tea. Then I said, "Sir, I think we are communicating." From then on we had a very effective conversation.

The simple fact is that no one who takes the trouble to study linguistics really believes that just because we bring our own background to the words, idioms and phrases we use, we cannot communicate at all. On the other hand we need to be warned: just because we know what *we* mean by a term does not mean that the person to whom we speak understands precisely the same thing. That would be very naive. In human conversation we have true communication, but it is never exhaustive. This is the third and only realistic possibility in our speaking to one another.

If we transfer the possibility of communication from the realm of human intercourse to that of the Divine-human, then the same principle applies. The biblical presentation indicates that because man is made in God's image, the problem of God communicating to him is not of an absolutely different order from that of man speaking to man. We are finite, God is infinite, but we can understand truly.

Love Is More Than a Word
This conception of the way in which God communicates gives a world which is different from the one in which modern man is struggling. It means quite simply that man no longer needs to destroy, nor to sink into apathy; there is a reason to live, build and love. Man is no longer adrift. We may demonstrate how different the two worlds are by considering the meaning of love. Modern man quite properly considers the conception of love to be overwhelmingly important as he looks at personality. Nevertheless, he faces a very real problem as to the meaning of love. Though modern man tries to hang everything on the word *love*, love can easily degenerate into something very much less because he really does not understand it. He has no adequate universal for love.

On the other hand, the Christian does have the adequate universal he needs in order to be able to discuss the meaning of love. Among the things we know about the Trinity is that the Trinity was before the creation of everything else and that love existed between the persons of the Trinity before the foundation of the world.[4] This being so, the existence of love as we know it in our makeup does not have an origin in chance, but from that which has always been.

Above the line of anthropology, God the Father loved God the Son before the creation of the world—this is on a horizontal plane. On the vertical plane God also loves me, who am below the line of anthropology. The word and act of love has crossed the line of anthropology downward. Then, also on the vertical plane, I am to love God. The word and act of love has crossed the line of anthropology upward. Finally, I am commanded by God to love my wife, children, neighbors, below the line of anthropology. Here is the word and act of love horizontally below the line of anthropology.

The relationships of love can be shown like this:

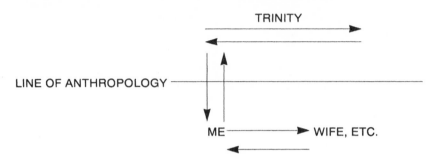

Two things follow from this. Firstly, I can know something truly of what it means when I am told that God the Father loves the Son. When I see a boy and a girl walking together arm in arm, obviously showing love towards each other, I do not know all that they feel towards one another; yet because I too love my woman, my looking at them is not as a dog would look at them. It is not exhaustive, but it is true understanding — there is true correlation. And when I talk about love existing in the Trinity before creation, I am not talking gibberish. Though I am very far from plumbing its depths when applied to God Himself, yet the word *love* and the reality of love when Christ spoke of the Father loving Him before the foundation of the world has true meaning for me.

Secondly, when I love my woman, its meaningfulness is not exhausted by the context of this one individual relationship alone, nor even the love of all men for all women, nor all finite love. The validity and meaning of love rest upon the reality that love exists between the Father and Son in the Trinity. When I say I love, instead of this being a nonsense word, it has meaning. It is rooted in what has always been in the personal relationship existing in the Trinity before the universe was created. Man's love is not a product of chance that has no fulfillment in what has always been. Love is a thing not only of meaning, but of beauty and wonder to be nourished in joy.

This then is the second great difference between Christianity and the new theology. The latter gives no basis for verifiable facts and knowing, including knowing the content of words used about God above the line of anthropology. Thus, such a word as *love* has no meaning or value beyond the realm of limited man. *It should be obvious by this time that Christianity and the new theology have no relationship except the use of a common terminology with different meanings.*

CHAPTER THREE

The Dilemma of Man

We have considered two areas in which Christianity and the new theology fundamentally disagree — personality and knowledge. There is one more area where disagreement could not be more radical, and that is the question of man and his dilemma. Anyone with sensitivity and concern for the world can see that man is in a great dilemma. Man is able both to rise to great heights and to sink to great depths of cruelty and tragedy. Modern man is desperately struggling with the concept of man in his dilemma. Most of the paintings of the crucifixion today, Salvador Dali's for example, are not of Christ dying on the cross in history. They are using the Christ-symbol to exhibit man in agony.

Of course, it is possible to try *not* to get involved in man's dilemma; but the only way not to get involved in the dilemma of man is by being young enough, well enough, having money enough, and being egotistic enough to care nothing about other human beings.

As we consider this question of man and his dilemma, only two possible explanations can be given. The first explanation suggests a *metaphysical cause*. This says, in effect, that man's problem is that he is too small, too finite to wrestle with the factors that confront him. The second explanation is quite different; it puts man's dilemma down to a *moral cause*. If the first explanation is right, then one is bound to conclude that man has always been in the same dilemma. Thus, for example, the new theology says that man has always been fallen man. This also means that there is no moral answer to the problem of evil and cruelty. Because man, whether somehow created by a curious thing called god or kicked up out of the slime by chance, has always been in this dilemma, the dilemma is part of what being "man" is. And if this is what man intrinsically is, and he has always been like this, then the French art historian and poet Baudelaire is right when he says, "If there is a God, He is the Devil." This statement was simply the logical deduction from the premise that man, with all his cruelty and suffering, is now as he always has been. At this point Baudelaire was consistent and refused to give any kind of romantic alternatives as an explanation. But the Bible says that this is not the situation.

One day I was talking to a group of people in the room of a young South African in Cambridge University. Among others, there was present a young Indian who was of Sikh background but a Hindu by religion. He started to speak strongly against Christianity, but did not really understand the problems of his own beliefs. So I said, "Am I not correct in saying that on the basis of your system, cruelty and noncruelty are ultimately equal, that there is no intrinsic difference between them?" He agreed. The people who listened and knew him as a delightful person, an "English gentleman" of the very best kind, looked up in amazement. But the student in whose room we met, who had clearly understood the implications of what the Sikh had admitted, picked up his kettle of boiling water with which he was about to make tea, and stood with it steaming over the Indian's head. The man looked up and asked him what he was doing, and he said with a cold yet gentle finality, "There is no difference between cruelty and noncruelty." Thereupon the Hindu walked out into the night.

If the metaphysical explanation to man's dilemma is given, it is not an abstraction. In such a case, all that moves man at his best is really meaningless.

The Scandal of the Cross

There is a serious commentary given on man and his dilemma in Albert Camus' book *The Plague*.[1] The story is about a plague brought by rats into the city of Oran at the beginning of the Second World War. On the surface it reads like an account of any city that might have been struck by such a tragedy. But Camus intends a deeper understanding. Therefore he confronts the reader with a serious choice: either he must join the doctor and fight the plague, in which case, says Camus, he will then also be fighting God; or he can join with the priest and not fight the plague, and thus be antihumanitarian. This is the choice; and this is the dilemma which Camus faced and which all those face who, like him, do not have the Christian answer.[2]

However, the new theology has no answer to the dilemma either. Its followers are caught equally in Camus' problem and Baudelaire's proposition. All that is reasonable in their position, based on observing the world as it is, says God is the Devil. Nevertheless, because they do not want to live with this conclusion, by an act of blind faith they say God is good. This, they say, is what the "scandal of the cross" is — to believe that God is good against all the evidence open to reason. But this is emphatically not the "scandal of the cross." The true scandal is that however faithfully and clearly one preaches the gospel, at a certain point the world, because it is in rebellion, will turn from it. Men turn away in order not to bow before the God who is there. This is the "scandal of the cross."

Modern theology may use the term *guilt*, but because it is not orientated in a true moral framework, it turns out to be no more than guilt-feelings. And as in their system they have no place for true guilt, the death of Jesus on the cross takes on an entirely different meaning. Following from this, the work of Christ and the ministry of the Church becomes one of two things: either a basis for sociological motivation, using undefinable religious terms; or a means for psychological integration, again using religious words. In both cases, the connotation words used are open to the control of the manipulators.

There is an opposite danger: that the orthodox Christian will fail to realize that at times guilt-feelings are present when no true guilt exists. Let us remember that the Fall resulted in division not only between God and man, and man and man, but between man and himself. Hence there are psychological guilt-feelings without true guilt. In such cases we must show genuine compassion. But where there is a real moral guilt before the God who is there, this must never be passed off or explained away as psychological, as the new theology does.

Another result of the position of the new theology is that there is no personal antithesis at the point of justification. For the new theologians there can never be a qualitative difference in man's relationship to God. The Christian view is that when a person casts himself on Jesus Christ as Savior, at that moment he has passed from death to life, from the kingdom of darkness to the kingdom of God's dear Son.[3] Justification means to be acquitted from true guilt and no longer to be condemned. This is an absolute personal antithesis. If on the other hand, there is no absolute antithesis between moral and immoral, cruel and noncruel, then the only difference is a quantitative one.

We may not play with the new theology even if we may think we can turn it to our advantage. This means, for example, we must beware of cooperation in evangelistic enterprises which force us into a position of accepting the new theology as Christian. If we do this, we have cut the ground from under the biblical concept of the personal antithesis of justification.

Because the new theology has no place for antithesis, and because for its proponents sin and guilt are, in the last analysis, a metaphysical and not a moral problem, they have either an implicit or explicit universalism regarding man's ultimate salvation. It is naive for evangelicals to regard this universalism as merely an unrelated corner of the neo-orthodox system. It may not always be explicit in the teaching of the new theologians, but we must see that the logic of their view concerning man's dilemma irresistibly drives them to this position. At this point their beliefs hang together very well. They have no final antithesis between right and wrong; therefore there can be no such thing as true moral guilt; therefore justification as a radically changed relationship with God can have no meaning; therefore no one is finally condemned. On the basis of their system, this is a perfectly consistent and necessary position to hold. Universalism is naturally related to what their system is.

Historic Christianity and Man's Dilemma

The historic Christian position is that man's dilemma has a moral cause. God, being nondetermined, created man as a nondetermined person. This is a difficult idea for anyone thinking in twentieth-century terms because most twentieth-century thinking sees man as determined. He is determined either by chemical factors, as the Marquis de Sade held and Francis Crick is trying to prove, or by psychological factors, as Freud and others have suggested, or by sociological factors, such as B. F. Skinner holds. In these cases, or as a result of a fusion of them, man is considered to be programmed. If this is the case, then man is not the tremendous thing the Bible says he is, made in the image of God as a personality who can make a free first choice. Because God created a true universe outside of Himself (not as an extension of His essence), there is a true history which exists. Man as created in God's image is therefore a significant man in a significant history, who can choose to obey the commandment of God and love Him, or revolt against Him.

This is the wonder of man and the wonder of history. It is the very opposite of the Zen-Buddhist statement which says, "The mind of man is like the wind in a pine tree in a Chinese ink drawing." In this, man is killed twice. He is only the wind in the pine tree, and even then only in a drawing. Christianity teaches the very reverse of what the Eastern thinker says. Man can understand and respond to the One who, having made him and communicated with him, called upon him to show that he loved Him by simple command: "Don't do this." The test could have been something else. No act of primitive magic is involved here. This is the infinite-personal God calling on personal man to act by choice. And it was a motivated command, ". . . for in the day that you eat of it you shall surely die,"[4] which would make no sense if man is only a machine. He could so act by choice because he was created to be different from the animal, the plant and the machine.

To ask that man should have been made so that he *was not able to revolt* is to ask that God's creation should have ceased after He created plants and animals. It is to ask that man should be reduced to machine programming. It is to ask that man as man should not exist.

If one begins to consider the Christian system as a total system, one must begin with the infinite-personal triune God who is there, and who was communicating and loving before anything else was. If one begins to consider how sinful man can return to fellowship with God, one must begin with Christ, His person and work. But if one begins to consider the differences between Christianity and rationalistic philosophy's answers, one must begin by understanding that man and history are now abnormal. It is not that philosophy and Christianity deal with completely different questions, but that historic Christianity and rationalistic philosophy differ in their answers — including the important point as to whether man and history are now normal or abnormal. They also differ in that rationalistic thinking starts with only the knowledge finite man can glean for himself.[5]

Christianity says man is now abnormal — he is separated from his Creator, who is his only sufficient reference point — not by a metaphysical limitation, but by true moral guilt. As a result he is now also separated from his fellowmen, and from himself. Therefore, when he is involved in cruelty, he is not being true to what he was initially created to be. Cruelty is a symptom of abnormality and a result of a moral, historic, space-time Fall.

What does a historic space-time Fall involve? It means that there was a period before man fell; that if you had been there, you could have seen Adam before he fell; that at the point when he revolted against God by making a free choice to disobey God's commandment, there was a tick of the clock. Take away the first three chapters of Genesis, and you cannot maintain a true Christian position nor give Christianity's answers.

CHAPTER FOUR

God's Answer to Man's Dilemma

With the Christian answer it is now possible to understand that there are true moral absolutes. There is no law behind God, because the furthest thing back is God. The moral absolutes rest upon God's character. The creation as He originally made it conformed to His character. The moral commands He has given to men are an expression of His character. Men as created in His image are to live by choice on the basis of what God is. The standards of morality are determined by what conforms to His character, while those things which do not conform are immoral.

God can know about things that are not actualized. For example, he knew all about Eve, but she was not actualized until He made her. The same thing can be true in the area of morals. When man sins, he brings forth what is contrary to the moral law of the universe and as a result he is morally and legally guilty. Because man is guilty before the Lawgiver of the universe, doing what is contrary to His character, his sin is significant and he is morally significant in a significant history. Man has true moral guilt. This is entirely different from the conception of modern thought, which states that actions do not lead to guilt — a view within which actions thus become morally meaningless. Even the

most degraded actions of sin have no final moral meaning. Ultimately "good" and "bad" actions alike are zero. This is an important factor in modern man seeing man as zero.

The Christian answer begins by saying that man is a moral
creature made in the image of the Creator; that there is a law in
the universe which, if broken, means that man is culpable. In this
view, man is morally significant both as far as God is concerned
and as far as his fellowmen are concerned. The modern non-
Christian answer denies the legitimacy of moral absolutes, refuses
to make any kind of final moral comment on man's actions, and
thus reduces cruel and noncruel acts to the same level. With this
answer not only is the concept of sin reduced to less than the biblical concept, but *man* is reduced to less than the biblical concept
of guilty man.

If the modern explanation is accepted, then there ceases to be
an answer to man's dilemma — man is as he was in the beginning
and ever will be. With the moral (in contrast to the metaphysical)
explanation of man's position in the universe and his consequent
dilemma following the Fall, there is a possible solution.

If there is true moral guilt in the presence of a personal God
(rather than a metaphysical intrinsic situation of what is and
always has been), then perhaps there will be a solution from
God's side. And God says to man that there is a solution. That
solution rests upon God saying that He is holy and He is love, and
in His love He has loved the world, and He sent His Son. Now in
history, there on Calvary's cross, in space and time, Jesus died.
And we should never speak of Jesus' death without linking it to
His person. This is the eternal Second Person of the Trinity. When
He died, with the division that man has caused by his revolt now
carried up into the Trinity itself, there in expiation, in propitiation
and substitution, the true moral guilt is met by the *infinite* value
of Jesus' death. Thus Jesus says: "It is finished."

Romans 3:26 is a verse that we tend to pass by too quickly in
the midst of the structure of the first three chapters of Romans.
These chapters tell us first why man is lost, and then the solution
in the propitiatory death of Jesus Christ. At this point Paul can
say: "that he himself might be just and *yet* (the force of the Greek
construction) the justifier of him who has faith in Jesus." On the
one hand, because of the infinite value of Christ's death, God
does not have to surrender His absolutely holy character; and on
the other, He does not have to violate man's significance in order

for Him to be able to pardon guilt and restore man's broken relationship to Himself. This is the very opposite of the denial of antithesis and significance in modern man's leap into the dark, which says that somehow we must believe, without reason, that God is love. A moral absolute remains, and yet there is a solution to man's dilemma.

There Need Be No Either-Or in La Peste
From the biblical answer flow four important facts.

Firstly, the God who is there is a good God.

Secondly, there is a hope of a solution to the dilemma of man.

Thirdly, there is a sufficient basis for morals. Nobody has ever discovered a way of having real "morals" without a moral absolute. If there is no moral absolute, we are left with hedonism (doing what I like) or some form of the social contract theory (what is best for society as a whole is right). However, neither of these alternatives corresponds to the moral motions that men have. Talk to people long enough and deeply enough, and you will find that they consider some things are *really* right and some things are *really* wrong. Without absolutes, morals as morals cease to exist, and humanistic man starting from himself is unable to find the absolute he needs. But because the God of the Bible is there, real morals exist. Within this framework I can say one action is right and another wrong, without talking nonsense.

Fourthly, there is an adequate reason for fighting wrong. The Christian never faces the dilemma posed in Camus' book *La Peste*. It simply is not true that he either has to side with the doctor against God by fighting the plague, or join with the priest on God's side and thus be much less than human by not fighting the plague.[1] If this were an *either-or* choice in life, it would indeed be terrible.[2] But the Christian is not confined to such a choice. Let us go to the tomb of Lazarus. As Jesus stood there, He not only wept, but He was *angry*. The exegesis of the Greek of the passages John 11:33 and 38 is clear.[3] Jesus, standing in front of the tomb of Lazarus, was *angry* at death and at the abnormality of the world — the destruction and distress caused by sin. In Camus' words, Christ hated the plague. He claimed to be God, and *He could hate the plague without hating Himself as God.*

A Christian can fight what is wrong in the world with compassion and know that as he hates these things, God hates them too. God hates them to the high price of the death of Christ.

But if I live in a world of nonabsolutes and would fight social injustice on the mood of the moment, how can I establish what social justice is? What criterion do I have to distinguish between right and wrong so that I can know what I should be fighting? Is it not possible that I could in fact acquiesce in evil and stamp out good? The word *love* cannot tell me how to discern, for within the humanistic framework love can have no defined meaning. But once I comprehend that the Christ who came to die to end "the plague" both wept and was angry at the plague's effects, I have a reason for fighting that does not rest merely on my momentary disposition, or the shifting consensus of men.

But the Christian also needs to be challenged at this point. The fact that he alone has a sufficient standard by which to fight evil, does not mean that he *will* so fight. The Christian is the real radical of our generation, for he stands against the monolithic, modern concept of truth as relative. But too often, instead of being the radical, standing against the shifting sands of relativism, he subsides into merely maintaining the *status quo*. If it is true that evil is evil, that God hates it to the point of the cross, and that there is a moral law fixed in what God is in Himself, then Christians should be the first into the field against what is wrong — including man's inhumanity to man.

CHAPTER FIVE

How Do We Know It Is True?

Those interested in my thoughts concerning "apologetics" will find these in Appendix A of this book.

All men on their own level face a problem. Confronted with the existence and form of the external universe and the "mannishness" of man, how does it fit together, and what sense does it make?

Imagine a book which has been mutilated, leaving just one inch of printed matter on each page. Although it would obviously be impossible to piece together and understand the book's story, yet few people would imagine that what was left had come together by chance. However, if the torn-off parts of each page were found in the attic and were added in the right places, then the story could be read and would make sense. The whole man would be relieved that the mystery of the book had been solved, and the whole man would be involved in the reading of the completed story; but man's reason would have been the first to tell him that the portions which were discovered were the proper solution to the problem of the ripped book.

Notice two things about this illustration. Firstly, the portions of each page left in the book could never tell what the story was about. Their importance would be as a test to determine whether

119

the pieces found in the attic were the right ones for that book. Secondly, the man who discovered the matching portions used his reason to show that they fitted the mutilated book. But then, on the level of his whole personality, he enjoyed reading and understanding the complete story of the original pieces and the added portions. This would particularly be the case if the *total* book opened the way to a restored communication with someone important to the reader.

So it is with Christianity: the ripped pages remaining in the book correspond to the abnormal universe and the abnormal man we now have. The parts of the pages which are discovered correspond to the Scriptures which are God's propositional communication to mankind, which not only touch "religious" truth but also the cosmos and history, which are open to verification. Neither the abnormal external world nor the abnormal "mannishness" of man can give the answer to the whole meaning of the created order; yet they are both important in knowing that the Scriptures, God's communication to man, are what they claim to be. The question is whether the communication given by God completes and explains the portions we had before and especially whether it explains what was obvious before, though without an explanation — that is, that the universe exists and the universe and the "mannishness" of man are not just a chance configuration of the printer's scrambled type. To put it another way, does the Bible's answer or does John Cage's chance music speak of what exists?

Rationalistically and autonomously man could not give a proper answer on the basis of the portion of the book that remained. Without the pages which were discovered, man would never have had the answer. Neither do we have a leap of faith, because the pieces match up in a coherent whole over the whole unified field of knowledge. With the propositional communication from the personal God before us, not only the things of the cosmos and history match up, but everything on the upper and lower stories matches too: grace and nature; a moral absolute and morals; the universal point of reference and the particulars, and the emotional and aesthetic realities of man as well.

Of course, the individual man will not see that they match up if he rejects the communication just because he has not thought it up himself. This would be much the same as the man in our illustration rejecting the pieces of the book found in the attic because he wanted to make up his own story.

The Nature of Proof

In dealing with the question of proof which has been raised by the illustration of the book, I want to suggest that scientific proof, philosophical proof and religious proof follow the same rules. We may have any problem before us which we wish to solve; it may concern a chemical reaction or the meaning of man. After the question has been defined, in each case proof consists of two steps:

A. The theory must be noncontradictory and must give an answer to the phenomenon in question.

B. We must be able to live consistently with our theory. For example, the answer given to the chemical reaction must conform to what we observe in the test tube. With regard to man and his "mannishness," the answer given must conform to what we observe in a wide consideration of man and how he behaves.

Specifically in relation to the question of man, does the Christian answer conform to and explain what we observe concerning man as he is (including my knowledge of myself as a man)? The Christian answer is that man is not dead; rather, that he was man and personal intrinsically from the time he was made by a personal source; and though at the beginning he was normal, he is now abnormal. The reader may well recall here the illustration of the water rising in the second valley and the material in the previous chapters which dealt with the personal source and with man's present abnormality.

Then there is the negative consideration. After a careful definition has weeded out the trivial, the other possible answers that do not involve a mystical leap of faith are of the following nature:

1. That the impersonal plus time plus chance have produced a personal man. But this theory is against all experience and thus usually the advocates of this theory end with a leap of faith, often hidden by the use of connotation words.

2. That man is not personal, but dead; that he is in reality a machine, and therefore personality is an illusion. This theory could fit the first criterion of being noncontradictory, but it will not fit the second, for man simply cannot live as though he were a machine. This may be observed as far back in the history of man as we have evidence — for example, from the art and artifacts of the caves or from man's burial rites. We have already given many examples of the way in which a man, such as a scientist in love, has been driven to a Jekyll and Hyde existence on the basis of this

conclusion. He is one thing in his laboratory, but something completely different at home with his wife and children. Included is the whole struggle of modern man, the despair shown by the acceptance of the irrational leap in a desperate attempt to have answers at the expense of reason, and the scream of the modern artists when they do not find a meaning for man. Although man may say that he is no more than a machine, his whole life denies it.

3. That in the future man will find another reasonable answer. There are, however, two overwhelming problems to this answer. Firstly, this could be said about any answer to anything and would bring all thought and science to an end. It must be seen to be an evasion and an especially weak reply if the person using it applies it only to this one question. Secondly, no one can live with this answer, for it simply is not possible to hold one's breath and wait until some solution is found in the future. Continually the individual makes moral judgments which affect himself and others, and he must be using some working hypothesis from which to start. Thus, if a person offers this seriously as an alternative theory, he should be prepared to go into deep freeze and stop making judgments which touch on the problem of man. Bertrand Russell, for example, should have stopped making sociological decisions which involved others. This position is only possible if one stops the clock.

4. That the scientific theory of relativity may in the future prove to be a sufficient answer for human life. But the scientific theory of relativity cannot be applied to human life in this way. The scientific theory is constantly being tested, both as a theory and by measurement. Therefore it does not mean that "anything goes," as it does when relativity is applied to human values. Moreover, in science the speed of light in a vacuum is considered an absolute standard. Therefore, scientific relativity does not imply that all scientific laws are in a constant state of flux. To use scientific relativity to buttress the concept of relativity in regard to human life and human values is completely invalid.

One might think of a few other attempts to find possible answers, but the possibilities are very few indeed.

In contrast to such answers, if the scope of the phenomena under consideration is large enough (that is, if it includes the existence of the universe and its form,[1] and the "mannishness" of man as he now is), Christianity, which begins with the existence of the infinite-personal God, man's creation in His image, and a space-time Fall, does offer a nonself-contradictory answer which explains the phenomena and which can be lived with, both in life and in scholarly pursuits.

I suggest that a serious question has to be faced as to whether the reason why modern men reject the Christian answer, or why they often do not even consider it, is *because they have already accepted, with an implicit faith, the presupposition of the uniformity of natural causes in a closed system.*

This does not mean that the Christian answer should be accepted for pragmatic reasons, but it does mean that the solution given in the Bible answers the problem of the universe and man, and nothing else does.

It should be added in conclusion that the Christian, after he becomes a Christian, has years of experimental evidence to add to all the above reasons. But we may stop at the same place as Paul does in Romans, chapter 1, by saying that the existence of the external universe and its form and the "mannishness" of man demonstrate the truth of the historic Christian position. He does not in Romans 1 go on to appeal to the Christian's experience. "For the wrath of God is revealed from heaven against all ungodliness and unrighteousness of men, who hold down the truth in unrighteousness; because that which may be known of God is manifest in them [the "mannishness" of man]. for God manifested it unto them. For the invisible things of him since the creation of the world are clearly seen, being perceived through the things that are made [the external world and its form], even his everlasting power and divinity, that they may be without excuse. "[2]

True Rationality But Not Only Rationality

Although rationality is important, it should never become exclusively so.[3] Rationality is not the end of the matter.[4] It is parallel to the problem of form and freedom in art. The artist, to be an artist, needs to be free. On the other hand, if there is no form to his painting, the artist loses all communication with the viewers. The form makes it possible for the artist to have freedom plus communication. In the same way, rationality is needed to open the door to a vital relationship to God.

The study of verbalized and nonverbalized communication enters here. What form is to the artist, words are to general communication. The use of words, clearly defined and dealt with rationally, gives form and certainty in communication. The same is true with carefully defined scientific symbols.

It is possible to add things to rational verbalization and thus to enrich it. For example, poetry undoubtedly adds something to prose form. In the Psalms something is communicated to us which would not be so in a bare prose account. The same thing is true when the artist paints a portrait. However, if there is an absolute divorce between the defined and rationally comprehended verbalization on one hand and (for example) *bare poetic form* on the other, no certain communication comes across to the reader. The most the reader can do is to use the bare poetic form as a quarry out of which to create something by his own emotions.

As long as a genuine continuity remains between the defined verbalization and what is added, then all kinds of enrichment can be brought in. But if there is discontinuity, then no one can say for certain what the added things mean. This is true in art, in experience, and even in the use of figures of speech. Figures of speech enhance communication, so long as they fit into a framework of defined speech which can be rationally considered. But if someone writes a book or a play composed only of figures of speech without any relation to a defined rational context, not only is communication lost, but the purpose of the figure of speech itself (to be enriching) is lost.

Therefore, it is not that rationality is exclusively important, but rather that rationality defines and provides a form for the whole. In the Scriptures there is a good example of this when John lays down as the only true test of the spirits and prophets something which has content and is rationally based: "Beloved, believe not every spirit, but prove the spirits, whether they are of God: because many false prophets are gone out into the world. Hereby know ye the Spirit of God: every spirit which confesseth that Jesus Christ is come in the flesh is of God: and every spirit that confesseth not Jesus is not of God: and this is the spirit of the antichrist."[5]

The Christian is not rationalistic; he does not try to begin from himself autonomously and work out a system from there on. But he *is* rational: he thinks and acts on the basis that A is A and A is not non-A. However, he does not end with only rationality, for in his response to what God has said his whole personality is involved. Yet, if the control of defined verbalization is lost, then he loses his way. There is no longer any means of testing the spirits, the prophets or experience. All of this then becomes merely the Greek "shade" in the upper story of the new theology to which we referred earlier.

It is therefore most important to get the balance between, on the one hand, the truly rational and, on the other, the involvement of the whole man at every level of his being as something which flows on from the first. Much can be added to the rational, but if we give up the rational everything is lost.

It will help us to clarify this if we go back to the earlier illustration of the ripped book. It is man's reason which is involved in knowing that the communication is the truth of what is; but then, it is the whole man who rejoices in the finding of the missing answer and in the reading of the now *combined* pieces. These combined pieces give knowledge of the infinite-personal God who is there and show how communication with Him may be restored. Reason began the process, and from then on the whole man was involved.

A number of years ago I was at a discussion group in Detroit. An older black pastor was there. We discussed many intellectual and cultural problems and the answers given by Christianity. One would have called the discussion "intellectual" rather than devotional. As he was leaving, the black pastor shook my hand and thanked me. If he had said, "Thank you for helping me to defend my people better," or "Thank you for helping me to be a better evangelist," I would have been very glad that what I had said had been helpful, and then possibly I would not have given it another thought. But what he actually said was, "Thank you for opening these doors to me; now I can worship God better." I will never forget him because he was a man who really understood. If this is not our own response first of all, and then the response of those whom we try to help, we have made a mistake somewhere.

Speaking Historic Christianity into the Twentieth-century Climate

CHAPTER ONE

Finding the Point of Tension

Communicating to One of My Kind
Communication means that an idea which I have in my mind passes through my lips (or fingers — in most art forms) and reaches the other person's mind. Adequate communication means that when it reaches the recipient's mind, it is substantially the same as when it left mine. This does not mean that it will be completely the same, but that he will nevertheless have substantially realized the point I wish to convey. The words that we use are only a tool for translating the ideas which we wish to communicate; we are not trying to convey merely a succession of verbal sounds.

Because we must use words in order to communicate ideas, there may be several language problems. The most obvious one arises between different language groups. If we want to speak to a man, we must first learn his language.

Another problem is that of time. In the course of history language changes in meaning; words may not have the same meaning today as they did in an earlier age. Language naturally changes its meaning as time passes, and this is uniquely true today with the great differences above and below the line of despair.

129

A further language barrier comes as we try to talk to people of a very different social background from ourselves, for example those in the deep slums.

In none of these cases do the language problems solve themselves automatically. If we wish to communicate, then we must take time and trouble to learn our hearers' use of language so that they understand what we intend to convey. This is particularly difficult today for us as Christians when we want to use a word like *God* or *guilt* in a strictly defined sense rather than as a connotation word, because the concepts of these words have been changed universally. In a case like this, either we must try to find a synonymous word without a false connotation, or else we have to define the word at length when we use it, so that we make sure our hearer understands as fully as possible what we are conveying. In this latter case we are no longer using the word as a technical word, in the sense that we assume a common definition.

I suggest that if the word (or phrase) we are in the habit of using is no more than an orthodox evangelical cliché which has become a technical term among Christians, then we should be willing to give it up when we step outside our own narrow circle and talk to the people around us. If, on the other hand, the word is indispensable, such as the word *God*, then we should talk at sufficient length to make ourselves clear. Technical words, if they are used without sufficient explanation, may mean that outsiders really do not hear the Christian message at all and that we ourselves, in our churches and missions, have become an introverted and isolated language group.

As we turn to consider in more detail how we may speak to people of the twentieth century, we must emphasize first of all that we cannot apply mechanical rules. We, of all people, should realize this, for as Christians we believe that personality really does exist and is important. We can lay down some general principles, but there can be no automatic application. If we are truly personal, as created by God, then each individual will differ from everyone else. Therefore each person must be dealt with as an individual, not as a case or statistic or machine. If we would work with these people, we cannot apply the things we have dealt with in this book mechanically. We must look to the Lord in prayer, and to the work of the Holy Spirit, for the effective use of these things.

Furthermore, we must remember that the person to whom we

are talking, however far from the Christian faith he may be, is an image-bearer of God. He has great value, and our communication to him must be in genuine love. Love is not an easy thing; it is not just an emotional urge, but an attempt to move over and sit in the other person's place and see how his problems look to him. Love is a genuine concern for the individual. As Jesus Christ reminds us, we are to love that individual "as ourselves." This is the place to begin. Therefore, to be engaged in personal "witness" as a duty or because our Christian circle exerts a social pressure on us, is to miss the whole point. The reason we do it is that the person before us is an image-bearer of God, and he is an individual who is unique in the world. This kind of communication is not cheap. To understand and speak to sincere but utterly confused twentieth-century people is costly. It is tiring; it will open you to temptations and pressures. Genuine love, in the last analysis, means a willingness to be entirely exposed to the person to whom we are talking.

The one before us is our kind. The Bible teaches that there are two humanities; yet, looking at it another way, there is only one humanity. There are two humanities in the sense that there are those still in rebellion against God, and there are those who have returned to God through Jesus Christ. But this should not dull us to the fact that God "hath made of one blood all nations of men for to dwell on all the face of the earth."[1] This does not just mean that the whole human race is biologically one, in the sense that we can reproduce together, but that we are all descended from Adam as a common ancestor. Thus, emotionally as well as intellectually, we must look at the man before us as *our kind*. This man is our counterpart; he is lost, but so once were we. We are one flesh, one blood, one kind.

Finally, as we consider how we are to communicate to man, we must bear in mind that we are speaking to him as a unit. We are not merely dealing with just one part of him called the "soul" in an attempt to get that to Heaven. We are conscious that the Bible teaches the unity of the personality. So as we try to communicate in this wholeness this must be reflected in our attitude, as well as in what we say.

Logical Conclusions
We can look now at some of the general principles to guide our communication with twentieth-century man.

Let us remember that every person we speak to, whether shop girl or university student, has a set of presuppositions, whether he or she has analyzed them or not. The dot in the diagram represents a person's non-Christian presuppositions; the arrow points to what would be the logical conclusion of those non-Christian presuppositions.

A MAN WITH HIS   ● ──────── ⊃   THE LOGICAL CONCLUSION
NON-CHRISTIAN   OF HIS NON-CHRISTIAN
PRESUPPOSITIONS   PRESUPPOSITIONS

If a man were completely logical to his presuppositions, he would come out at the line on the right. If he arrived there in thinking and life, he would be consistent to his presuppositions.

But, in fact, no non-Christian can be consistent to the logic of his presuppositions. The reason for this is simply that a man must live in reality, and reality consists of two parts: the external world and its form, and man's "mannishness," including his own "mannishness." No matter what a man may believe, he cannot change the reality of what is. As Christianity is the truth of what is there, to deny this, on the basis of another system, is to stray from the real world:

THE REAL WORLD—   THE LOGICAL CONCLUSION
THE EXTERNAL WORLD   ⊂──────── ⊃   OF A MAN'S NON-CHRISTIAN
AND MAN HIMSELF   PRESUPPOSITIONS

Every man, therefore, irrespective of his system, is caught. As he tries intellectually to extend his position in a logical way and then live within it, he is caught by the two things which, as it were, slap him across the face. Without indicating that his psychology or philosophy is correct, Carl Gustav Jung has correctly observed that two things cut across every man's will—the external world with its structure, and those things which well up from inside himself. Non-Christian presuppositions simply do not fit into what God has made, including what man is. This being so, every man is in a place of tension. Man cannot make his own universe and then live in it.

The Bible takes this point a step further when it says that, even in Hell, a man cannot be consistent to his non-Christian presuppositions; "If I make my bed in hell, behold, thou [God] art there."[2] Man will be separated from communion with God in Hell, but no one is going to be able to form Hell to make their own universe in a limited area. Man there will still be in the universe of God. Hence, even in Hell, a man cannot be consistent to his non-Christian presuppositions.

In this present life it is the same. It is impossible for any non-Christian individual or group to be consistent to their system in logic or in practice. Thus, when you face twentieth-century man, whether he is brilliant or an ordinary man of the street, a man of the university or the docks, you are facing a man in tension; and it is this tension which works on your behalf as you speak to him. If I did not know this from the Word of God and personal experience, I would not have the courage to step into the circles I do. A man may try to bury the tension and you may have to help him find it, but somewhere there is a point of inconsistency. He stands in a position which he cannot pursue to the end; and this is not just an intellectual concept of tension, it is what is wrapped up in what he is as a man.

Torn by Two Consistencies
Christian apologetics do not start somewhere beyond the stars. They begin with man and what he knows about himself. When a man is lost, he is lost against all that there is, including what he is. Therefore, when he stands before God in judgment, God, in order to point out how false his position has been, will only need to refer to what he as an individual has known of the external world and "mannishness." As far as morals are concerned, man will only have to be judged according to the standards he himself has laid down in condemning others, for, as Paul makes clear, he then proceeds deliberately to break even his own standards.[3]

Hence, the person before you is not in a vacuum. He knows something of the external world, and he knows something of himself.

Every person is somewhere along the line between the real world and the logical conclusion of his or her non-Christian presuppositions. Every person has the pull of two consistencies, the pull towards the real world and the pull towards the logic of his system. He may let the pendulum swing back and forth between them, but he cannot live in both places at once. He will be living nearer to the one or to the other, depending on the strength of the pull at any given time. To have to choose between one consistency or the other is a real damnation for man. *The more logical a man who holds a non-Christian position is to his own presuppositions, the further he is from the real world; and the nearer he is to the real world, the more illogical he is to his presuppositions.*

The Tensions Are Felt in Differing Strengths

We have said that every person, however intelligent or lacking in intelligence, has stopped somewhere along the line towards the consistent conclusion of his own position. Some people are prepared to go further from the real world than others, in an attempt to be more logical to their presuppositions. The French existentialists Camus and Sartre exhibited this:

THE REAL WORLD— | CAMUS SARTRE | THE LOGICAL CONCLUSION
THE EXTERNAL WORLD | | OF A MAN'S NON-CHRISTIAN
AND MAN HIMSELF | | PRESUPPOSITIONS

Sartre said that Camus was not sufficiently consistent on the basis of their mutual presuppositions. The reason for this was because Camus never gave up "hope," centered in random personal happiness, though it went against the logic of his position. Or, as was stated when Camus received the Nobel prize, because he never gave up the search for morals, though the world seemed to be without meaning. These are the reasons why, of the two, Camus was more loved in the intellectual world. He never got the real world sorted out, as we have seen from his book *The Plague*, but he was nearer to it than Sartre.

Sartre was correct to say that Camus was illogical to their presuppositions; but, as we saw before, he could not be consistent either. When he signed the Algerian Manifesto, taking a position as though morals have real meaning, he too was being inconsistent to his presuppositions. Thus Sartre was also in tension.

Each person may move up or down the line at different times in their lives, according to their circumstances, but most people more or less stabilize at one point. Every non-Christian, whether he is sleeping under the bridges in Paris or is totally bourgeois, is somewhere along the line.

THE REAL WORLD— | | THE LOGICAL CONCLUSION
THE EXTERNAL WORLD | | OF A MAN'S NON-CHRISTIAN
AND MAN HIMSELF | | PRESUPPOSITIONS

This is not an abstraction, for each of these persons is created in the image of God, and thus is in tension because, within himself, there are things which speak of the real world. Men in different cultures have different standards for morals, but there is no one who does not have some moral motions. Follow a modern girl through her day. She may seem totally amoral. But if you were to get to know her you would find that, at some point, she felt the pull of morals. Love may carry different expressions, but all men have some motions of love. The individual will feel this tension in different ways — with some it will be beauty, with some it will be significance, with some it will be rationality, with some it will be the fear of nonbeing.

Man today seeks to deflect this tension by saying that he is no more than a machine. But if he were no more than a machine, he would find no difficulty in proceeding step by step down the line to the logical conclusion of his non-Christian presuppositions. Man is not a machine, however, even if he says he is.

Suppose that a satellite were put into orbit around the earth with a camera that was able to photograph everything on the world's surface. If this information was then fed back to a giant computer that did not need programming, it might calculate that everything behaved mechanically. But the final observer is not a computer but the individual man. There is always one person in the room who does not allow everything to be seen as machine-like; it is myself, the observer, because I know myself.

Christians must be careful at this place. Though the Bible says men are lost, it does not say they are nothing. When a man says he is a machine or nothing, he makes himself less than the Bible's view of fallen man.

Therefore, the first consideration in our apologetics for modern man, whether factory-hand or research student, is to find the place where his tension exists. We will not always find it easy to do this. Many people have never analyzed their own point of tension. Since the Fall man is separated from himself. Man is complicated, and he tries to bury himself in himself. Therefore, it will take time and it will cost something to discover what the person we are speaking to often has not yet discovered for himself. Down inside of himself man finds it easy to lie to himself. We, in love, looking to the work of the Holy Spirit, must reach down into that person and try to find where the point of tension is.

CHAPTER TWO

From the Point of Tension to the Gospel

Why There Is a Place for Conversation[1]
If the man before you were logical to his non-Christian presuppositions, you would have no point of communication with him. It would be impossible to have communication if he were consistent. But in reality no one can live logically according to his own non-Christian presuppositions, and consequently, because he is faced with the real world and himself, in *practice* you will find a place where you can talk. He would not be where he is, suspended between the real world and the logical conclusions of his presuppositions, if he were consistent. The only reason he can be at the point of tension, nearer to the real world than his presuppositions would logically indicate, is because, to some extent, he is not logical; and the nearer he is to the real world, the more illogical he is to his presuppositions. As an illustration: it is illogical for John Cage to pick mushrooms as he does, in a universe which, he says, is intrinsically chance, but, illogically, he does pick them in that way; and thus, you could start talking to him concerning the inadequacy of his system, with its chance music, in relationship to his mushrooms.

In *practice* then, we do have a point for conversation, but this point is not properly to be spoken of as "neutral." There are no neutral facts, for facts are God's facts. However, there is common ground between the Christian and non-Christian because regardless of a man's system, he has to live in God's world. If he were consistent to his non-Christian presuppositions he would be separated from the real universe and the real man, and conversation and communication would not be possible.[2]

In this way, it does not seem to me that presuppositional apologetics should be seen as ending conversation with the people around us. On the other hand, to try to work below the line of despair without a clear and defined concept of presuppositional apologetics is simply to destroy the possibility of helping twentieth-century people. There is no use talking today until the presuppositions are taken into account, and especially the crucial presuppositions concerning the nature of truth and the method of attaining truth.

Giving and Taking Blows

When we have discovered, as well as we can, a person's point of tension, the next step is to push him towards the logical conclusion of his presuppositions:

THE REAL WORLD—
THE EXTERNAL WORLD
AND MAN HIMSELF

THE LOGICAL CONCLUSION
OF A MAN'S NON-CHRISTIAN
PRESUPPOSITIONS

We ought not to try first to move a man away from the logical conclusion of his position but towards it, in the direction of the arrow. We should try to move him in the natural direction his presuppositions take him. We are pushing him towards the place where he ought to be, had he not stopped short.

As I seek to do this, I need to remind myself constantly that this is not a game I am playing. If I begin to enjoy it as a kind of intellectual exercise, then I am cruel and can expect no real spiritual results. As I push the man off his false balance, he must be able to feel that I care for him. Otherwise I will only end up destroying him, and the cruelty and ugliness of it all will destroy me as well. Merely to be abstract and cold is to show that I do not really believe this person to be created in God's image and therefore one of my kind. Pushing him towards the logic of his presuppositions is going to cause him pain; therefore, I must not push any further than I need to.

If we find the man ready to receive Christ as Savior, then by all means we should not talk about presuppositions but tell him the glorious good news. The whole purpose of our speaking to twentieth-century people in the way I have outlined is not to make them admit that we are right in some personally superior way, nor to push their noses in the dirt, but to make them see their need so that they will listen to the gospel. As soon as the person before us is ready to listen to the gospel, we do not push him any further — it is horrible to be propelled in the direction of meaninglessness against the testimony of the external world and the testimony of oneself.

As we get ready to tell the person God's answer to his or her need, we must make sure that the individual understands that we are talking about real *truth*, and not about something vaguely religious which seems to work psychologically. We must make sure that he understands that we are talking about *real guilt* before God, and we are not offering him merely relief for his guilt-feelings. We must make sure that he understands that we are talking to him about *history*, and that the death of Jesus was not just an ideal or a symbol but a fact of space and time. If we are talking to a person who would not understand the term "space-time history" we can say: "Do you believe that Jesus died in the sense that if you had been there that day, you could have rubbed your finger on the cross and got a splinter in it?" *Until he understands the importance of these three things, he is not ready to become a Christian.*

Push him towards the logic of his position in the area of his own real interests. If he is interested in science, we will push him to the logical conclusion of his position in science. If it is art, then gently and yet firmly we push him from the point of tension to the end of his presuppositions. At all points in the conversation, we must allow him to ask any question he wants. We cannot say, on the one hand, that we believe in the unity of truth and then, on the other hand, suddenly withdraw from the discussion and tell him to believe on blind authority. He has a right to ask questions. It is perfectly true that not all Christians proceed in this way with all modern people, and yet people are brought to Christ by them. For every person who is saved we should be very thankful. But to withdraw by saying or implying, "Keep quiet and just believe" may later lead to spiritual weakness, even if the person does become a Christian, for it will leave crucial questions unanswered. Therefore, in the midst of our attempts to press our case, we must be ready to receive blows as well. The more he is a true twentieth-century man the more important it is, if you wish to see him become a Christian, that you should accept the blows of the questions in the name of Jesus Christ, and in the name of truth. On the other hand, keep pressing him back, for *he* must keep answering questions, too. As we take time to study both the modern world in which we live and, more particularly, our Bible, we shall come to know more and more answers. We must have faced the question, "Is Christianity true?" for ourselves. We must be men of the Scriptures, so that we can know what the content of the biblical system is. Every day of our lives we should be studying the Scriptures to make sure that what we are presenting really is the Christian position, and that we are presenting it as well as possible in our day.

Taking the Roof Off

Let us think of it in a slightly different way. Every man has built a roof over his head to shield himself at the point of tension:

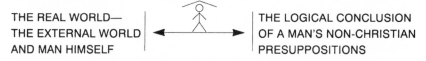

THE REAL WORLD—
THE EXTERNAL WORLD
AND MAN HIMSELF

THE LOGICAL CONCLUSION
OF A MAN'S NON-CHRISTIAN
PRESUPPOSITIONS

At the point of tension the person is not in a place of consistency in his system, and the roof is built *as a protection against the blows of the real world*, both internal and external. It is like the great shelters built upon some mountain passes to protect vehicles from the avalanches of rock and stone which periodically tumble down the mountain. The avalanche, in the case of the non-Christian, is the real and the abnormal, fallen world which surrounds him. The Christian, lovingly, must remove the shelter and allow the truth of the external world and of what man is to beat upon him. When the roof is off, each man must stand naked and wounded before the truth of what is.

The truth that we let in first is not a dogmatic statement of the truth of the Scriptures, but the truth of the external world and the truth of what man himself is. This is what shows him his need. The Scriptures then show him the real nature of his lostness and the answer to it. *This, I am convinced, is the true order for our apologetics in the second half of the twentieth century for people living under the line of despair.*

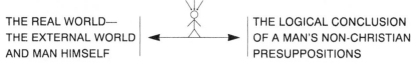

THE REAL WORLD—		THE LOGICAL CONCLUSION
THE EXTERNAL WORLD	← →	OF A MAN'S NON-CHRISTIAN
AND MAN HIMSELF		PRESUPPOSITIONS

It is unpleasant to be submerged by an avalanche, but we must allow the person to undergo this experience so that he may realize his system has no answer to the crucial questions of life. He must come to know that his roof is a false protection from the storm of what is; and then we can talk to him of the storm of the judgment of God.

Removing the roof is not some kind of optional exercise. It is strictly biblical in its emphasis. In the thinking of the twentieth-century man the concept of judgment and of Hell is nonsense, and therefore to begin to talk here is to mumble in a language which makes no contact with him. Hell or any such concept is unthinkable to modern man because he has been brainwashed into accepting the monolithic belief of naturalism which surrounds him. We of the West may not be brainwashed by our State, but we are brainwashed by our culture. Even the modern radicals are radicals in a very limited circle.

Before men passed below the line of despair they knew for the most part that they were guilty, but it rarely entered their minds that they were dead as well. By contrast, modern man hardly ever considers himself to be guilty, but he often acknowledges that he is dead. The Bible says that both these things are true. Man in revolt against the holy God who is there is guilty and is already under God's wrath. Because he is guilty, he is separated from his true and only reference point and therefore he is dead as well. The Bible does not say man will become lost, but that he *is* lost. The chasm in biblical teaching does not come at death but at the point of conversion, when the individual passes from death to life. This is the point of personal antithesis; before that, man is dead indeed.

Hence we begin to deal with "modern man" by preaching at the place where he can understand. Often he understands the horrible point of meaninglessness. Often he recognizes the tension between the real world and the logic of his presuppositions. Often he appreciates the horror of being dead and yet still alive. The Word of God is overwhelmingly clear in its teaching that there are two aspects of lostness: present and future. When I accept Christ as Savior, I pass from death to life, *and therefore before that time I am clearly dead.* Therefore, when modern man feels dead, he is experiencing what the Word of God tells him he is. In himself he will not be able to define his deadness, for he does not know what his deadness is — and even less does he know the solution to it. However, he is aware of one thing, and that is that he is dead. It is our task to tell him that the present death he knows is moral death and not just metaphysical lostness, and then to tell him God's solution. But we begin with the present lostness with which he wrestles. This is not adding to the gospel; it is applying in practice the depths of the truth of the Word of God, that man in revolt is purposeless and dead.

This is what we mean by taking the roof off But we cannot ever think this to be easy. The hardest thing of all is that when we have exposed modern man to his tension, he still may not be willing for the true solution. Consequently, we may seem to leave him in a worse state than he was in before. But this is the same as the evangelism of the past. Whenever the evangelist preached the reality of Hell, men who did not believe were more miserable after hearing his preaching than if they had never heard him. We are in the same position. We confront men with reality; we remove their protection and their escapes; we allow the avalanches to fall. If they do not become Christians, then indeed they are in a worse state than before we spoke to them.

CHAPTER THREE

Applying the Gospel

How Dare We Do It?

How dare we deal with men in this way? Only for one reason — because Christianity is truth. If we are *not* functioning in the area that this is absolute truth, such evangelism is cruel beyond measure. But if this is truth, if it is true that this man before me is separated from God and lost now and for eternity, then even though in individual cases men do not accept Christ and are left worse off than when I began, I must nevertheless have the courage so to speak. If there is a thesis, there is an antithesis. If there is that which is true truth, there is that which is error. If there is true Christian salvation (in contrast to the concept of salvation in the new theology), there is lostness.

When I began to approach individuals in this way, some years ago now, my wife said to me, "Are you not afraid that someone will commit suicide one day?" Since then we have had one girl who tried to do this; fortunately she did not die and later on made a profession of faith. But even if she had succeeded, after walking in the mountains and crying before God, I would have begun the same way with the next person who came.

We cannot do this until we have personally faced the question as to whether the Judeo-Christian system is true in the way we have been speaking of truth. When we are certain about this for ourselves, then if we love men we shall have the courage to lift the roof off other people's lives and expose them to the collapse of their defenses. We ourselves, as we face these people, must have the integrity to continue to live open to the questions: Does God exist? Is the content of the Judeo-Christian system truth?

The more comprehending we are as we take the roof off, the worse the man will feel if he rejects the Christian answer. In a fallen world, we must be willing to face the fact that however lovingly we preach the gospel, if a man rejects it he will be miserable. It is dark out there. I think one reason I am able to talk to this kind of twentieth-century person is because I understand something of just how dark it can be. Men must know that with integrity we have faced the reality of the dark path they are treading.

Once at Cambridge University a postgraduate student said to me, in front of a group that had gathered in his room, "Mr. Schaeffer, I heard you speak last year. Since then I have been preparing a paper and I would like to read it to you. I dare read it to you because I think you understand. Sir, I am in horror of great darkness." There is no romanticism as one seeks to move a man in the direction of honesty. On the basis of his system you are pushing him further and further towards that which is not only totally against God, but also against himself. You are pushing him out of the real universe. Of course it hurts, of course it is dark in the place where a man, in order to be consistent to his non-Christian presuppositions, must deny what is there in this life as well as in the next.

Often it takes much more time to press him towards the logical conclusion of his position than it does later take to give him the answer. Luther spoke of the Law and the Gospel; and the Law, the need, must always be adequately clear first. Then one can give the Christian answer because he knows his need for something; and one can tell him what his deadness really is, and the solution in the total structure of truth. But if we do not take sufficient time to take the roof off, the twentieth-century man will not comprehend what we are trying to communicate, either what his death is caused by, or the solution. We must never forget that the first part of the gospel is not "Accept Christ as Savior," but "God is there." Only then are we ready to hear God's solution for man's *moral* dilemma in the substitutionary work of Christ in history.

When we have reached this point with a man, we discover that however complicated the modern man may be under the line of despair, however sophisticated or cultured or filled with knowledge, when he sees his need the good news is the same as it has always been. The wonderful thing is that at this point not only can the same ideas be given, but even the same words used to all men.

I recall a time some years ago when two people professed belief in Christ on the same day. One was a very intelligent doctor, and the other a very simple Swiss peasant. In my previous conversations with them, the peasant would have understood little of my talks with the doctor. Yet on this day, when both of them had come to understand their need, as I spoke first to one and then to the other, I was able to use not only the same ideas, but exactly the same words in telling each one the answer to the need. There is no point in being complicated once the intelligent or the simple man understands his need; the same ideas and even the same words are all that is needed.

The problem which confronts us as we approach modern man today is *not* how we are to change Christian teaching in order to make it more palatable, for to do that would mean throwing away any chance of giving the real answer to man in despair; rather, it is the problem of how to communicate the gospel so that it is understood.

Faith in the Biblical Sense
In the first place, Christian faith turns on the reality of God's existence, His being there.[1] Then it also turns on an acceptance of the fact that man's dilemma is moral and not metaphysical. Each person must face these two things on his own level as a matter of truth.

The Philippian jailer asked Paul and Silas, "What must I do to be saved?" The passage which follows is: "Believe on the Lord Jesus, and thou shalt be saved, thou and thy house. And they spake the word of the Lord unto him, with all that were in his house."[2]

What Paul and Silas said in reply to the question was not spoken in a vacuum. Because of the earthquake and the remarkable way Paul and Silas behaved in prison, the jailer had reason to be aware of the existence of a personal God — one who acts in history, answers prayers, and gives men reality in their lives. But this was not all. The whole city had been in an uproar because of all that Paul and Silas had been saying and doing *before* they were put into prison. Finally, it seems from the preciseness of the jailer's question and from what we know elsewhere of Paul's preaching that the jailer had heard the Christian message from Paul himself.

After he had taken them to his house, we read that Paul and Silas spoke to him and his household further of the things of the Lord. Only after this — which we have no reason to think was merely a few minutes' conversation — did they all believe.

True Christian faith rests on content. It is not a vague thing which takes the place of real understanding, nor is it the strength of belief which is of value. *The true basis for faith is not the faith itself, but the work which Christ finished on the cross.* My believing is not the basis for being saved — the basis is the work of Christ. Christian faith is turned outward to an objective person: "Believe on the Lord Jesus, and thou shalt be saved."

Once the truth of God's existence is known to us, and we know that we have true moral guilt before a holy God, then we should be glad to know the solution to our dilemma. The solution is from God's side, not ours.

Now the content of God's propositional promises begins to be wonderful to us. Paul and Silas made such a propositional promise to the jailer, and in the Bible God gives such propositional promises more generally. For example, John 3:36 reads: "He that believeth on the Son has everlasting life: and he that believeth not the Son shall not see life, but the wrath of God abideth on him." There is a strong antithesis here. The second part of the verse speaks of man's present and future lostness; the first part of the verse gives God's solution. The call to Christian believing rests on God's propositional promises. We are to consider whether these things are true, but then we are faced with a choice — either we believe Him, or we call God a liar and walk away, unwilling to bow to Him.

As a man is faced with God's promises, Christian faith means bowing twice: Firstly, he needs to bow in the realm of Being (metaphysically) — that is, to acknowledge that he is a creature before the infinite-personal Creator who is there. Secondly, he needs to bow in the realm of morals — that is, to acknowledge that he has sinned and therefore that he has true guilt before the God who is there. If he has true moral guilt before an infinite God, he has the problem that he, as finite, has no way to remove such a guilt. Thus what he needs is a nonhumanist solution. Now he is faced with God's propositional promise, "Believe on the Lord Jesus, and thou shalt be saved."

What remains is the meaning of "believe on the Lord Jesus." What does it mean to believe on, to cast oneself on, Christ? I would suggest there are four crucial aspects. More detail could be considered, but these are crucial. They are not slogans to be repeated by rote and they do not have to be said in these words, but the individual must have come to a positive conclusion and affirmation concerning them, if he is to believe in the biblical sense:

1. Do you believe that God exists and that He is a personal God, and that Jesus Christ is God — remembering that we are not talking of the *word* or *idea* god, but of the infinite-personal God who is there?

2. Do you acknowledge that you are guilty in the presence of this God — remembering that we are not talking about guilt-feelings, but true moral guilt?

3. Do you believe that Jesus Christ died in space and time, in history, on the cross, and that when He died His substitutional work of bearing God's punishment against sin was fully accomplished and complete?

4. On the basis of God's promises in His written communication to us, the Bible, do you (or have you) cast yourself on this Christ as your personal Savior — not trusting in anything you yourself have ever done or ever will do?

But note with care that God's promise, "He that believeth on the Son has everlasting life," rests upon: God's being there; Christ being the Second Person of the Trinity whose death therefore has infinite value; my not coming presumptuously in thinking I can save myself, but casting myself on the finished work of Christ and the written promises of God. My faith is simply the empty hands by which I accept God's free gift.

John Bunyan in *Pilgrim's Progress* has Hopeful say it this way: "He [Faithful] bid me go to him and see. Then I said it was presumption. He said, no, for I was invited to come.[3] Then he gave me a book of Jesus' inditing, to encourage me the more freely to come; and he said concerning that book, that every jot and tittle thereof stood firmer than heaven and earth. Then I asked him further how I must make my supplication to him; and he said, Go and thou shalt find him upon a mercy-seat, where he sits all year long to give pardon and forgiveness to them that come. I told him that I knew not what to say when I came; and he bid me say to this effect: God be merciful to me a sinner, and make me to know and believe in Jesus Christ; for I see, that if his righteousness had not been, or I have not faith in that righteousness, I am utterly cast away. Lord, I have heard that thou art a merciful God, and hast ordained that thy Son Jesus Christ should be the Saviour of the world; and moreover, that thou art willing to bestow him upon a poor sinner as I am — and I am a sinner indeed. Lord, take therefore this opportunity and magnify thy grace in the salvation of my soul through thy Son Jesus Christ." Bunyan says that Hopeful did not understand at once, but soon he did and said: "From all which, I gathered that I must look for righteousness in his person, and for satisfaction for my sins by his blood; that what he did in obedience to his Father's law, and in submitting to the penalty thereof, was not for himself but for him that will accept it for his salvation, and be thankful."[4]

This is what "believing on the Lord Jesus" means. If a man has believed in this way, he has God's promise that he is a Christian.[5]

Of course, *becoming* a Christian is just the beginning, but we will think more about that in the last section of this book.

After a person has become a Christian, four things will help him:

1. A regular study of the Bible, which is God's communication to us.

2. Regular prayer. Now that our guilt has been removed, there is no barrier between us and God and we are able to talk freely with Him. There are two kinds of praying we shall need to practice: special times of prayer, and the constant looking to the Lord as we go about our daily tasks.

3. Talking to others about the God who exists and His solution to man's dilemma.

4. Regular attendance at a church where the Bible is believed. This does not mean every church, but one that is true to the content of the Bible, and one which does not just recite the right words, but where there is a living of the truth in community and compassion to those in the church and to those outside of it.

Pre-evangelism Is No Soft Option

CHAPTER ONE

Commending the Christian Faith
to Our Generation

Defense of the Faith

There are two purposes of Christian apologetics. The first is
defense. The second is to communicate Christianity in a way that
any given generation can understand.

Defense is proper and necessary because in every age historic
Christianity will be under attack. Defense does not mean being on
the defensive. One must not be embarrassed about the use of the
word *defense*. The proponents of any position who are alive to
their own generation must give a sufficient answer for it when
questions are raised about it. Thus, the word defense is not used
here in a negative sense, because in any conversation, in any
communication which is really dialogue, answers must be given
to objections raised.

Such answers are necessary in the first place for myself as a
Christian if I am going to maintain my intellectual integrity, and if
I am to keep united my personal, devotional and intellectual life.
In the second place, these answers are necessary for the sake of
those for whom I have a responsibility.

It is unreasonable to expect people of the next generation in
any age to continue in the historic Christian position, unless they

151

are helped to see where arguments and connotations directed against Christianity and against them as Christians, by their generation, are fallacious. We must prepare Christian young people to face the monolithic twentieth-century culture by teaching them what the particular attack in our generation is, in contrast to the attacks of previous generations.

I find that everywhere I go — both in the United States and in other countries — children of Christians are being lost to historic Christianity. This is happening not only in small groups in small geographical areas, but everywhere. They are being lost because their parents are unable to understand their children, and therefore cannot really help them in their time of need. This lack of understanding is not only on the part of individual parents, but often also of churches, Christian colleges and Christian missions. Some Christian colleges (and I am not talking of "liberal" colleges) lose many of the best students before they graduate. We have left the next generation naked in the face of the twentieth-century thought by which they are surrounded.

So then, the defense, for myself and for those for whom I am responsible, must be a conscious defense. We cannot assume that because we are Christians in the full biblical sense, and indwelt by the Holy Spirit, automatically we shall be free from the influence of what surrounds us. The Holy Spirit can do what He will, but the Bible does not separate His work from knowledge; nor does the work of the Holy Spirit remove our responsibility as parents, pastors, evangelists, missionaries or teachers.

Communication of the Faith

Having said that, however, Christian apologetics should never be restricted to guarding against attack. We have a responsibility to communicate the gospel to our generation.

Christian apologetics is not like living in a castle with the drawbridge up and occasionally tossing a stone over the walls. It is not to be based on a citadel mentality — sitting inside and saying, "You cannot reach me here." If the Christian adopts this attitude, either in theory or in practice, his contacts with those who have accepted twentieth-century thought will stop. Apologetics should not be merely an academic subject, a new kind of scholasticism. It should be thought out and practiced in the rough and tumble of living contact with the present generation. Thus, the Christian should not be interested only in presenting a nicely balanced system on its own, like some Greek metaphysical system, but rather in something which has constant contact with reality — the reality of the questions being asked by his own and the next generation.

No one can become a Christian unless he understands what Christianity is saying. Many pastors, missionaries and Christian teachers seem to be helpless as they try to speak to the educated people and the mass of people about them. They do not seem to face the fact that it is our task to speak to *our* generation; the past has gone, the future is not yet here. *So the positive side of apologetics is the communication of the gospel to the present generation in terms that they can understand.*

The purpose of "apologetics" is not just to win an argument or a discussion, but that the people with whom we are in contact may become Christians and then live under the Lordship of Christ in the whole spectrum of life.

It is important to remember, first of all, that we cannot separate true apologetics from the work of the Holy Spirit, nor from a living relationship in prayer to the Lord on the part of the Christian. We must understand that eventually the battle is not just against flesh and blood.

However, the biblical emphasis that knowledge is needed prior to salvation will influence us in attaining that knowledge which is needed to communicate the gospel. Historic Christianity has never separated itself from knowledge. It insists that all truth is one, and we must live and teach this even if twentieth-century thought and theology deny it.

The invitation to act comes only after an adequate base of knowledge has been given. This accords with the reason John gave for writing his Gospel: "Many other signs therefore did Jesus in the presence of his disciples which are not written in this book. But these are written that ye may believe that Jesus is the Christ, the Son of God: and that believing ye may have life in his name."[1] The word "sign" is related to the historic events of the life, death and resurrection of Christ as put forth in this Gospel. In twentieth-century language we could translate "sign" as "space-time proof": "Many other space-time proofs therefore did Jesus." Note first that these space-time proofs which, by their very nature, are observable were set forth as having taken place in the presence of the disciples who observed them. And not only that, but that they were written down in verbalized form. This means, of course, that these space-time proofs can be considered on the basis of the normal use of language as set forth in grammars and lexicons.

The order in these verses is important. Firstly, these are space-time proofs in written form, and consequently capable of careful consideration. Then, secondly, these proofs are of such a nature as to give good and sufficient evidence that Christ is the Messiah as prophesied in the Old Testament, and also that He is the Son of God. So that, thirdly, we are not asked to believe until we have faced the question as to whether this is true on the basis of the space-time evidence.

The same kind of groundwork of true knowledge is set forth in the Prologue to the Gospel of Luke:[2] "Forasmuch as many have taken in hand to draw up a narrative concerning those matters which have been fulfilled among us" (there are things which have happened in history, in the space-time before "us"), "even as they delivered them unto us, which from the beginning were eyewitnesses" (this history is open to verification by eyewitnesses) "and ministers of the word, it seemed good to me also, having traced the course of all things accurately from the first, to write unto thee in order, most excellent Theophilus" (what is open to verification can also be communicated verbally, in writing) "that thou mightest know the truth concerning the things (or words) wherein thou wast instructed." There is no leap in the dark, for it is possible to "know the truth." Only when we have understood this introduction are we ready for the rest of the Gospel of Luke, beginning in the next verse: "There was in the days of Herod, King of Judaea, a certain priest. . . ." We know from the Prologue that Luke is dealing with a framework of historic truth, and we are to place Herod, Zacharias and Christ within this space-time framework.

Knowledge precedes faith. This is crucial in understanding the Bible. *To say (as a Christian should) that only that faith which believes God on the basis of knowledge is true faith, is to say something which causes an explosion in the twentieth-century world.*

CHAPTER TWO

The Importance of Truth

Some time ago I was speaking at Oxford University to a group of theological students on the subject of communicating the gospel to those people who are dominated by the consensus of twentieth-century thinking. When I had finished speaking, a Canadian post-graduate student stood up and said, "Sir, if we understand you correctly, you are saying that pre-evangelism must come before evangelism. If this is so, then we have been making a mistake at Oxford. The reason we have not been reaching many of these people is because we have not taken enough time with pre-evangelism." I said that I totally agreed.

Truth Stands Before Conversion
Before a man is ready to become a Christian, he must have a proper understanding of truth, whether he has fully analyzed his concept of truth or not. All people, whether they realize it or not, function in the framework of some concept of truth. Our concept of truth will radically affect our understanding of what it means to become a Christian. We are concerned, at this point, not with the *content* of truth so much as with the *concept* of what truth is.

Some who consider themselves real Christians have been infil-

155

trated by the twentieth-century thought-forms. In reference to conversion, in a Christian sense, truth must be first. The phrase "accepting Christ as Savior" can mean anything. We are not saying what we are trying to say unless we make completely clear that we are talking about objective truth when we say Christianity is true and therefore that "accepting Christ as Savior" is not just some form of "upper-story leap."

Truth and Spirituality
Just as this matter of objective truth needs to be stressed before we can do effective evangelism, so the same thing must be considered before we can talk about true spirituality. From the biblical viewpoint, spirituality is not fragmented. Therefore, it has to be distinguished from modern concepts of spirituality, both in the West and the East, and, unhappily, from some evangelical concepts. It is not fragmented because it concerns the whole man in his whole moment-by-moment life. Over against this true biblical view, some evangelicalism has been Platonic in the sense that it has placed too much emphasis on the soul in contrast to the whole person, including the body and the intellect.

It is very important to realize, over against modern concepts of "spiritual experience," that the biblically-based experience rests firmly on truth. It is not only an emotional experience, nor is it contentless.

We can think of true spirituality as having three parts. The indispensable beginning is to consider who (or what) "is there," and how I can have a relationship to him (or it). That something must be understood and defined. You cannot have a personal relationship with something unknown. Then, having understood who it is with whom I am to have a personal relationship and how I may have it, comes the actual step of entering into that relationship. The Bible calls this being converted, "born again," and this is a step which a person can take only as an individual. We cannot be born again in groups, but only one at a time. But to say that this is an individual matter is not the same as to say it is individualistic. The words may sound alike, but they are worlds apart. This gives the basis for a whole sociological and cultural concept.

True spirituality cannot be abstracted from truth at one end, nor from the whole man and the whole culture at the other. If there is a true spirituality, it must encompass all. The Bible insists that truth is one — and it is almost the sole surviving system in our generation that does.

To avoid confusion, let us notice what this emphasis on the unity of truth does *not* involve. First of all, from the biblical viewpoint, truth is not ultimately related to orthodoxy. Orthodoxy is important, and I am known as a man who is a convinced orthodox theologian. But truth is not ultimately related to orthodoxy. Secondly, truth is not related ultimately to the Creeds either. I, also, believe the historic Christian Creeds are important, but we must realize that, while the Creeds are important, truth is not finally related to them. Truth is related to something back of both orthodoxy and the Creeds.

Thirdly, truth is not *ultimately* related even to the Scriptures. Let me explain. Though I firmly believe what the early Church and the reformers taught concerning the nature of the Scriptures, and though I would emphasize that what they have to say concerning the Scriptures is crucially important, yet again, truth is finally related to something behind the Scriptures. The Scriptures are important, not because they are printed in a certain way nor bound in a certain kind of leather, nor because they have helped many people. This is not the basic reason for the Scriptures being overwhelmingly important. The Bible, the historic Creeds, and orthodoxy are important because God is there, and, finally, that is the only reason they have their importance.

The force of this was brought home to me several years ago when a young Swiss-German architect was reporting at one of our Farel House seminars in Switzerland on Max Planck's last essays. He pointed out that Planck, speaking in terms of his discipline, which was physics and not religion, said that modern man has had to move the screen back several times in our generation, and the question he posed was: what will be the final screen? Planck was saying that we do not know what the final screen will be in the material structure of the universe. This idea of a final screen started to bore away in my mind as a Christian, and as one speaking into the twentieth-century world. What is the final screen of truth?

The answer can only be the existence of God and who He is. Therefore, Christian truth is that which is in relationship to what exists and ultimately to the God who exists. And true spirituality consists of being in the correct relationship to the God who is there, first in the once-for-all act of justification, secondly by being in that correct relationship as a continuing moment-by-moment reality. This is the biblical emphasis on true spirituality. It is a continuing moment-by-moment proper relationship with the God who exists.

The God Behind Truth

I have chosen to use this expression "God is there" as being equivalent to "God exists," not because I am unaware of the theological discussions today, nor because I have met anyone who, holding to the truth of the Bible, believes in a three-story universe, but in order to meet the problem of the modern theology, which denies that God is there in the historical biblical sense. We must have the courage to say that God is there, or, to use different terminology, that the final environment of what is there is God Himself, the One who has created everything else.

Let us notice carefully that in saying God is there, we are saying God exists, and not just talking about the *word* god, or the *idea* god. We are speaking of the proper relationship to the living God who exists. In order to understand the problems of our generation, we should be very alive to this distinction.

Semantics (linguistic analysis) for a certain period made up the heart of modern philosophical study in the Anglo-Saxon world. Though the Christian cannot accept this study as a philosophy, there is no reason why he should not be glad for the concept that words need to be defined before they can be used in communication. As Christians, we must understand that there is no word so meaningless as the word *god* until it is defined. No word has been used to teach absolutely opposite concepts as much as the word *god*. Consequently, let us not be confused. There is much "spirituality" about us today that relates itself to the *word* god or to the *idea* god; but this is not what we are talking about. Biblical truth and spirituality is not a relationship to the *word* god, or to the *idea* god. It is a relationship to the One who is there. This is an entirely different concept.

Following on from the discussion as to who or what God is, springs the second fundamental question of today, "Who or what am I?" In order to make it possible to have a meaningful relationship between God and man, an answer to both questions must be given.

The answer we give here profoundly affects our idea of the form of the relationship between God and man. Whether we regard this relationship as mechanical, deterministic or — infinitely more wonderful — personal will turn upon our answers to the questions "Who is the God who is there?" and "Who am I?"

Many sensitive people today are really struggling for their lives, asking the question, "What is the purpose of man?" In fact, modern man has not come up with a satisfactory answer to this question in any of his fields of thinking. It does not matter much whether he has approached it along the lines of naked rationalism or the leap into the dark of modern secular and theological mysticism; twentieth-century man has failed to answer this question.

When someone asks me the Christian answer to this question of purpose, the reason for man's existence, I always take them to the first commandment of Christ. In passing, let us note that there is no reason to think that the first commandment — "Thou shalt love the Lord thy God with all thy heart, and with all thy soul, and with all thy mind, and with all thy strength"[1] — is merely a first commandment uttered by Jesus. We know it is not so because He quoted it from the last book of Moses, the book of Deuteronomy. But we can say something more. Surely it is the first commandment because it is the one that expresses the purpose of man and, individually, my purpose.

But it is not enough to quote this on its own. Without the answer given by historic Christianity that God is really there, such an answer can only be another cliché to the honest enquirer, just one more twentieth-century "religious answer"; and we cannot blame him if he stops listening. When I hear this first commandment to love the God who is there with everything that I am, it carries with it a total concept of life and of truth. A man can only love a God who exists and who is personal and about whom he has knowledge. So the fact that this God has communicated is also of supreme importance. But this commandment carries something more; it tells me something very fundamental and exciting about *myself.*

There is indeed something to be excited about if we know the dilemmas of our generation. If you could see the sober, sensitive men and women who come to our chalet asking the questions, "who, or what, am I?" with real longings, you would realize there is something electrifying to know about "myself."

As far as the modern mentality is concerned, it is shattering to be told that there is nothing intrinsically nonsensical in calling upon me to love the God who is there, and that God is of such a nature and that I am of such a nature as to make this a valid proposition. Those who understand what is involved will not dismiss this as "something I have heard since I was little." To think through the implications is totally exciting. The God who is there is of such a nature that He can be loved, and I am of such a nature that I can love; and thus this first commandment, or basic purpose of man, is the very opposite of a nonsense statement. I know what man is, and I know who I am.

Personal and Corporate Living into the Twentieth-century Climate

CHAPTER ONE

Demonstrating the Character of God

Salvation Does Not End with the Individual

We have examined the tension which a non-Christian is bound to feel — the tension between the real world and the logical conclusion of a man's non-Christian presuppositions. If we are honest, Christians, too, have a question to face. As people watch us, individually and corporately, and hear our presuppositions, what do they see with regard to our consistence to our presuppositions?

THE MAN, NOW THE   THE LOGICAL CONCLUSION

CHRISTIAN, AND HIS ————————▶ OF OUR CHRISTIAN

PRESUPPOSITIONS   PRESUPPOSITIONS

In this concluding section I want to pursue the question of a reality which is visible to a watching world.

As Christians, we must consider what the logical conclusions of *our* presuppositions are. Here we are speaking of apologetics, not abstractly, not scholastically, not as a subject taught in a Christian school, but as practiced in the battles of our generation. Christian apologetics must be able to show intellectually that Christianity speaks of *true truth*; but it must also *exhibit* that it is not just a theory. This is needed for the defense of the flock of Christ, and also in the positive sense of reaching out to those who are honestly asking questions. What is observable, both individually and corporately, is also included in Christian apologetics. Christians should always have comprehended and considered this; but it is overwhelmingly important in view of the thought-forms of our generation to show that Christianity is not just a better dialectic.

As orthodox evangelicals we have often made the mistake of stopping with individual salvation. Historically the word *Christian* has meant two things. First, the word *Christian* defines a person who has accepted Christ as Savior. This is decidedly an individual thing. But there is a second consideration as well. It concerns that which flows from individual salvation. While it is true that there is an individual salvation, and this is the beginning of the Christian life, yet nevertheless individual salvation should show itself also in *corporate* relationships. This is the Bible's clear teaching concerning the Church and what we find, in some measure, as we consider the Church at its strongest through the ages.

When man fell, various divisions took place. The first and basic division is between man who has revolted and God. All other divisions flow from that. We are separated from God by our guilt — true moral guilt. Hence we need to be justified upon the basis of the finished substitutionary work of the Lord Jesus Christ. Yet it is quite plain from the Scriptures and from general observation that the separations did not stop with the separation of man from God. For, secondly, man was separated from himself. This gives rise to the psychological problems of life. Thirdly, man was separated from other men, leading to the sociological problems of life. Fourthly, man was separated from nature.

According to the teaching of the Scriptures, the finished work of the Lord Jesus Christ is meant eventually to bring healing to each of these divisions: healing which will be perfect in every aspect when Christ comes again in history in the future.

In justification, there is a relationship which is already perfect. When the individual accepts Christ as his Savior, on the basis of the finished work of Christ, God as Judge declares that his guilt is gone immediately and forever. With regard to the other separations, it is plain from the scriptural teaching and from the struggles of God's people throughout the best years of the Church that in this present life the blood of Christ is meant to bring *substantial* healing now. Individual salvation comes with justification, and guilt is gone at once. Then comes a future day when my body will be raised from the dead, and the other separations will be healed just as completely. Now, in the present life, when men can observe us, there is to be a *substantial* healing of these other divisions. *Substantial* is the right word to use because it carries with it two ideas. Firstly, it means that it is not yet perfect. Secondly, it means that there is reality.

The Visible Quality
The world has a right to look upon us and make a judgment. We are told by Jesus that as we love one another the world will judge, not only whether we are His disciples, but whether the Father sent the Son.[1] The final apologetic, along with the rational, logical defense and presentation, is *what the world sees* in the individual Christian and in our corporate relationships together. The command that we should love one another surely means something much richer than merely organizational relationship. Not that we should minimize proper organizational relationship, but one may look at those bound together in an organized group called a church and see nothing of a substantial healing of the division between people in the present life.

On the other hand, while there is "the invisible Church" (that is, everyone who is a Christian living anywhere in the world), yet the Church is not to be hidden away, in an unseen area, as though it does not matter what men see. What we are called to do, upon the basis of the finished work of Christ in the power of the Spirit through faith, is to exhibit a substantial healing, individual and then corporate, so that people may observe it. This too is a portion of the apologetic: a presentation which gives at least some demonstration that these things are not theoretical, but real; not perfect, yet substantial. If we only speak of and exhibit the individual effects of the gospel, the world, psychologically conditioned as it is today, will explain them away. What the world cannot explain away will be a substantial, corporate exhibition of the logical conclusions of the Christian presuppositions. It is not true that the New Testament presents an individualistic concept of salvation. Individual, yes — we must come one at a time; but it is not to be individualistic. First there must be the individual reality, and then the corporate. Neither will be perfect in this life, but they must be real. I have discovered that hard twentieth-century people do not expect Christians to be perfect. They do not throw it in our teeth when, individually or corporately, they find less than perfection in us. They do not expect perfection, but they do expect reality; and they have a right to expect reality, upon the authority of Jesus Christ.

There must be communion and community among the people of God: not a false community that is set up as though human community were an end in itself; but in the local church, in a mission, in a school, wherever it might be, true fellowship must be evident as the outcome of original, individual salvation. This is the real Church of the Lord Jesus Christ — not merely organization, but a group of people, individually the people of God, drawn together by the Holy Spirit for a particular task either in a local situation or over a wider area. The Church of the Lord Jesus should be a group of those who are redeemed and bound together on the basis of true doctrine. But subsequently they should show together a substantial "sociological healing" of the breaches between men which have come about because of the results of man's sin.

The Christian sociological position is that the sociological problems which exist, regardless of what they may be, are a result of the separation that has come between men because of sin. Now the world should be able to see in the Church external marks which exhibit that there is a substantial sociological healing possible in the present generation. We can never expect the testimony of a previous generation to be sufficient for our own time. We can point to the wonders of past achievements, but men have a right to say, "This is our moment, this is our history, what about today?" It is not enough for the Church to be engaged with the State in healing social ills, though this is important at times. But when the world can turn around and see a group of God's people exhibiting substantial healing in the area of human relationships in their present life, then the world will take notice. Each group of Christians is, as it were, a pilot plant, showing that something can be done in the present situation, if only we begin in the right way.

Corporate living in the early Church was very strong at this point. It was not perfect, but it was strong. The testimony has come down to us that one of the things that shook the Roman Empire was that as they looked at these Christians — a cross section of the wide sociological spectrum in the Roman Empire from slaves to their masters, and including some of Caesar's household — non-Christians were forced to say, "Behold, how they love each other." And this was not in a vacuum, but loving each other in the circle of truth.

Realism in Exhibition
We must look to the Son of God, moment by moment, for these things; such things cannot be done in our own strength. We must allow Him to bear His fruit through us. We can proclaim "orthodoxy" in the flesh, and we can compromise in the flesh. But our calling is a different calling: it is to exhibit God and His character, by His grace, in this generation. We need to show Him forth as personal, as holy, and as love. It is possible in the flesh to be both orthodox and dead — or loving and compromising. What is not possible in the flesh is simultaneously to exhibit both the justice of God and the love of God — this can only be done through the work of the Holy Spirit. And yet anything less is not a picture of God, but only a caricature of the God who exists.

Demonstrating God's character must be existential. The existentialists are right at this place, though they are wrong when they say that history is not going anywhere. As far as living is concerned, we are on the knife-edge of time. What will matter is our relationship to the Lord Jesus, individually and then corporately, at this existential moment. What counts, as men look upon us individually and corporately, is whether we are exhibiting God and His character *now*. The Christian position is not static, but is living.

Christ says, "Be ye therefore perfect, even as your Father which is in heaven is perfect."[2] How could a perfect God say, "Just sin a little bit"? This would be impossible. The standard is God's own perfection. And yet the Word of God does not leave us with a romantic notion that we must either have total perfection in this life or, if not, that we must smash everything and have nothing. I am firmly convinced that many wonderful things have been destroyed because people have had a preconceived and romantic notion in their minds as to what the perfect thing should be, would settle for nothing else, and thus have smashed what could have been.

How glad we should be for the Apostle John when he says, "My little children, these things write I unto you, that ye sin not. And if any man sin, *we* have an advocate with the Father."[3] There is a tremendous and wonderful implication in that word *"we."* John, the beloved apostle, places himself among us. On the one hand, we must stand against all standards lower than perfection. The standards are not arbitrary, but are those which the holy God who exists has given us in the Bible, and we are to take them with total seriousness. Anything less than the totality of these standards will not do. Sin is not to be minimized either in the individual or the corporate life. Antinomianism in theory or practice is always wrong and destructive.

Yet, on the other hand, we must stand against all the romantic concepts of perfection in this life. The Bible does not promise us perfection in this life, except in the area of justification. It does not promise us in this life perfection morally, physically, psychologically or sociologically. There are to be moral victories and growth, but that is different from perfection. John could say "we." Paul could indicate his own lack of perfection.[4] There can be physical healing, but that does not mean that the one healed is then a perfect physical specimen. The day Lazarus was raised from the dead he may have had a headache, and certainly one day he died again. People can be wonderfully helped psychologically, but that does not mean that they will then be totally integrated personalities. The Christian position is understanding that on this side of the resurrection the call *is* to perfection, and yet at the same time not to smash and destroy what we cannot bring again to life — just simply because it is less than the perfections that we romantically build in our thinking. For example, how many women have I found — and how many men — — who have stomped on a perfectly good marriage until it was dead, just because they had a romantic concept of what marriage should or could be, either physically or emotionally.

Personality Is Central
We have been speaking about those things which are vitally important with regard to the logical conclusions of the Christian presuppositions. So far we have spoken about two: the *corporate* and the *substantial*. Now we will add the third: the *personal*.

The Christian system is consistent as no other system that has ever been. It is beautiful beyond words, because it has that quality that no other system completely has — you begin at the beginning, and you can go to the end. It is as simple as that. *And every part and portion of the system can be related back to the beginning.*

Whatever you discuss, to understand it properly, you just go back to the beginning and the whole thing is in its place. The beginning is simply that God exists and that He is the personal-infinite God. Our generation longs for the reality of personality, but it cannot find it. But Christianity says personality is valid because personality has not just appeared in the universe, but rather is rooted in the personal God who has always been.

All too often, when we are talking to the lost world, we do not begin at the beginning and therefore the world stops listening. Without this emphasis on personality we cannot expect people really to listen, because without this the concept of salvation is suspended in a vacuum.

If we understand this, we understand the meaning of life. The meaning of life does not end with justification, but is seen in the reality that when we accept Christ as our Savior in the true biblical sense, our personal relationship with the personal God is restored. Every place we turn in Christianity we find that we are brought face to face with the wonder of personality — the very opposite of the dilemma and the sorrow of modern man who finds no meaning in personality. Consider the words of Paul, "The grace of the Lord Jesus Christ, and the love of God, and the communion of the Holy Ghost be with you all."[5] It is the personal to which we are brought. First of all there is the personal relationship with God Himself — this is the most wonderful, and is not just in Heaven, but is substantially real in practice now. When we understand our calling, it is not only true but beautiful — and it should be exciting. It is hard to understand how an orthodox, evangelical, Bible-believing Christian can fail to be excited. The answers in the realm of the intellect should make us overwhelmingly excited. But more than this, we are returned to a personal relationship with the God who is there. If we are unexcited Christians, we should go back and see what is wrong. We are surrounded by a generation that can find "no one home" in the universe. If anything marks our generation, it is this. In contrast to this, as a Christian I know who I am; and I know the personal God who is there. I speak, and He hears. I am not surrounded by mere mass, nor only energy particles, but He is there. And if I have accepted Christ as my Savior, then though it will not be perfect in this life, yet moment by moment, on the basis of the finished work of Christ, this person to person relationship with the God who is there can have reality to me.

CHAPTER TWO

The Legal, But Not Only the Legal

Today most non-Christians exclude any real notion of law. They do this because they have no *absolute* anywhere in the universe, and without an absolute one cannot really have any morals as morals. For them, everything is relative; they have no real *circle* of law. For them there is no circle inside which there is right, in contrast to that which is outside the circle and therefore wrong. To the Christian this is not so. God does exist, and He has a character; there are things which are outside the commandments He has given us as the expression of His character. For example, there is therefore a proper legal circle in regard to the visible Church. The visible Church should be a true Church. It will not be a perfect Church, but it should be a true one. And marriage is the proper circle for sexual relationships. The new morality, following the new theology and lacking the Christian epistemology, the Christian Scripture, and the Christian God, can find no real legal circle and so finds no way to set boundaries.

The fault of orthodoxy is that though it has a legal circle, it tends too often to act as though merely to be within the legal circle is enough. We should be thankful for the legal circle — a real absolute, something we can know and within which we can function — because it means that we do not have to act on the assumption that we can, or must, weigh all the results of our acts out to infinity, when, being finite, we cannot see the results of our acts more than one or two steps ahead. Having to act as a finite god is painful. But what a tragedy to think that because we are in the proper legal circle, everything is finished and done — as though marriage, the Church, and other human relationships are static and that only the legal circle is important.

Even in justification, many Christians who are perfectly orthodox in doctrine look back upon their justification as though it were the end of all, at least until death comes. It is not. Birth is essential to life, but the parent is not glad only for the birth of his child. He is thankful for the living child that grows up. Whoever saw a couple get engaged simply because they wanted to enjoy the marriage ceremony? What they want to do is to live together. So it is with becoming a Christian. In one way you can say that the new birth is everything; in another way you can say that really it is very little. It is everything because it is indispensable to begin with, but it is little in comparison with the living existential relationship. The legal circle of justification does not end statically; it opens to me a living person-to-person communication with the God who exists.

In marriage, in the Church, and in other human relationships the same thing applies — the proper legal relationship must be there, but if it is static it becomes a dusty monument. It is no longer beautiful. It becomes a flower that dies under a glass. It can only be beautiful if inside the proper legal circle we have a personal relationship which speaks of the personal God who is there. This is our calling, not only to exhibit something substantially real to a watching world, but to enjoy it ourselves. I am called to love God with all my heart and soul and mind, and I am called to love my neighbor as myself: each person involved in the proper circle and in the proper relationship.

If we say that personality is not an intrusion in the universe but central, the world has a right to see the Christians both individually and corporately living on a personal level. Men must see that we take personality seriously enough, by the grace of God, to act upon it.

There must be an observable indication of this in the midst of the daily life in this present abnormal world, or we have denied the central Christian presupposition.

Human People in Our Culture

When we use the phrase, "it is only human," we are usually referring to something sinful. In this sense, the Christian should feel a
calling *not* to be "human"; but in a more profound sense, the
Christian is called to exhibit the characteristics of true humanity,
because being a man is not intrinsically being sinful man, but
being that which goes back before the Fall, to man made in the
image of God.

Therefore, Christians in their relationships should be the most
human people you will ever see. This speaks for God in an age of
inhumanity and impersonality and facelessness. When people
look at us their reaction should be, "These are human people";
human because we know that we differ from the animal, the plant
and the machine, and that personality is native to what has always
been. This is not something only to put forward intellectually —
when people observe us their reaction should be: "These *are*
human people!"

If they cannot look upon us and say, "These are real people,"
nothing else is enough. Far too often young people become Christians and then search among the Church's ranks for real people,
and have a hard task finding them. All too often evangelicals are
paper people.

If we do not preach these things, talk about them to each other,
and teach them carefully from the pulpit and in the Christian
classroom, we cannot expect Christians so to act. This has always
been important, but it is especially so today because we are surrounded by a world in which personality is increasingly eroded. If
we who have become God's children do not show Him to be personal in our lives, then in practice we are denying His existence.
People should see a beauty among Christians in their practice of
the centrality of personal relationships — in the whole spectrum of
life and in the whole culture. This is equivalent today, when many
think both man and God are dead, to the songs of wonder and
exultation in the Old Testament, sung because God is a living
God and not a lifeless idol.

On the final day of a series of lectures I was giving at a Christian
college some years ago, the president of the Student Council handed
me the following letter written on Student Council stationery:

Dear Dr. Schaeffer,
You have helped me a great deal this week to spot some of the rea-

sons for my rebellion against both the evangelical form of orthodoxy, and to some degree against God. For this I can't thank you enough, nor can I thank God enough for helping me to see myself a little more clearly. The difficulty, of course, comes in the implementation of my conclusions into my own being, though I trust this will occur.

I am also concerned about the effect that your messages may have on the rest of the campus and on evangelicalism as a whole. You have asserted that Christianity is both a system, orthodoxy, and a personal association with Christ. As such there are some absolutes which we as Christians can depend on and demand of others if they are to be considered truly Christian. With this I agree, although I may not hold to all the absolutes which you have indicated are necessary for the Christian "system." But the matter which is of concern to me is that there are many here at (— — —) and in evangelicalism who, because they believe they have true truth, impose their own societal and evangelical, subcultural absolutes on those of us who have had "the roof blown off." The result is that students are often forced into either accepting evangelicalism, with all of its absolutes, be they Victorian or early twentieth-century, or out into total despair. Believe me, sir, when I say there are many at (— — —) in this position. In fact, this is what has finally driven many into neo-orthodoxy and skepticism.

This brings me to my final point which is simply this: Now that you have succeeded in "blowing the roof off" for some students, and have instructed evangelicalism to go and do likewise, would you please tell us how evangelicalism can eliminate some of these extraneous absolutes which make orthodoxy (as we know it) almost impossible to swallow. How can evangelicals really become the salt of the earth when many of their absolutes forbid them to even come into contact with the earth? How does the evangelical house clean out enough dust to make it the orthodox house, and then perhaps we will be relevant to the twentieth-century man?

Very Sincerely,

(— — —)

Student Council President.

I do not think that I would agree with this student in all the details involved, but I do agree that there is much dust to clear out. Our task is to deal with the dust, but not to burn down the house in order to remove it.

The Question of Apologetics

Since *The God Who Is There* was originally published, questions have been asked about my views concerning what is often called "apologetics." I will try to clarify this under three headings: *Apologetics, Rationalism,* and *Evangelism and Lifestyle.*

Apologetics
The answer as to whether I am an apologete depends on how the concept of apologete, or apologetics, is defined.

First, I am not an apologete if that means building a safe house to live in, so that we Christians can sit inside with safety and quiescence. Christians should be out in the midst of the world as both witnesses and salt, not sitting in a fortress surrounded by a moat.

Second, I would quote what has been a part of the text of *The God Who Is There* on page 120 from its original edition onward:

> As we turn to consider in more detail how we may speak to men of the twentieth century, we must emphasize first of all that we cannot apply mechanical rules. We, of all people, should realize this, for as Christians we believe that personality really does exist and is impor-

tant. We can lay down some general principles, but there can be no automatic application. If we are truly personal, as created by God, then each individual will differ from everyone else. Therefore each man must be dealt with as an individual, not as a case or statistic or machine. If we would work with these people, we cannot mechanically apply the things of which we have been speaking in this book. We must look to the Lord in prayer, and to the work of the Holy Spirit, for effective use of these things.

In the light of this, I have been mystified at times about what has been said concerning "Schaeffer's apologetics."

I do not believe there is any one apologetic which meets the needs of all people. And, as I said in the text of *The God Who Is There*, I did not (and do not) mean that what I wrote in that book should ever be applied mechanically, as a set formula. There is no set formula that meets everyone's need, and if only applied as a mechanical formula, I doubt if it really meets anyone's need — short of an act of God's mercy.

Human nature being what it is, I am sure some people have read *The God Who Is There* or have come to L'Abri and have gone away thinking that what they have learned can be applied mechanically as a formula. I, and we at L'Abri, have tried to do everything we can to dispel this. The quotation I gave from *The God Who Is There* above says this clearly.

When we have the opportunity to talk to the non-Christian, what (if not the formula mentality) should be the dominant consideration? I think this should be love. I think these things turn on love and compassion to people not as objects to evangelize, but as people who deserve all the love and consideration we can give them, because they are our kind and made in the image of God. They are valuable, so we should meet them in love and compassion. Thus, we meet the person where he or she is.

Consequently, if I were with Paul and Silas in the Philippian jail, and the Philippian jailer said to me, "Sir, what must I do to be saved?" for me to start talking about epistemology would be horrible. I would say what Paul said: "Believe on the Lord Jesus Christ, and you shall be saved," because the jailer was, on the basis of previous knowledge and events, ready for that answer.[1]

Now on the other hand, if we are dealing with someone who has honest problems and who really believes that truth is truth — things are true and things are false (and that previously was the generally accepted concept almost everywhere) — it would then be a different need. In that situation, if he or she had questions on the historicity of Christ's resurrection and so on, we would deal with those questions — because he or she already accepts that truth is truth.

What I try to do in *The God Who Is There* is to show that when we get to those holding the concept that there is no such thing as objective (or universal) truth, we can still keep talking. We can move further back and keep talking in the way they need. I do not believe that there is any one system of apologetics that meets the need of all people, any more than I think there is any one form of evangelism that meets the need of all people. It is to be shaped on the basis of love for the person as a person.

If we are to deal with people where they are (whether they can express their position in a sophisticated way or not), we have got to have enough genuine love for them and concern, as a human being, that we would take seriously what they are preoccupied with. We tend to give a person a prepackaged answer instead of having the compassion of Christ, which is to take the person where they are and actually step into their world in order to talk in a meaningful way to them. And if that world is that of the Philippian jailer, good; if it is that of the one who believes truth is truth, good; but if it is the person who is lost in relativity, we can give them the Christian answers there as well.

If people do not have "modern" intellectual questions, there is no need of dealing with such questions; but we must acknowledge that in our generation almost everybody has them. I walked out of the restaurant one morning a few weeks ago, and there was a girl sitting with a cup of coffee reading Skinner's book *Beyond Freedom and Dignity*. She represents millions. We have millions and millions facing these questions, and in fact I think today the majority of the community have such questions. And they do not have to be university graduates. I have worked with shipyard workers, mill workers, all kinds of people (as well as, when I was younger, personally working on farms, a huckster wagon, in factories, and so on), and I am convinced that these people often have the same questions as the intellectual; the only thing is that they do not articulate them, or if they do articulate them it is not in the same terminology. I know these people, and I am convinced that the things we are talking about can be talked about to almost anyone — all one has to do is to shift gears in language. Incidentally, that too is love.

The middle-class family wonders why things have changed — they realize the problem of relativism, though they perhaps would not use that term. They are brought up against the relativism when their daughter goes off to sleep with someone, and it is clear that she does not see this as either wrong nor a surprising thing to do. They also see the law changing and do not know why, but are troubled. They too are asking the same questions. They too are either below "the line of despair" or comprehending its existence in some at least vague way. Love means dealing with them at the place where they are.

For the "modern person" we can keep talking in a way which helps because in contrast to the concept that everything is relative, we know that there are good, adequate and sufficient reasons to know that the Christian answers are truth. I do not believe that there is a leap of faith needed; there are good and sufficient reasons to know why Christianity is true — and more than that, that is the Bible's insistence. The Bible's emphasis is that there are good and sufficient reasons to *know* that Christianity is true, so much so that we are disobedient and guilty if we do not believe it.

The Christian system (what is taught in the whole Bible) is a unity of thought. Christianity is not just a lot of bits and pieces — there is a beginning and an end, a whole system of truth, and this system is the only system that will stand up to all the questions that are presented to us as we face the reality of existence. Some of the other systems answer some of the questions, but leave others unanswered. I believe it is only Christianity that gives the answers to all the crucial questions.

What are those questions? The questions are those which are presented to us as we face the reality of existence. God shuts us up to reality. We cannot escape the reality of what is, no matter what we say we believe or think.

This reality of which I speak falls into two parts: the fact that the universe truly exists and it has a form, and then what I would call the "mannishness" of man — which is my own term for meaning that man is unique. People have certain qualities that must be explained.

God has shut up all people to these things, and I always like to go back to the statement of Jean-Paul Sartre, though he had no answer for his own statement, and that is that the basic philosophic question is that something is there. Things do exist, and this demands an explanation for their existence. I would then go beyond Sartre's statement to one by Einstein. Einstein said that the most amazing thing about the universe is that we can know something truly about it. In other words, it has a form that is comprehensible, even though we cannot exhaust it. And then I would say beyond that — no matter what people say they are, they are what they are; that is, man is unique as made in the image of God. Any system of thought, to be taken seriously, has to at least try to explain these two great phenomena of the universe and man. In other words, we are talking about objective truth related to reality and not just something within our own heads.

Now I would like to add a corollary to this: In *Whatever Happened to the Human Race?*, and especially the extensive notes of the fifth chapter, there is a third thing, and that is the way the Bible measures up to history. Once we say that, this is very exciting. It is very exciting because other religions are not founded in history, they are "out there" somewhere, or you can think of them as inside of your own head — whichever way you are looking at it. On the other hand, the Bible claims to be rooted in history. Whether we are considering the history of the Old Testament, whether we are considering the history of Christ, including the resurrection, or Paul's journeys, it is insisted on as real history. So now we have three interwoven parts. Usually I have dealt with the first two because I think they are the two which touch more the twentieth-century person, but the third is also there. We have to face the reality of the universe and its having an existence and having a form. We have to face the reality in the uniqueness of man. We are able to discuss the fact that the Bible is rooted in history.

I would repeat, God shuts everyone up to the fact of reality, and everyone has to deal with the reality that is.

When we turn to the Bible, the Bible says that on the basis of God's created world and on the basis of who we are, there are good and sufficient reasons to know the biblical answers are true. People come to the knowledge that this is adequate on different levels, depending on their intelligence, their education, their personality, the way their mind works; but at some point they come to the place where indeed they have what to them should be good and sufficient and adequate answers.

So what you have is the flow of the totality of reality — instead of being focused on religious things only, it is religious things as a part of reality. And instead of this concept being contrary to the

Bible, it is the way the Bible is written. It is not "just a religious book"; the Bible is rooted in space-time history and speaks of the totality of reality.

The glory of the Bible is that it is enough for every age and it is enough for every person. When you consider the early chapters of Genesis on through Deuteronomy, given about 1500 B.C. to Moses, it gave truth to those people in that day. Now we come to our age, and we know a lot that those people did not know about the cosmos, all kinds of things, and those same chapters (and the rest of the Bible) are enough to give truth to us. If Christ does not come back for another 500 years the people then will know more than we do now, and the Bible will give truth to them. So, whether it is the individual, no matter what his level of education, sophistication, etc., or whether it is the age we live in with the knowledge we have, the Bible is enough to give the answer to the questions raised by reality.

When people refuse God's answer, they are living against the revelation of the universe and against the revelation of themselves. They are denying the revelation of God in *who* they themselves are. I am not saying that non-Christians do not live in the light of real existence. I am saying that they do not have any answer for living in it. I am not saying that they do not have moral motions, but they have no basis for them. I am not saying that the person with a non-Christian system (even a radical system like Buddhism or Hinduism or the modern Western thinking of chance) does not know that the object exists — the problem is that they have no system to explain the subject-object correlation. As a matter of fact, this is their damnation, this is their tension, that they have to live in the light of their existence, the light of reality — the total reality in all these areas — and they do live there, and yet they have no sufficient explanation for any of these areas. So, the wiser they are, the more honest they are, the more they feel that tension, and that is their present damnation.

There is nowhere that people can go that they can escape the things of grace that God has given them to shut them in, in the reality that exists. And if we love people enough, and we have compassion enough, we can usually find ways to talk to them, no matter how deep in the well they are. That is what I am saying. It is not that we use a universal formula to reach people, either in evangelism or in apologetics.

When we say a person is lost we usually think of evangelically lost, that he or she is a sinner and needs to accept Christ as Savior. But what we must realize is that these people do not know that they are lost evangelically. How could they? They do not believe there is right and wrong, they do not believe there is a God, they do not believe there is an absolute, there is no reason for them to think of themselves as a sinner. Few believe in guilt anymore. There is only "sickness," or "guilt-feelings," or "sociological nonconformity." There is no such thing as true guilt. How much meaning does our talking about accepting Christ as Savior have for such a person? But our whole generation has a second sense of being lost which is valid, and that is they are without meaning in the world, without purpose, without morals, without a basis for law, no final principles, no final answers for anything. They know they are lost in this way. When we turn to the Bible, the Bible makes plain that indeed they are lost in both senses — they are lost evangelically; but without God, they are lost in the modern sense as well.

This lostness is answered by the existence of a Creator. So Christianity does not begin with "accept Christ as Savior." Christianity begins with "In the beginning God created the heavens (the total of the cosmos) and the earth." That is the answer to the twentieth century and its lostness. At this point we are then ready to explain the second lostness (the original cause of all lostness) and the answer in the death of Christ.

In summary: God in His grace has shut us up by the totality of reality to the biblical answers — i. e., there are good, adequate and sufficient reasons to know that the Christian answers are truth — so much so that if we do not bow to those answers, the Bible says we are disobedient and guilty.

Those who object to the position that there are good, adequate, and sufficient reasons to *know with our reason* that Christianity is true are left with a *probability position* at some point. At some point and in some terminology they are left with a leap of faith. This does not say that they are not Christians, but it means that they are offering *one more probability* to twentieth-century relativistic people to whom everything is only probability. They are offering one more leap of faith without reason (or with the severe diminishing of reason) to a generation that has heard a thousand leaps of faith proposed in regard to the crucial things of human life. I would repeat that what is left is that Christianity is a probability.

Of course, faith is needed to become a Christian, but there are two concepts concerning faith. The two ideas of faith run like this: One idea of faith would be a blind leap in the dark. A blind leap in which you believe something with no reason (or no adequate reason), you just believe it. This is what I mean by a blind leap of faith. The other idea of faith, which has no relationship with this, none whatsoever, is that you are asked to believe something and bow before that something on the basis of good and adequate reasons. There is no relationship between those two concepts of faith.

The biblical concept of faith is very much the second and not the first. You are not asked to believe in a blind leap of faith. The Bible teaches that there are good and sufficient reasons to know that these things are true. If you examine the ministry of Paul and also of Christ, you find they endlessly answered questions. There was no concept here of "Keep quiet, just believe"; it just does not exist. Paul answered the questions of the Jews, he answered the questions of the non-Jews, he was always answering questions; and the book of Romans certainly answered the questions of those without the Bible as well as of those with it.

There are good and sufficient reasons to know that these things are true. We have already dealt with the fact of reality and everybody having to deal with reality: (1) the existence of the universe and its form; (2) the distinctiveness of man; and (3) you can relate these to a third thing, and that is the examination of the historicity of Scripture.

But now we can ask another question. If it is so that there are good and sufficient reasons to know that Christianity is true, why doesn't everybody accept the sufficient answers?

We must realize that Christianity is the easiest religion in the world, because it is the only religion in which God the Father and Christ and the Holy Spirit do everything. God is the Creator; we have nothing to do with our existence, or the existence of other things. We can shape other things, but we cannot change the fact of existence. We do nothing for our salvation because Christ did it all. We do not have to do anything. In every other religion we have to do something — everything from burning a joss stick to sacrificing our firstborn child to dropping a coin in the collection plate — the whole spectrum. But with Christianity we do not do anything; God has done it all: He has created us and He has sent His Son; His Son died and because the Son is infinite, therefore

He bears our total guilt. We do not need to bear our guilt, nor do we even have to merit the merit of Christ. He does it all. So in one way it is the easiest religion in the world.

But now we can turn that over because it is the hardest religion in the world for the same reason. The heart of the rebellion of Satan and man was the desire to be autonomous; and accepting the Christian faith robs us not of our existence, not of our worth (it gives us our worth), but it robs us completely of being autonomous. We did not make ourselves, we are not a product of chance, we are none of these things; we stand there before a Creator plus nothing, we stand before the Savior plus nothing — it is a complete denial of being autonomous. Whether it is conscious or unconscious (and in the most brilliant people it is occasionally conscious), when they see the sufficiency of the answers on their own level, they suddenly are up against their innermost humanness — not humanness as they were created to be human, but human in the bad sense since the Fall. That is the reason that people do not accept the sufficient answers and why they are counted by God as disobedient and guilty when they do not bow.

People are living against the revelation of themselves. They are denying the revelation of God they themselves and all reality are. They are denying it and yet they have to live with it. When the person comes to see that there are good and sufficient reasons, then he or she is faced with a problem; either they bow before those good and sufficient reasons, *and bow to the Person behind the reasons*, or they refuse to bow.

It is not that the answers are not good, adequate and sufficient. Unless one gives up one's autonomy, one *cannot* accept the answers.

Rationalism
At times some have said my way of discussing "apologetics" is a form of rationalism.

First, a definition of words is helpful: A *rationalist* is someone who thinks man can begin with himself and his reason plus what he observes, without information from any other source, and come to final answers in regard to truth, ethics and reality. In contrast to the words *rationalist* or *rationalism*, *rationality* concerns the validity of thought, or the possibility to reason.

Some who have said I am a rationalist also speak of my being Aristotelian — that is, that my thinking has been influenced by

Aristotle. Those who do this usually (if not always) would hold the position that thought in terms of antithesis was originated by Aristotle. Thought in terms of antithesis means the concept that if a certain thing is true, the opposite is not true; or if a certain thing is right, the opposite is wrong. It would be well here for you to rethink all I have said about antithesis in *The God Who Is There* and also in *Escape from Reason*. In *The God Who Is There*, my Note 5 on Section III, Chapter 3, in regard to Heidegger, is important concerning this discussion.

Heidegger and others who hold the view that rational thought in terms of antithesis began with Aristotle have no historic basis for this. Rational thought as antithesis is not rooted in Aristotle, it is rooted in reality: first, the reality of the objective existence of God in antithesis to His not existing; second, the reality that God is a personal-infinite God to whom not all things are the same, in antithesis to an impersonal or limited God, or one who does not differentiate in the areas of truth or morals; third, the reality of the objective existence of that which God created in contrast to what He did not create; fourth, that which people do or make or paint or think, etc., in contrast to what does not exist. In morals, antithesis rests upon what conforms to God's character, in contrast to what opposes it.

Further, our minds are so created by God that we think in antithesis: so much so that the only way a person can deny antithesis is on the basis of antithesis. It is not surprising that God made our minds to think in the category of antithesis, for this fits the reality of His existence and the reality of His creation.

When certain people speak of those who hold to rationality (in regard to the Christian answers being adequate and sufficient) as being Aristotelian or rationalistic, they themselves should go back and think through as to whether they are not trapped in irrationality, not only in this discussion, but in other areas as well.

As I said above, a rationalist is a person who thinks man and his reason can come to final answers without information from any other source. No one stresses more than I that people have no final answers in regard to truth, morals or epistemology without God's revelation in the Bible. This is true in philosophy, science and theology. Rationalism can take a secular or theological form. In both, the rationalist thinks that on the basis of man's reason, plus what he can see about him, final answers are possible. My books stress that man cannot generate final answers from himself. First, even without the Fall, man was finite and needed the knowledge God gave him (revelation). Second, on this side of the Fall this is even more necessary.

At this point, I would suggest you reread my illustration of the torn book in *The God Who Is There*. As Christians, we do have the answers to the questions posed by reality. But we have not thought up these answers, we did not generate the answers, we are not the origin of the answers — we know them from God's revelation. This is the very opposite of rationalism.

On the other hand, the Bible does not say man is a zero. This view would be that since the Fall man cannot do anything, he just sits there and suddenly there is a strike of lightning out of the sky and he is a Christian. But the Bible does not say that. As I have said, the Bible stresses that the individual is guilty before God if he does not bow in the light of the adequacy of the biblical answers to the questions posed by reality. The individual has the responsibility of bowing before the answers which reason indicates to be sufficient *and necessary*.[2]

The work of the Holy Spirit and the responsibility I have as made in the image of God cannot be put into a Cartesian, mathematical formula. But that is different from saying, on one hand, that man can find the final answers by his finite (and fallen) reason alone, or, on the other hand, that man as he now is, is a zero. The Bible rejects both of these positions.

And as we speak of the balance of the work of the Holy Spirit and the person's responsibility to be humble enough to give up his or her autonomy to bow to the adequate answers, so also as we give the adequate and sufficient answers (which we did not generate, but which we have from the Bible), we must consciously pray for the Lord's work as these adequate answers are given. Giving the answers does not stand in a dichotomy with our being careful not to minimize the work of the Holy Spirit. When I am talking to an individual or sitting on a platform talking to 5,000 people and answering questions, very often, more often than most people know, I am praying for them. There is no contradiction between such prayer with expectancy that the Lord will answer that prayer, and showing that the Bible gives such good, adequate, sufficient, and necessary answers to the questions raised by reality that the hearers are truly disobedient and guilty if they do not bow.

Evangelism and Lifestyle

People often say, "What are you?" and I at times have said, "Well, basically I am an evangelist." But sometimes I do not think people have understood that does not mean that I think of an evangelist in contrast to dealing with philosophic, intellectual or cultural questions with care.

I am not a professional, academic philosopher—that is not my calling, and I am glad I have the calling I have, and I am equally glad some other people have the other calling. But when I say I am an evangelist, it is not that I am thinking that my philosophy, etc. is not valid—I think it is. For example, the answer I give in *He Is There and He Is Not Silent*, I think, is the real answer in regard to epistemology. That is not to say that all my answers are correct. Nor is it to say that the more academically oriented philosopher cannot deal with more of the necessary details. But what I am saying is that all the cultural, intellectual or philosophic material is not to be separated from leading people to Christ. I think my talking about metaphysics, morals and epistemology to certain individuals is a part of my evangelism just as much as when I get to the moment to show them that they are morally guilty and tell them that Christ died for them on the cross. I do not see or feel a dichotomy: *this* is my philosophy and *that* is my evangelism. The whole thing is evangelism to the people who are caught in the second lostness we spoke of—the second lostness being that they do not have any answers to the questions of meaning, purpose, and so on.

We always should realize, and I cannot say it often enough, that Christianity is a creation-centered teaching. It is not that suddenly for some strange reason out of nowhere if you accept Christ as Savior you are in. That is a part of a total structure. Christianity is a *system,* and I would say that I have no apology for using the word *system,* though it must not be allowed to be a mere academic system or theoretical or dead intellectualism. In the proper sense of the word, God is systematic in His creation and revelation.

It has got to be the whole man coming to know this is truth, acting upon it, living it out in his life, and worshiping God. But it is a system, it begins with the fact that there is a Creator, there is the God, the triune God who has existed forever. He has created all things, so there is nothing autonomous from Him.

Thus apologetics, as I see it, should not be separated in any way from evangelism. In fact, I wonder if "apologetics" which does not lead people to Christ as Savior, and then on to their living under the Lordship of Christ in the whole of life really is Christian apologetics. There certainly is a place for an academic study of a subject called "apologetics," as the defense and the credibility of Christianity, but if it does not lead the students to use that material in the way I have spoken about in the previous sentence, one can ask its value.

There certainly is a place for a study of philosophy as a scholarly discipline in great detail. That too can be a Christian's calling. But if the total course does not give answers so that the students are left with more than probability in regard to Christianity, it is much less than a course in philosophy can and should be.

To me there is a unity of all reality, and we can either say that every field of study is a part of evangelism (especially useful to certain people in the world); or we can say that there is no true evangelism that does not touch all of reality and all of life.

There are those who would approve (and praise) the "lifestyle," the emphasis on community, at L'Abri, but who would strenuously differ with what is taught here. Their disapproval usually falls somewhere under what I have dealt with above under the headings of *Apologetics, Rationalism* and *Evangelism and Lifestyle.*

Certainly there is no perfection of community at L'Abri, but we are thankful for what there has been (and is) in it of reality and beauty.

To us what there has been of the reality of community *is living truthfully* upon what the truth is. Without the certainty of that truth, and the content of that truth, the call for community would float in midair and be one more utopia. What there has been of the reality of community rests upon what is taught here.

Our calling is not primarily to an alternate lifestyle. Considering what the Bible teaches, what is crucial is not the word *community,* nor the form the practice of community takes.

Our primary calling is to truth as it is rooted in God, His acts and revelation; and, if it is indeed truth, it touches all of reality and all of life, including an adequate basis for, and some practice of, the reality of community.

1981

The Problem of the Middle-class Church in the Latter Half of the Twentieth Century

It is my hope that this book may be useful in helping orthodox evangelicalism so that it will be a thing of strength and beauty in the second half of the twentieth century.

In order for evangelicalism to be this, three principles must be observed:

1. The full doctrinal position of historic Christianity must be clearly maintained.

2. Every honest question must be given an honest answer. It is unbiblical for anyone to say, "Just believe."

3. There must be an individual and corporate exhibition that God exists in our century, in order to show that historic Christianity is more than just a superior dialectic or a better point of psychological integration.

There are two sections of our society to which, by and large, we have failed to communicate — the intellectuals on the one hand, and the workers on the other. The problem of being largely middle-class in our churches becomes really pressing both because of this, and also when we realize that we are losing children of Christian parents because they no longer accept their middle-class background in either home or local church.

In the two increasingly important areas of ideas and the application of morals, the majority of churches have little to say either to intellectuals or workers or, too often, to the young people from Christian homes.

Working in Switzerland, we have had many Christians' children who are honestly confused, coming from many different countries. They find so often that the answers they have been given simply do not touch the problems which are *their* problems. But this observation is gleaned not only from the many people who come to us in Switzerland, but also from traveling over much of the Western world, lecturing in many different places.

It is therefore my considered opinion that if the Church today is really concerned to break out of its middle-class format and meet the intellectuals, workers and young people where they are, it must make an honest and courageous attempt to implement all three of the principles above. It is as we who are working together in L'Abri Fellowship have sought by the grace of God, even though totally inadequately, to put them into practice that we have seen many twentieth-century men and women reached by the gospel. It would be our conclusion that all three points are imperative, wherever the Church is serious in wanting to speak to these of our generation.

We do not think that the material and outlook in this book is shut up to a few exotic Christian works appealing to an international group of intellectual and creative people. A number of those who have spent time to grasp this material are now using it with the uneducated with very encouraging results. For this we are thankful.

But even more, we are convinced that a comprehending use of this material would be helpful also within the "middle-class" churches and institutions which make up so much of evangelicalism and orthodoxy today. Firstly, it would give a new dimension of wealth in Christ to those churches, missions, and institutions. Secondly, it would be much harder for those round about to write them off as a subculture, representing largely only yesterday. Thirdly, they would protect their own next generation. The Christians have been in danger not only of not understanding, but of not taking seriously the problems of their children.

I must say that I am deeply troubled not only by what I find amongst our Western churches, but also by what I come up against among Christian converts from overseas. On many occasions as I have been lecturing to international groups, I have felt torn to bits for those from overseas who have been educated in mission schools and then sent out naked into the twentieth-century world.

The work of the Holy Spirit should never be minimized, but nowhere in the Scriptures do we find the work of the Holy Spirit an excuse for laziness and lack of love on the part of those with Christian responsibility. Nor is the Holy Spirit ever old-fashioned in the bad meaning of that term.

A word of warning here. To grasp and apply the principles we have been seeking to lay down is not just to memorize a static framework or terminology; this could be just one more dead thing. One of the joys in our work is to see how many young people and more mature teachers are carrying this thinking into their own academic disciplines and the arts, and are developing them along the lines of their own fields of interest.

As we seek to meet the problems there are two things which we must strenuously seek to avoid, whether we are engaged in teaching, missionary work or in some aspect of the life of the local church.

First: settling down and accepting the present situation simply because of the inertia caused by those who speak of the problem of the churches' young people and speak much of missions, but who simply do not want to question the familiar because it is painful to do so. The problem is that the evangelical, orthodox churches, institutions and programs are today often under the control of those who are in this category. This control is both organizational and financial. Thus, there is a tendency not to "rock the boat." This responsibility cannot be met by the young people themselves, nor by the young ministers and young missionaries alone.

Mature Christians, and Christians in places of responsibility, must summon the courage to distinguish, under the Holy Spirit, between unchangeable biblical truth and the things which have merely become comfortable for us. Often one hears people speak of "the simple gospel only," when in reality they do not really care enough for those outside the churches, or their own children for that matter, to be willing to face what preaching the simple gospel may mean in a changing and complex situation.

Second: the development of an intellectual and cultural snobbishness or elitism. This can easily come about unless we help one another not to fall into it. Such an attitude grieves the Holy Spirit, destroys rather than builds, and is as offensively ugly as anything can be.

We will make mistakes, but by God's grace we must strive to avoid either of these two errors or a choice between them.

After considerable thought and the practical experience of trying it out in several countries, I would suggest the following two concepts be borne in mind as we train our young people to take their full part in the Christian work of our time.

First of all, it must be remembered that those who make up the body of the churches and the institutions are also the lambs of God. They need care and help just as much as do the intellectuals, the creative people, and the young people who are becoming twentieth-century people. When a pastor accepts the call to go to a particular church, his call is to minister to the whole congregation. Those who care nothing about the new problems are to be fed and shepherded. Therefore, the general preaching and teaching in the middle-class evangelical church should not be of such a nature as to confuse, hurt or undernourish them.

On the other hand, nothing should be preached or taught in the general services and classes which will have to be unlearned when young people and others read and discuss the deeper problems or go away to university. I would suggest that all Sunday school, Bible class and educational material should be prepared with this in mind. We should ask ourselves the question, "Is the material of such a nature that it could be extended by eighteen years of honest study without it proving false?"

This will mean more attention to the preparation of sermons, lesson material, Bible study notes, and so on. Not everyone will be equally adept at this, but each could be helped if Christian schools, seminaries and theological colleges, Bible schools, missionary training institutes, and publishing houses would set up a program in order to avoid making the old mistakes and omissions and add some to their staff who had been trained to think in a total cultural apologetic. The program could be set up to be operative at a given date, say in three years' time.

Thus, my first suggestion would be: the general teaching and preaching should be of such a nature as to feed and care for those who make up the body of the congregation or institution, yet keeping in mind that nothing is given which must be unlearned as deeper problems are later met.

Second, I would suggest that special times be set aside in the Church, institution or mission, so that those who are in, or are coming into, the twentieth-century problems can get what they need. The occasion could be a talk, discussion or seminar. It would be valuable if those claiming no affiliation to the Church could be brought into the discussion as well. It does not have to be a big gathering or extensively publicized, but rather the gathering together of those in the Church and outside the Church who wish to get on. Nor does this getting on have to be purely intellectual, for if one goes deep enough into the intellectual questions one comes to the deep spiritual problems and realities. And when one goes deep enough spiritually, one touches on the real intellectual problems and realities.

Men and women trained in this way will then have the opportunity, as they go overseas or into unfamiliar territories at home, of understanding what are the twentieth-century problems people face.

So it seems to me that a course in homiletics or apologetics which does not consciously seek to implement these two suggestions today is really a preparation for failure and sorrow.

Christian conferences, etc., could have a place for caring for those considerations on a deeper and extended level. Surely, too, those who have a responsibility for Christian radio programs and television could at least find small corners for those who, in many places, make up the majority of the population.

In this way all could be fed, and, if introduced not too rapidly, but rather with much emphasis on spiritual growth and love as well as understanding, in most cases there would not have to be two "churches" under one roof, nor an explosion.

Yet, I would say, some ripples are worthwhile rather than allowing those outside and our own young people who are longing for real answers to choke in the all-too-present dustiness.

The Practice of Truth

With regard to the first of the principles of which we spoke at the beginning of Appendix B (*The full doctrinal position of historic Christianity must be clearly maintained*), it seems to me that the central problem of evangelical orthodoxy in the second half of the twentieth century is the problem of the *practice* of this principle. This is especially so when we take into account the spiritual and intellectual mentality which is dominant in our century. Any consideration of methods and programs must be secondary to a consideration of this central problem.

If a clear and unmistakable emphasis on truth, in the sense of antithesis, is removed, two things occur: firstly, Christianity in the next generation as true Christianity is weakened; and secondly, we shall be communicating only with that diminishing portion of the community which still thinks in terms of the older concept of truth. We are not minimizing the work of the Holy Spirit. We should remember, however, that our responsibility is so to communicate that those who hear the gospel will understand it. If we do not communicate clearly on the basis of antithesis, many will respond to their own interpretation of the gospel, in their own relativistic thought-forms, including a concept of psychological

195

guilt-feelings rather than of true moral guilt before the holy, living God. If they do respond in this way, they have not understood the gospel; they are still lost, and we have defaulted in our task of preaching and communicating the gospel to our generation.

The unity of orthodox or evangelical Christianity should be centered around this emphasis on *truth*. It is always important, but doubly so when we are surrounded by so many for whom the concept of truth, in the sense of antithesis, is considered to be totally unthinkable.

In such a setting the problem of communication is serious; it can only be overcome by negative statements that clearly say what we do *not* mean, so that the twentieth-century man understands the positive statements we *do* mean. Moreover, in an age of synthesis, men will not take our protestations of truth seriously unless they see by our actions that we *practice* truth and antithesis in the unity we try to establish, and in our activities. Without this, in an age of relativity, we cannot expect the evangelical, orthodox Church to mean much to the surrounding culture or even to the Church's own children. What we try to say in our teaching and evangelism will be understood in the twentieth-century thought-form of synthesis. Both a clear comprehension of the importance of truth and a clear practice of it, even when it is costly to do so, is imperative if our witness and our evangelism are to be significant in our own generation and in the flow of history.

It would seem to me that some evangelicals are jettisoning any serious attempt to exhibit truth and antithesis. There has been a tendency to move from a lack of seriousness ecclesiastically concerning truth to the same tendency in matters of wider cooperation. This often finishes up by denying, in practice if not in theory, the importance of doctrinal truth as such.

Many evangelicals who are rightly disturbed by the new theology's view of the Scriptures and universalism and who try to meet it at these points of error in fact never go far enough back in order to establish a clear line of truth and error which will hold weight for the next generation. Inevitably the next generation tends to go further in the direction already established and, if this is already towards synthesis, they will move with it ever closer to the new theology. Therefore, to avoid this, we must be careful to consider what truth and antithesis mean *in practice* in ecclesiastical matters and in evangelism.

Thus it must be said that in spite of (and even because of) one's commitment to evangelism and cooperation among Christians, I can visualize times when the only way to make plain the seriousness of what is involved in regard to a service or an activity where the gospel is going to be preached is *not* to accept an official part if men whose *doctrine* is known to be an enemy are going to be invited to participate officially. In an age of relativity, the *practice* of truth when it is costly is the only way to cause the world to take seriously our protestations concerning truth. Cooperation and unity that do not lead to purity of life and purity of doctrine are just as faulty and incomplete as an orthodoxy which does not lead to a concern for, and a reaching out towards, those who are lost.

There is an opposite danger to be avoided. Some of those who have contended for truth have cut the ground from under this position, not only by a loss of beauty and love but even, in practice, by a loss of truth in speaking about men.

All too often the only antithesis we have exhibited to the world and to our own children has been our *talking* about holiness or our *talking* about love, rather than the practice of holiness and love together as truth, in antithesis to what is false in theology, in the Church, and the surrounding culture.*

*Based on a talk given at the Berlin Congress on the Bible.

Glossary

Absolute. A concept which is not modifiable by factors such as culture, individual psychology or circumstances, but which is perfect and unchangeable. Used as an antithesis of relativism.

Agnostic. A person who does not know, or who thinks it is impossible to know, whether there is a God.

Anthropology. That which deals only with man, his relationship with himself and with other men, such as the studies of psychology, and sociology, and nothing beyond man.

Antinomianism. Holding that, under the gospel dispensation, the moral law is of no use or obligation.

Antiphilosophy. Many of the modern forms of philosophy which have given up any attempt to find a rational unity to the whole of thought and life.

Antithesis. Direct opposition of contrast between two things. (As in "joy" which is the antithesis of "sorrow.")

Apologetics. That branch of theology having to do with the defense and communication of Christianity.

Archetype. The psychologist Jung interpreted dream symbols that have appeared throughout the history of man and called them archetypes.

Atheist. A person who believes that there is no God.

Authenticate oneself. A term used by existentialists whereby man validates the genuineness of his existence by an act of the will or a feeling of dread.

Being. A term denoting the area of existence.

Communication. The transmitting of ideas and information.

Connotation. The implication of meanings to words other than the definition of the word.

Cosmology. Theory of the nature and principles of the universe.

Dada. The name given to a modern art movement originating in Zurich in 1916. The name, chosen at random from a French dictionary, means "rocking horse."

Determinism. The doctrine that human action is not free, but results from such causes as psychological and chemical makeup which render free-will an illusion.

Dialectic. The principle of change which takes place by means of triadic movement. A thesis has its opposite, an antithesis. The two opposites are resolved in a synthesis, which in turn becomes a thesis and the process goes on.

Dichotomy. Division into two totally separated parts. In this book, used for the total separation of the rational and logical in man from both meaning and faith.

Epistemology. That part of philosophy concerned with the theory of knowledge, its nature, limits and validity.

Existential. Relating to and dealing with moment-by-moment human existence. Empirical reality as opposed to mere theory.

Existentialism. A modern theory of man that holds that human experience is not describable in scientific or rational terms. Existentialism stresses the need to make vital choices by using man's freedom in a contingent and apparently purposeless world.

Final Experience. Term used by Karl Jaspers to denote a crucial experience which is great enough to give hope of meaning.

Humanism. There are two meanings: (1) Any philosophy or system of thought that begins with man alone, in order to try to find a unified meaning to life; (2) that part of humanistic thinking in the above wider sense that stresses the hope of an optimistic future for mankind.

Impressionism. Movement in the visual arts in which the classical tendencies of nineteenth-century French painting culminated and from which modern art has sprung. Its aim was to reproduce, by means of a careful analysis of color, the effect of light upon objects in nature.

Linguistic Analysis. Branch of philosophy which desires to preserve philosophy from confusion of concepts by showing the use of these concepts in their natural language context. It sees the task of philosophy as clarifying what lies on the surface rather than offering explanations.

Logic. The science of correct reasoning. The predictable and inevitable consequence of rational analysis. In classical logic it could be asserted that "A" is "A" and that "A" cannot equal "non-A."

Logical Positivism. Name given to an analytic trend in modern philosophy which holds that all metaphysical theories are strictly meaningless because, in the nature of the case, unverifiable by reference to empirical facts.

"Mannishness" of Man. Those aspects of man, such as significance, love, rationality and the fear of nonbeing, which mark him off from animals and machines and give evidence of his being created in the image of a personal God.

Methodology. Study of the procedures and principles whereby the question of truth and knowledge is approached.

Monolithic. Constituting one undifferentiated whole. In terms of modern culture, giving a unified message.

Mysticism. There are two meanings: (1) A tendency to seek direct communion with ultimate reality of "the divine" by immediate intuition, insight or illumination; (2) a vague speculation without foundation.

Neo-orthodoxy. Name given to the theology of men who have particularly applied the dialectical methodology of Hegel and Kierkegaard's "leap" to the Christian faith.

Nihilism. A denial of all objective grounds for truth. A belief that existence is basically senseless and useless, leading often to destructive tendencies in society or in the individual.

Pantheism. Doctrine that God and nature are identical. The universe is an extension of God's essence rather than a special creation.

Pragmatism. A system of thought which makes the practical consequences of a belief the sole test of truth.

Presupposition. A belief or theory which is accepted before the next step in logic is developed. Such a prior postulate often consciously or unconsciously affects the way a person subsequently reasons.

Propositional Truth. Truth which can be communicated in the form of a statement in which a predicate or object is affirmed or denied regarding a subject.

Rational. Whatever is related to or based upon man's power to reason consistently.

Rationalism. Cf. Humanism, first meaning.

Romantic. A view of life that has no base in fact, being the product of an exaggerated optimism.

Semantics. (1) Science of the study of the development of the meaning and uses of words and language; (2) the exploitation of the connotations and ambiguities in words.

Substantial. A term used to denote the extent of healing in the relationships of man with God, with his fellowman, and within himself which should be seen in the life of a Christian — not perfect and yet visible in reality.

Surrealism. An art form which produces fantastic or incongruous imagery by means of unnatural juxtapositions and combinations, related to Dada plus the subconscious.

Synthesis. The combination of the partial truths of a thesis and its antithesis into a higher stage of truth; cf dialectic.

"Upper Story." Term used to denote that which, in modern thinking, deals with significance or meaning, but which is not open to contact with verification by the world of facts which constitute the "lower story."

Validity. Something which has been authenticated by reference to well-grounded and sufficient evidence.

Verbalization. The putting of a proposition into words.

Verification. The procedure required for the establishment of the truth or falsity of a statement.

BOOK TWO

ESCAPE FROM REASON

Foreword

If a man goes overseas for any length of time, we would expect
him to learn the language of the country to which he is going.
More than this is needed, however, if he is really to communicate
with the people among whom he is living. He must learn another
language — that of the thought-forms of the people to whom he
speaks. Only so will he have real communication with them and
to them. So it is with the Christian Church. Its responsibility is
not only to hold to the basic, scriptural principles of the Christian
faith, but to communicate these unchanging truths "into" the generation in which it is living.

Every generation of Christians has this problem of learning
how to speak meaningfully to its own age. It cannot be solved
without an understanding of the changing existential situation
which it faces. If we are to communicate the Christian faith effectively, therefore, we must know and understand the thought-forms
of our own generation. These will differ slightly from place to
place, and more so from nation to nation. Nevertheless there are
characteristics of an age such as ours which are the same wherever we happen to be. It is these that I am especially considering
in this book. And the object of this is far from being merely to

satisfy intellectual curiosity. As we go along, it will become clear how far-reaching are the practical consequences of a proper understanding of these movements of thought.

Some may be surprised that in analyzing the trends in modern thought in this book I should begin with Aquinas and work my way forward from there. But I am convinced that our study must be concerned at one and the same time with both history and philosophy. If we are to understand present-day trends in thought, we must see how the situation has come about historically and also look in some detail at the development of philosophic thought-forms. Only when this has been done are we ready to go on to the practical aspects of how to communicate unchanging truth in a changing world.

One

Nature and Grace

The origin of modern man could be traced back to several periods. But I will begin with the teaching of a man who changed the world in a very real way. Thomas Aquinas (1225-1274) opened the way for the discussion of what is usually called "nature and grace." It may be set out diagrammatically like this:

GRACE
NATURE

This diagram may be amplified as follows, to show what is included on the two different levels:

GRACE, THE HIGHER:	God the Creator; heaven and heavenly things; the unseen and its influence on the earth; man's soul; unity
NATURE, THE LOWER:	The created; earth and earthly things; the visible and what nature and man do on earth; man's body; diversity

Up until this time, man's thought-forms had been Byzantine. The heavenly things were all-important, and were so holy that they were not pictured realistically. For instance, Mary and Christ were never portrayed realistically. Only symbols were portrayed. So if you look up at one of the later Byzantine mosaics in the baptistry at Florence it is not a picture of Mary that you see, but a symbol representing Mary.

On the other hand, simple nature — trees and mountains — held no interest for the artist, except as part of the world to be lived in. Mountain climbing, for instance, simply had no appeal as something to be done for its own sake. As we shall see, mountain climbing as such began only with the new interest in nature. So prior to Thomas Aquinas there was an overwhelming emphasis on the heavenly things, very far-off and very holy, pictured only as symbols, with little interest in nature itself. With the coming of Aquinas, we have the real birth of the humanistic elements of the Renaissance.

Aquinas's view of nature and grace did not involve a complete discontinuity between the two, for he did have a concept of unity between them. From Aquinas's day on, for many years there was a constant struggle for a unity of nature and grace and a hope that rationality would say something about both. It must be said that Thomas Aquinas certainly would not have been pleased with all that was extended from his writings as the years passed.

There were very good things that resulted from the birth of Renaissance thought. In particular, nature received a more proper place. From a biblical viewpoint nature is important because it has been created by God, and is not to be despised. The things of the body are not to be despised when compared with the soul. The things of beauty are important. Sexual things are not evil of themselves. All these things follow from the fact that in nature God has given us a good gift, and the man who regards it with contempt is really despising God's creation. As such he is despising, in a sense, God Himself, for he has contempt for what God has made.

Pollution and the Death of Man: The Christian View of Ecology deals in detail with the biblical view concerning nature.

Aquinas and the Autonomous
While there were good things that resulted from Renaissance thought, at the same time we are now able to see the significance

of the diagram of nature and grace in a different way. While there were good results from giving nature a better place, it also opened the way for much that was destructive. In Aquinas's view the will of man was fallen, but the intellect was not. From this incomplete view of the biblical Fall flowed subsequent difficulties. Out of this as time passed, man's intellect was seen as autonomous.

This sphere of the autonomous growing out of Aquinas takes on various forms. One result, for example, was the development of natural theology. In this view, natural theology is a theology that could be pursued independently from the Scriptures. Aquinas certainly hoped for unity and would have said that there was a correlation between natural theology and the Scriptures. But the important point in what followed was that a really autonomous area was set up.

From the basis of this autonomous principle, philosophy also became increasingly free, and was separated from revelation. Therefore philosophy began to take wings, as it were, and fly off wherever it wished, without relationship to the Scriptures. This does not mean that this tendency was never previously apparent, but it appears in a more total way from this time on.

Nor did it remain isolated in what developed out of Thomas Aquinas's philosophic theology. Soon it began to enter the arts.

Today we have a weakness in our educational process in failing to understand the natural associations between the disciplines. We tend to study all our disciplines in unrelated parallel lines. This tends to be true in both Christian and secular education. This is one of the reasons why evangelical Christians have been taken by surprise at the tremendous shift that has come in our generation. We have studied our exegesis as exegesis, our theology as theology, our philosophy as philosophy; we study something about art as art; we study music as music, without understanding that these are things of man, and the things of man are never unrelated parallel lines.

There are several ways in which this association between theology, philosophy and the arts emerged following Aquinas.

Painters and Writers
The first artist to be influenced was Cimabue (1240-1302), teacher of Giotto (1267-1337). Aquinas lived from 1225 to 1274; clearly then these influences were quickly felt in the field of art. Instead of all the subjects of art being above the dividing line

between nature and grace in the symbolic manner of the Byzantine, Cimabue and Giotto began to paint the things of nature as nature. In this transition period the change did not come all at once. Hence there was a tendency at first to paint the lesser things in the picture naturalistically, but to continue to portray Mary, for example, as a symbol.

Then Dante (1265-1321) began to write in the way that these men painted. Suddenly everything started to shift on the basis that nature was important. The same development can be seen in the writers Petrarch (1304-1374) and Boccaccio (1313-1375). Petrarch was the first man we hear of who ever climbed a mountain just for the sake of climbing a mountain. This interest in nature as God made it is, as we have seen, good and proper. But Aquinas had opened the way to an autonomous humanism, an autonomous philosophy; and once the movement gained momentum, there was soon a flood.

Nature Versus Grace

The vital principle to notice is that as nature was made autonomous, nature began to "eat up" grace. Through the Renaissance, from the time of Dante to Leonardo da Vinci, nature gradually became more and more autonomous. It was set free from God as the humanistic philosophers began to operate ever more freely. By the time the Renaissance reached its climax, nature had eaten up grace.

This can be demonstrated in various ways. We will begin with a miniature entitled *Grandes Heures de Rohan*, painted about 1415. The story it portrays is a miracle story of the period. Mary and Joseph and the baby, fleeing into Egypt, pass by a field where a man is sowing seed, and a miracle happens. The grain grows up within an hour or so and is ready for harvesting. When the man goes to harvest it, the pursuing soldiers come by and ask, "How long ago did they pass by?" He replies that they passed when he was sowing the seed and so the soldiers turn back. However, it is not the story that interests us, but rather the way in which the miniature is laid out. First of all, there is a great difference in the size of the figures of Mary and Joseph, the baby, a servant, and the donkey which are at the top of the picture and which dominate it by their size, and the very small figures of the soldier and the man wielding the sickle at the bottom of the picture. Second, the message is made clear, not only by the size of the upper figures, but also by the fact that the background of the upper part of the miniature is covered with gold lines. Hence there is a total pictorial representation of nature and grace.

This is the older concept, with grace overwhelmingly important, and nature having little place.

In Northern Europe Van Eyck (1370-1441) was one who opened the door for nature in a new way. He began to paint real nature. In 1410, a very important date in the history of art, he produced a tiny miniature. It measures only about five inches by three inches. But it is a painting with tremendous significance because it contains the first real landscape. It gave birth to every background that came later during the Renaissance. The theme is Jesus' baptism, but this takes up only a small section of the area. There is a river in the background, a very real castle, houses, hills and so on — this is a real landscape; nature has become important. After this, such landscapes spread rapidly from the north to the south of Europe.

Soon we have the next stage. In 1435, Van Eyck painted the *Madonna of the Chancellor Rolin* — now in the Louvre in Paris. The significant feature is that Chancellor Rolin, facing Mary, is the same size as she is. Mary is no longer remote, the Chancellor no longer a small figure, as would have been the case with the donors at an earlier period. Though he holds his hands in an attitude of prayer, he has become equal with Mary. From now on the pressure is on: how is this balance between nature and grace to be resolved?

Another man of importance, Masaccio (1410-1428), should be mentioned at this point. He makes the next big step in Italy after Giotto, who died in 1337, by introducing true perspective and true space. For the first time, light comes from the right direction. For example, in the marvellous Carmine Chapel in Florence, there is a window which he took into account as he painted his pictures on the walls, so that the shadows in the paintings fall properly in relation to the light from this window. Masaccio was painting true nature. He painted so that his pictures looked as though they were "in the round"; they give a feeling of atmosphere, and he has introduced real composition. He lived only until he was twenty-seven; yet he almost entirely opened the door to nature. With Masaccio's work, as with much of Van Eyck's, the emphasis on nature was such that it could have led to painting with a true biblical viewpoint.

Coming on to Filippo Lippi (1406-1469), it is apparent that nature begins to "eat up" grace in a more serious way than Van Eyck's *Madonna of the Chancellor Rolin*. Only a very few years before that, artists would never have considered painting Mary in a natural way at all—they would have painted only a symbol of her. But when Filippo Lippi painted the Madonna in 1465 there is a startling change. He has depicted a very beautiful girl holding a baby in her arms, with a landscape that you cannot doubt was influenced by Van Eyck's work. This Madonna is no longer a far-off symbol; she is a pretty girl with a baby. But there is something more we need to know about this painting. The girl he painted as Mary was his mistress, and all Florence knew it was his mistress. Nobody would have dared to do this just a few years before. Nature was killing grace.

In France, in about 1450, Fouquet (c. 1416-1480) painted the king's mistress, Agnes Sorel, as Mary. Everyone knowing the court and who saw it knew that this was the king's current mistress. Fouquet painted her with one breast exposed. Whereas before it would have been Mary feeding the baby Jesus, now it is the king's mistress with one breast exposed—and grace is dead.

The point to be stressed is that it is destructive when nature is made autonomous. As soon as one accepts the concept of an autonomous realm, one finds that the lower element begins to eat up the higher. In what follows I shall be speaking of these two elements as the "lower story" and the "upper story."

Leonardo da Vinci and Raphael

The next man to examine is Leonardo da Vinci. He brings a new factor into the flow of history, and comes closer to being a modern man than any before him. His dates are important (1452-1519), because they overlapped with the beginning of the Reformation. Leonardo da Vinci is also very much a part of a significant shift in philosophic thinking. Cosimo the elder, of Florence, who died in 1464, was one of the first to see the importance of Platonic philosophy. Thomas Aquinas had introduced Aristotelian thinking. Cosimo began to champion Neoplatonism. Ficino (1433-1499), the greatest Neoplatonist, taught Lorenzo the Magnificent (1449-1492). By the time of Leonardo da Vinci, Neoplatonism was a dominant force in Florence. It became a dominant force for the simple reason that they needed to find some way to put something in the "upper story." They introduced

Neoplatonism in an attempt to reinstate ideas and ideals — that is, universals:

GRACE — UNIVERSALS

NATURE — PARTICULARS

A universal is that which would give meaning and unity to all the particulars. The particulars are all the individual things — each individual thing is a particular.

A painting that illustrates this is *The School of Athens* by Raphael (1483-1520). In the room in the Vatican where this picture is located, there is on one wall a mural which represents the Roman Catholic Church. This Raphael balances with *The School of Athens*, representing classical pagan thought, on the opposite wall. In *The School of Athens* itself Raphael portrays the difference between the Aristotelian element and the Platonic. The two men stand in the center of the picture and Aristotle is spreading his hands downwards (emphasizing the particulars), while Plato is pointing upwards (emphasizing the ideas and ideals, the universals).

This problem can be put in another way. Where do you find a unity when you set diversity free? Once the particulars are set free, how do you hold them together? Leonardo grappled with this problem. He was a Neoplatonist painter and, many people have said — I think quite properly — the first modern mathematician. He saw that if you begin with an autonomous rationality, what you come to is mathematics (that which can be measured), and mathematics only deals with particulars, not universals. Therefore you never get beyond mechanics. As a man who realized the need for a unity, he understood that this would not do. So he tried to paint the soul. The soul in this context is not the Christian soul; the soul is the universal — the soul, for example, of the sea or of the tree.

SOUL — UNITY

MATHEMATICS — PARTICULARS — MECHANICS

One of the reasons Leonardo never painted very much was simply that he tried to draw in order to be able to paint the universal. He never succeeded.

A modern writer, Giovanni Gentile, one of the greatest Italian philosophers until his death some years ago, said that Leonardo died in despondency because he would not abandon the hope of a rational unity between the particulars and the universal.[1] To have escaped this despondency, Leonardo would have had to have been a different man. He would have had to let go his hope of unity above and below the line. Leonardo, not being a modern man, never gave up the hope of a unified field of knowledge. He would not, in other words, give up the hope of educated man, who, in the past, has been marked by this insistence on a unified field of knowledge.

Two

A Unity of Nature and Grace

At this point it is important to note a historical relationship between the Renaissance and the Reformation. Calvin was born in 1509. His *Institutes* were written in 1536. Leonardo died in 1519, the same year as the Leipzig Disputation between Luther (1483-1546) and Dr. Eck. The king who took Leonardo to France at the close of his life was Francis I, the same king to whom Calvin addressed his *Institutes*. We come therefore to an overlapping of the Renaissance with the Reformation.

To this problem of unity of which we have been speaking, the Reformation gave an entirely opposite answer from that of the Renaissance. It repudiated both the Aristotelian and the Neoplatonic presentation. What was the Reformation answer? It rejected the old and growing humanism in the Roman Catholic Church, and it rejected the concept of an incomplete Fall resulting in man's autonomous intellect and the possibility of a natural theology which could be pursued independently from the Scriptures. The Reformation accepted the biblical picture of a total Fall. The whole man had been made by God, but now the whole man is fallen, including his intellect and will. Only God was autonomous.

This was true in two areas. First of all, there was nothing autonomous in the area of final authority. For the Reformation, final and sufficient knowledge rested in the Bible — that is, Scripture alone, in contrast to Scripture plus anything else parallel to the Scriptures, whether it be the Church or a natural theology. Second, there was no idea of man being autonomous in the area of salvation. In the Roman Catholic position there was a divided work of salvation — Christ died for our salvation, but man had to merit the merit of Christ. Thus there was a humanistic element involved. The reformers said that there is nothing man can do; no autonomous or humanistic religious or moral effort of man can help. One is saved only on the basis of the finished work of Christ as He died in space and time in history, and the only way to be saved is to raise the empty hands of faith and, by God's grace, to accept God's free gift — faith alone. It was Scripture alone and faith alone.

Christians need to notice, at this point, that the Reformation said "Scripture alone" and not "the revelation of God in Christ alone." If you do not have the view of the Scriptures that the reformers had, you really have no content to the word *Christ* — and this is the modern drift in theology. Modern theology uses the word without content because *Christ* is cut away from the Scriptures. The Reformation followed the teaching of Christ Himself in linking the revelation Christ gave of God to the revelation of the written Scriptures.

The Scriptures give the key to two kinds of knowledge — the knowledge of God, and the knowledge of men and nature. The great Reformation confessions emphasize that God revealed His attributes to man in the Scriptures and that this revelation was meaningful to God as well as to man. There could have been no Reformation and no Reformation culture in Northern Europe without the realization that God had spoken to man in the Scriptures and that, therefore, we know something truly about God, because God has revealed it to man.

It is an important principle to remember, in the contemporary interest in communication and in language study, that the biblical presentation is that though we do not have exhaustive truth, we have from the Bible what I term "true truth." In this way we know true truth about God, true truth about man, and something truly about nature. Thus on the basis of the Scriptures, while we do not have exhaustive knowledge, we have true and unified knowledge.

The Reformation and Man

We thus know something wonderful about man. Among other things, we know his origin and who he is — he is made in the image of God. Man is not only wonderful when he is "born again" as a Christian; he is also wonderful as God made him in His image. Man has value because of who he was originally before the Fall, who he is by his creation.

Some years ago I was lecturing in Santa Barbara and was introduced to a boy who had been on drugs. He had a good-looking sensitive face, long curly hair, sandals on his feet, and was wearing blue jeans. He came to hear my lecture and said, "This is brand-new; I've never heard anything like this." So he was brought along again the next afternoon, and I greeted him. He looked me in the eyes and said, "Sir, that was a beautiful greeting. Why did you greet me like that?" I said, "Because I know who you are — I know you are made in the image of God." We then had a tremendous conversation. We cannot deal with people like human beings, we cannot deal with them on the high level of true humanity, unless we really know their origin — who they are. God tells man who he is. God tells us that He created man in His image. So man is something wonderful.

But God tells us something else about man — He tells us about the Fall. This introduces the other element which we need to know in order to understand man. Why is he so wonderful and yet so flawed? Who is man? Who am I? Why can man do these things that make man so unique, and yet why is man so horrible? Why is it?

The Bible says that you are wonderful because you are made in the image of God, but that you are flawed because at a space-time point of history man fell. The reformers knew that man was separated from God because of man's revolt against God. But the reformers, and the people who following the Reformation built the culture of Northern Europe, knew that while man is morally guilty before the God who exists, man is not *nothing*. Modern man tends to think that he is nothing. The reformers knew they were the very opposite of nothing, because they knew they were made in the image of God. Even though they were fallen and, without the nonhumanistic solution of Christ and His substitutionary death, were separated from God and would go to Hell, this still did not mean that they were nothing.

When the Word of God, the Bible, was listened to, the Reformation had tremendous results, both in people individually becoming Christians, and in general culture.

What the Reformation tells us, therefore, is that God has spoken in the Scriptures concerning both the "upstairs" and "downstairs." He has spoken in a true revelation concerning nature, the cosmos and man. Therefore, the reformers had a real unity of knowledge. They simply did not have the Renaissance problem of nature and grace! They had a real unity, not because they were clever, but because they had a unity on the basis of what God had revealed in both areas. In contrast to humanism there was, for the Reformation, no autonomous portion.

This did not mean that there was no freedom for art or science. It was quite the opposite; there was now possible true freedom within the revealed form. But though art and science have freedom, they are not autonomous — the artist and the scientist are also under the revelation of the Scriptures. As we shall see, whenever art or science has tried to be autonomous, a principle has always manifested itself — nature "eats up" grace. Thus art and science themselves soon began to be meaningless.

The Reformation had some tremendous results, and made possible the culture which many of us love — even though our generation is now throwing it away. The Reformation confronts us with an Adam who was, to use twentieth-century thought-forms, an unprogrammed man — he was not set up as a punch card in a computer system. One thing that marks twentieth-century man is that he cannot visualize this, because modern man is infiltrated by a concept of determinism. But the biblical position is clear — man cannot be explained as totally determined and conditioned. This was the position that built the concept of the dignity of man. People today are trying to hang on to the dignity of man, but they do not know how to, because they have lost the truth that man is made in the image of God. Adam was an unprogrammed man, a significant man in a significant history, and he could change history.

You have then, in Reformation thought, a man who is somebody. But you also have him in revolt; and he really revolts — it is not "a piece of theatre." And because he is an unprogrammed man and really revolts, he has true moral guilt. Because of this, the reformers understood something else. They had a biblical understanding of what Christ did. They understood that Jesus died on the cross in substitution and as a propitiation in order to save men from their true guilt. We need to learn that when we begin to tamper with the scriptural concept of true moral guilt, whether it be psychological tampering, genetic tampering, theological tampering or any other kind of tampering, our view of what Jesus did will no longer be scriptural. Christ died for man who had true moral guilt because man had made a real and true choice.

More About Man

We must now see something else about man. To do this, we must notice that everything in the biblical system goes back to God. I love the biblical system as a system. While we might not like the connotation of the word *system*, because it sounds rather cold, this does not mean that the biblical teaching is not a system. Everything goes back to the beginning, and thus the Christian system has a unique beauty and perfection because everything is under the apex of the system. Everything begins with the kind of God who is "there." This is the beginning and apex of the whole, and everything flows from this in a noncontradictory way. The Bible says God is a living God, and it tells us much about Him; but most significantly perhaps, for twentieth-century man, it speaks of Him as both a personal God and an infinite God. This is the kind of God who is "there," who exists. Furthermore, this is the only system, the only religion, that has this kind of God. The gods of the East are infinite by definition, in the sense that they encompass all — the evil as well as the good — but they are not personal. The gods of the West were personal, but they were very limited. The Teutonic, the Roman and the Greek gods were all the same — personal but not infinite. The Christian God, the God of the Bible, is personal-infinite.

This personal-infinite God of the Bible is the Creator of all else. God created all things, and He created them out of nothing. Therefore everything else is finite, everything else is the creature. He alone is the infinite Creator. This can be set out as follows:

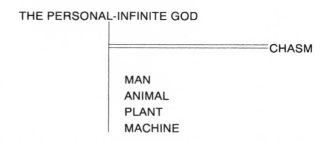

He created man, the animals, the flowers, and the machine. On the side of His infinity, man is as separated from God as is the machine. But, says the Bible, when you come on to the side of man's personality, you have something quite different. The chasm is at a different point:

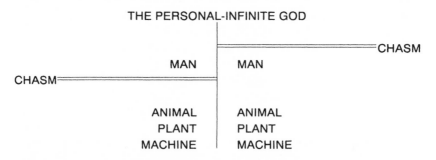

So man, being made in the image of God, was made to have a personal relationship with Him. Man's relationship is upward and not merely downward. If you are dealing with twentieth-century people, this becomes a very crucial difference. Modern man sees his relationship downward to the animal and to the machine. The Bible rejects this view of who man is. On the side of personality you are related to God. You are not infinite but finite; nevertheless you are truly personal; you are created in the image of the personal God who exists.

Reformation, Renaissance and Morals

There are many practical results of these differences between Renaissance and Reformation thought. Illustrations could be given from a wide field. For example, the Renaissance set women free. So did the Reformation — but with a great difference. Jacob Burckhardt's work *The Civilization of the Renaissance in Italy,*

published in Basel in 1860, is still a standard work on these subjects. He points out that the women of the Renaissance in Italy
were free, but at the great cost of general immorality. Burckhardt
(1818-1897) takes pages to illustrate this point.

Why was this so? It goes back to the then current view of
nature and grace. These things are never merely theoretical,
because men act the way they think:

LYRIC POETS — "SPIRITUAL LOVE" — IDEAL LOVE

NOVELISTS AND COMIC POETS — SENSUAL LOVE

In the upper section you have the lyric poets who taught "spiritual love" and ideal love. Then, below, you have the novelists
and the comic poets who taught sensual love. There was a flood
of pornographic books. This element of the Renaissance period
did not stop with the books themselves, but carried over into the
kind of lives men lived. The autonomous man found himself
looking into a dualism. Take Dante, for example. He fell in love
with one woman at first sight, and he loved her all his life. Then
he married another woman who bore his children and washed his
dishes.

The simple fact is that this nature-grace division flowed over
into the whole structure of Renaissance life, and the autonomous
"lower story" always consumed the "upper."

The Whole Man
The Reformation's biblical view was, and is, very different. It is
not a Platonic view. The soul is not more important than the body.
God made the whole man, and the whole man is important. The
doctrine of the bodily resurrection of the dead is not an old-fashioned thing. It tells us that God made the whole man, God loves
the whole man, and the whole man is important. The biblical
teaching, therefore, opposes the Platonic, which makes the soul
(the "upper") very important and leaves the body (the "lower")
with little importance at all. The biblical view also opposes the
humanist position, where the body and autonomous mind of man
become important, and grace becomes very unimportant and all
universals, all absolutes, are lost.

The biblical position, stressed at the Reformation, says that neither the Platonic view nor the humanist view will do. First, God

made the whole man and He is interested in the whole man. Second, when the historic space-time Fall took place, it affected the whole man. Third, on the basis of Christ's work as Savior, and having the knowledge that we possess in the revelation of the Scriptures, there is redemption for the whole man. In the future, the whole man will be raised from the dead and will be redeemed perfectly. And Paul says in Romans 6 that even in the present life we are to have a substantial reality of the redemption of the whole man. This is to be on the basis of the shed blood of Christ and in the power of the Holy Spirit through faith, even though it will not be perfect in this life. There is the real Lordship of Christ over the whole man. This is what the reformers understood and what the Bible teaches. In Holland, for example, more than in Anglo-Saxon Christianity, they emphasized that this meant a Lordship of Christ in culture.

So it means that Christ is equally Lord in both areas:

<u>GRACE</u>
NATURE

There is nothing autonomous — nothing independent from the Lordship of Jesus Christ and the authority of the Scriptures. God made the whole man and is interested in the whole man, and the result is a unity.

Thus, at the same time as the birth of modern man in the Renaissance there was the Reformation's answer to the humanistic Renaissance man's dilemma. By contrast, the dualism in Renaissance man has brought forth the modern forms of humanism, with modern man's sorrows.

Three

Early Modern Science

Science was very much involved in the situation that has been outlined. What we have to realize is that early modern science was started by those who lived in the consensus and setting of Christianity. A man like J. Robert Oppenheimer (1904-1967), for example, who was not a Christian, nevertheless understood this. He said that Christianity was needed to give birth to modern science.[1] Alfred North Whitehead (1861-1947) stressed the same thing. Christianity was necessary for the beginning of modern science for the simple reason that Christianity created a climate of thought which put men in a position to investigate the form of the universe.

Jean-Paul Sartre (1909-1980) states that the great philosophic question is that something exists rather than that nothing exists. No matter what man thinks, he has to deal with the fact and the problem that something is there. Christianity gives an explanation of why it is objectively there. In contrast to Eastern thinking, the Hebrew-Christian tradition affirms that God has created a true universe outside of Himself. When I use this term "outside of Himself," I do not mean it in a spatial sense; I mean that the universe is not an extension of the essence of God. It is not just a dream of God. There is something *there* to think about, to deal with, and to investigate which has objective reality. Christianity gives a certainty of objective reality and of cause and effect, a certainty that is strong enough to build on. Thus the object, and history, and cause and effect really exist.

Further, many of the early scientists had the same general outlook as that of Francis Bacon (1561-1626), who said in *Novum Organum Scientiarum*: "Man by the Fall fell at the same time from his state of innocence and from his dominion over nature. Both of these losses, however, can even in this life be in some part repaired; the former by religion and faith, the latter by the arts and sciences." Therefore science as science (and art as art) was understood to be, in the best sense, a religious activity. Notice in the quotation the fact that Francis Bacon did not see science as autonomous, for it was placed within the revelation of the Scriptures at the point of the Fall. Yet, within that "form," science (and art) was free and of intrinsic value before both men and God.

The early scientists shared the outlook of Christianity in believing that there is a reasonable God, who had created a reasonable universe; and thus man, by use of his reason, could find out the universe's form. As well as Francis Bacon, Copernicus (1475-1543), Galileo (1564-1642), Kepler (1571-1630), Faraday (1791-1867), and Maxwell (1831-1879) looked upon the universe, and carried on this work as scientists, in this framework.

These tremendous contributions, which we take for granted, launched early modern science. It is a very real question whether the scientists of today, who function without these assurances and motivations, would, or could, have ever begun modern science. Nature had to be freed from the Byzantine mentality and returned to a proper biblical emphasis, and the Renaissance played a part in this; but it was the biblical mentality which gave birth to modern science.

Early science was natural science in that it dealt with natural things, but it was not naturalistic, for, though it held to the uniformity of natural causes, it did not conceive of God and man as caught in the machinery. The early modern scientists held the conviction, first, that God gave knowledge to men in the Bible — knowledge concerning Himself and also concerning the universe and history — and, second, that God and man were not a part of the machinery and could affect the working of the machine of cause and effect. There was cause and effect, but in an open system. God could work into the cause and effect system, and people are not total prisoners in the machine. So there was not an autonomous situation in the "lower story."

Science thus developed, a science which dealt with the real, natural world, but which had not yet become naturalistic.

Kant and Rousseau
After the Renaissance-Reformation period the next crucial stage was reached at the time of Rousseau (1712-1778) and of Kant (1724-1804), although there were of course many others in the intervening period who could well be studied.

By the time we come to Kant and Rousseau, the sense of the autonomous is fully developed. So we find now that the problem was formulated differently. This shift in the wording of the formulation shows, by itself, the development of the problem. Whereas previously men had spoken of nature and grace, by the eighteenth century there was no idea of grace — the word did not fit any longer. Rationalism was now well-developed and entrenched, and there was no concept of revelation in any area. Consequently the problem was now defined, not in terms of "nature and grace," but of "nature and freedom":

FREEDOM

NATURE

This is a titanic change, expressing a secularized situation. Nature has totally devoured grace, and what is left in its place "upstairs" is the word *freedom.*

Kant's system broke upon the rock of trying to find a way, any way, to bring the phenomenal world of nature into relationship with the noumenal world of universals. The line between the upper and lower stories is now much thicker — and is soon to become thicker still.

At this time, we find that nature is now really so totally autonomous that determinism begins to emerge. Previously determinism had almost always been confined to the area of physics, or, in other words, to the machine portion of the universe. Now gradually determinism in one form or another is applied to people.

But though a determinism was involved in the lower story,

there was still an intense longing after human freedom. However, human freedom was seen as autonomous also. In the above diagram, freedom and nature are both now autonomous. The individual's freedom is seen not only as freedom without the need of redemption, but as absolute freedom.

The fight to retain freedom is carried on by Rousseau to an extreme. He and those who follow him express in their literature and art a casting aside of civilization as that which is restraining man's freedom. This is the birth of the Bohemian ideal. These thinkers feel the pressure "downstairs" of man as a machine. Naturalistic science becomes a very heavy weight — an enemy. Freedom is beginning to be lost. So these men, who are not really modern men as yet — and so have not accepted the fact that they are only machines — begin to hate science. They long for freedom even if the freedom makes no sense, and thus autonomous freedom and the autonomous machine stand facing each other.

What is autonomous freedom? It means a freedom in which the individual is the center of the universe. Autonomous freedom is a freedom that is without restraint. Therefore, as man begins to feel the weight of the machine pressing upon him, Rousseau and others swear and curse, as it were, against the science which threatens their human freedom. The freedom that they advocate is autonomous in that it has nothing to restrain it. It is freedom without limitations. It is freedom that no longer fits into the rational world. It merely hopes and tries to will that the finite individual man will be free — and that which is left is individual *self-expression*.

To appreciate the significance of this stage of the formation of modern man, we must remember that up until this time the schools of philosophy in the West, from the time of the Greeks onward, had three important principles in common.

The first is that they were rationalistic. By this is meant that man begins absolutely and totally from himself, gathers information concerning the particulars, and formulates the universals. This is the proper use of the word *rationalistic*, and the way I am using it in this book.

Second, they all believed in the rational. This word had no relationship to the word *rationalism*, and must not be confused with it. They acted upon the basis that man's aspiration concerning the validity of reason was well-founded. They thought in terms of antithesis. If a certain thing was true, the opposite was not true. In morals, if a thing was right, the opposite was wrong. This is something that goes as far back as you can go in man's thinking. There is no historical basis for the later Heidegger's (1889-1976) position that the pre-Socratic Greeks, prior to Aristotle, thought differently. As a matter of fact, it is the only way man can think. Antithetical thought was not begun by Aristotle — it ultimately rests on the reality that God exists in contrast to His not existing, and on the reality of His creating what exists in contrast to what does not exist — and then to His creating people to live, observe and think in the reality. To apply the name Aristotelian to the use of reason and antithesis is mistaken.

The sobering fact is that the only way one can reject thinking in terms of an antithesis and the rational is on the basis of the rational and the antithesis. When a man says that thinking in terms of an antithesis is wrong, what he is really doing is using the concept of antithesis to deny antithesis. That is the way God has made us, and there is no other way to think. Therefore, the basis of classical logic is that A is A and is not non-A. The understanding of what is involved in this methodology of antithesis, and what is involved in casting it away, is very important in understanding contemporary thought.

The third thing that men had always hoped for in philosophy was that they would be able to construct a unified field of knowledge. At the time of Kant, for example, men were tenaciously hanging on to this hope, despite the pressure against it. They hoped that by means of rationalism plus rationality they would find a complete answer — an answer that would encompass all of thought and all of life. With minor exceptions, this aspiration marked all philosophy up to and including the time of Kant.

Modern Modern Science
Before we move on to Hegel, who marks the next significant stage towards modern man, I want to take brief note of the shift in science that occurred along with this shift in philosophy we have been discussing. This requires a moment's recapitulation.

The early scientists believed in the uniformity of natural causes. What they did not believe in was the uniformity of natural causes *in a closed system*. That little phrase makes all the difference in the world. It makes the difference between natural science and a science that is rooted in naturalistic philosophy. It makes all the difference between what I would call modern science and what I would call modern modern science. It is important to notice that this is not a failing of science as science, but rather that the uniformity of natural causes in a closed system has become *the dominant philosophy* among scientists.

Under the influence of the presupposition of the uniformity of natural causes in a closed system, the machine does not merely embrace the sphere of physics; it now encompasses everything. Earlier thinkers would have rejected this totally. Leonardo da Vinci understood the way things were going. We saw earlier that he understood that if you begin rationalistically with mathematics, all you have is particulars and therefore you are left with mechanics. Having understood this, he hung on to his pursuit of the universal. But by the time to which we have now come in our study, the autonomous lower story has eaten up the upstairs completely. The modern modern scientists insist on a total unity of the downstairs and the upstairs, and the upstairs disappears. Neither God nor freedom are there anymore — everything is in the machine. In science the significant change came about therefore as a result of a shift in emphasis from the uniformity of natural causes to the uniformity of natural causes in a closed system. This shift did not come because of newly discovered facts, but because of a shift in their presuppositions — a shift to the worldview of materialism or naturalism.

One thing to note carefully about the men who have taken this direction — and we have now come to the present day — is that *these men* still insist on unity of knowledge. These men still follow the classical ideal of unity. But what is the result of their desire for a unified field? We find that they no longer include in their naturalism physics only; now psychology and social science are also in the machine. They say there must be unity and no division. But the only way unity can be achieved on this basis is simply by ruling out freedom.

Thus we are left with a deterministic sea without a shore. The result of seeking for a unity on the basis of the uniformity of natural causes in a closed system is that freedom does not exist. In fact, love no longer exists; significance, in the old sense of man's longing for significance, no longer exists. In other words, what has really happened is that the line has been removed and put up above everything — and in the old "upstairs" nothing exists.

GOD ~~LOVE~~ ~~MORALS~~
~~FREEDOM~~ ~~SIGNIFICANCE~~ ~~MAN~~

NATURE—PHYSICS, SOCIAL SCIENCES
AND PSYCHOLOGY—DETERMINISM

Nature, having been made autonomous, has eaten up both grace and freedom. An autonomous lower story will always eat up the upper. The lesson is: Whenever you make such a dualism and begin to set up one autonomous section below, the result is that the lower consumes the upper. This has happened time after time in the last few hundred years. If you try artificially to keep the two areas separate and keep the autonomous in one area only, soon the autonomous will embrace the other.

Modern Modern Morality
This, of course, has repercussions in the sphere of morality. The twentieth-century pornographic writers all trace their origin to the Marquis de Sade (1740-1814). The twentieth century now treats him as a very important man — he is no longer just a dirty writer. A generation ago, if anyone was found with one of his books in England he was liable to have difficulties with the law. Today he has become a great name in drama, in philosophy, in literature. All the nihilistic "black" writers, the writers in revolt, look back to de Sade. Why? Not only because he was a dirty writer, or even that he has taught them how to use sexual writing as a vehicle for philosophic ideas, but also basically he was a chemical determinist. He understood the direction that things would have to take when man is included in the machinery. The conclusions he drew were these: If man is determined, then what *is*, is right; if all of life is only mechanism — if that is all there is — then morals really do not count. Morals become only a word for a sociological framework. Morals become a means of manipulation by society in the midst of the machine. The word *morals* by this time is only a semantic connotation word for nonmorals. What *is*, is right.

This leads to the second step — man is stronger than woman. Nature has made him so. Therefore, the male has the right to do what he wishes to the female. The action for which they put de Sade in prison, both under the Monarchy and the Republic — taking a prostitute and beating her for his own pleasure — was by nature right. We get our word *sadism* from this. But it must not be forgotten that it is related to a philosophic concept. Sadism is not only pleasure in hurting somebody. It implies that what is, is right and what nature decrees in strength is totally right.

Men like Francis Crick (1916-) with his genetic determinism, and Freud (1856-1939), at the point of psychological determinism, are only saying what the Marquis de Sade has already told us — we are part of the machine. But if this is so, the Marquis de Sade's formula is inescapable — what is, is right. We are watching our culture put into effect the fact that when you tell men long enough that they are machines, it soon begins to show in their actions. You see it in our whole culture — in the theatre of cruelty, in the violence in the streets, in the death of man in art and life. These things, and many more like them, come quite naturally from the historical and philosophic flow which we are tracing.

What is wrong? When nature is made autonomous, it soon ends up by devouring God, grace, freedom and eventually man. You can hang on to freedom for a while, desperately using the *word* freedom like Rousseau and his followers, but freedom becomes nonfreedom.

Hegel

We come now to the next step of significance following Kant. We have said that there were three points that classical philosophy and thought had held on to — rationalism, rationality, and the hope of a unified field of knowledge. Prior to Hegel (1770-1831), all philosophic pursuit had proceeded something like this: Someone had tried to construct a circle which would encompass all of thought and all of life. The next man said that this was not the answer, but that he would provide one. The next man said, "You have failed, but I will give you the answer." The next man said, "Not at all; this is it," and the next said, "No!" and so on. It is hardly surprising that the study of the history of philosophy causes no great joy!

But by Kant's time the rationalistic rational possibilities are exhausted. Beginning with rationalistic presuppositions, the upper and lower "stories" are by his time in such great tension that they are ready to separate totally. Kant and Hegel are the doorway to modern man.

What did Hegel say? He argued that attempts had been made for thousands of years to find an answer on the basis of antithesis, and they had not come to anything. Philosophic humanistic thought had tried to hang on to rationalism, rationality and a unified field, and it had not succeeded. Thus, he said, we must try a new suggestion. The long-term effect of this new approach of Hegel's has been that Christians today do not understand their children. It may sound strange, but it is true. What Hegel changed was something more profound than merely one philosophic answer for another. He changed the rules of the game in two areas: *epistemology*, the theory of knowledge and the limits and validity of knowledge; and *methodology*, the method by which we approach the question of truth and knowing.

His thinking led to this: Let us no longer think in terms of antithesis. Let us think rather in terms of thesis — antithesis, with the answer always being synthesis. All things are relativized. In so doing, Hegel changed the world. A central reason Christians do not understand their children is because their children no longer think in the same framework in which their parents think. It is not merely that they come out with different answers. The methodology has changed — that is, the very method by which they arrive at, or try to arrive at, truth has changed.

It is not because rationalistic man *wanted* to make this change. It was made out of desperation, because for hundreds of years rationalistic thought had failed. A choice was made, and the choice consisted in holding on to rationalism at the expense of rationality.

It is true that Hegel is usually classified as an idealist. He hoped for a synthesis which somehow would have some relationship to reasonableness, and he used religious language in his struggle for this, but this ended only in religious words rather than in a solution.

He opened the door to that which is characteristic of modern man: truth as truth is gone, and synthesis (the both-and), with its relativism, reigns.

The basic position of man in rebellion against God is that man is at the center of the universe, that he is autonomous — here lies his rebellion. Man will keep his rationalism and his rebellion, his insistence on total autonomy or partially autonomous areas, even if it means he must give up his rationality.

Kierkegaard and the Line of Despair

The man who follows Hegel, Kierkegaard (1813-1855), is the real modern man because his thinking led to what Leonardo and all other thinkers had rejected. His thinking led to putting aside the hope of a unified field of knowledge.

The formulation had been, first,

$$\frac{\text{GRACE}}{\text{NATURE}}$$

secondly,

$$\frac{\text{FREEDOM}}{\text{NATURE}}$$

It now became:

$$\frac{\text{FAITH}}{\text{RATIONALITY}}$$

In the following diagram, the line is a time line. The higher levels are earlier, the lower levels are later. The steps represent different disciplines.

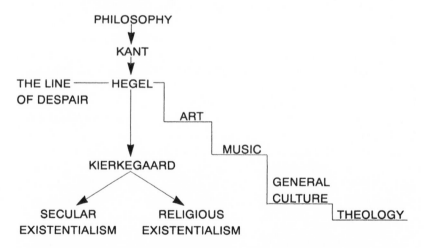

This new way of thinking spread in three different ways. In the first place it spread geographically, from Germany outward. Consequently Holland and Switzerland knew it before England, and America continued thinking in the old way much longer.

Second, it spread by classes. The intellectual was first affected.

Then, through the mass media, it passed down to the workers. What it left was a middle class that was not touched by it and often is still not touched by it. This middle-class group is, in many ways, a product of the Reformation; it is something to be thankful for as a source of stability. But now people in this group often do not understand the basis of its stability. They do not understand why they think in the old way; they are continuing to act out of habit and memory after they have forgotten why the old form was valid. Often they still think in the right way — to them truth is truth, right is right — but they no longer know why. So how can they understand their twentieth-century children who think in the new way, who no longer think that truth is truth nor that right is right?

The mass of people have received the new way of thinking through the mass media without analyzing it. It is worse for them because they have been smashed in the face by it, because the cinema, television, the books they read, the press, magazines have been infiltrated by the new thought-forms in an unanalyzed way. In between the intellectuals and the working classes, you find a pocket — the middle class. Undoubtedly, one of our difficulties is that most of our churches are in this upper-middle-class bracket, and the reason why Christians are not understanding their own children is because the children are being educated into the other way of thinking. It is not merely that they think different things. They think differently. Their thinking has changed in such a way that when you say Christianity is true, the sentence does not mean to them what it means to you.

The third way this has spread is by disciplines as shown in the preceding diagram: philosophy, then art, then music, then general culture, which can be divided into a number of areas. Theology comes last. In art, for example, you have the great Impressionists, Van Gogh (1853-1890), Gauguin (1848-1903), and Cezanne (1839-1906). Then you have the post-Impressionists. And here you come into the modern world. In music, Debussy (1862-1918) is the door. In literature you can think of a man like the early T. S. Eliot (1888-1965). The man who opened the door in theology is Karl Barth[2] (1886-1968).

I call this line in the diagram the line of despair. I do not mean by this that everybody under the line cries, although some, like the painter Francis Bacon (1909-) do cry. Giacometti (1901-1966) cried — he died crying.

What is this despair? It arises from the abandonment of the hope of a unified answer for knowledge and life. Modern man continues to hang on to his rationalism and his autonomous revolt even though to do so he has had to abandon any rational hope of a unified answer. Previously, educated men would not give up rationality and the hope of the unified field of knowledge. Modern man has given up his hope of unity and lives in despair — the despair of no longer thinking that what has always been the aspiration of men and women is at all possible.

Four

The Leap

The line of despair step has brought us to Kierkegaard (1813-1855) and the leap of faith. With Kant we noticed that the line between nature and universals had widened considerably. What Kierkegaard's leap did was to put away the hope of any unity. After Kierkegaard we are left with this:

OPTIMISM MUST BE NONRATIONAL

ALL RATIONALITY = PESSIMISM

The hope of a connecting link between the two spheres has disappeared. There is no permeation of interchange; there is a complete dichotomy between the upper and lower stories. The line between the upper and lower stories has become a concrete horizontal, ten thousand feet thick, with highly charged barbed wire fixed in the concrete.

What we are left with now runs something like this: Below the line there is rationality and logic. The upper story becomes the nonlogical and the nonrational. There is no relationship between them.

In other words, in the lower story, on the basis of all reason, man as man is dead. You have simply mathematics, particulars, mechanics. Man has no meaning, no purpose, no significance. There is only pessimism concerning man as man. But up above, on the basis of a nonrational, nonreasonable leap, there is a nonreasonable faith which gives optimism. This is modern man's total dichotomy.

The trouble with those of us who come out of a Christian background, or middle-class background, is that we cannot easily feel the thickness of this line in the way that it would be understood by the twentieth-century man on the left bank in Paris, or at London University. We, coming out of our background, think there must be some interchange, but the answer of our age is, "No, there has never been and there never will be." When man thought there was an interchange it was just an illusion. On the basis of all reason, man is meaningless. He has always been dead as far as rationality and logic are concerned. It was a vain hope that man thought he was not dead.

This is what it means to say man is dead. It does not mean he was alive and died. He was always dead, but did not know enough to know that he was dead.

Secular Existentialism
From Kierkegaard there are two extensions — secular existentialism and religious existentialism.

Secular existentialism divides into three main streams: Jean-Paul Sartre (1905-1980) and Camus (1913-1960) in France, Jaspers (1883-1969) in Switzerland, Heidegger (1889-1976) in Germany. First, Jean-Paul Sartre. Rationally the universe is absurd, and you must try to authenticate yourself. How? By authenticating yourself by an act of will. So if you are driving along the street and see someone in the pouring rain, you stop your car, pick him up and give him a lift. It is absurd. What does it matter? He is nothing, the situation is nothing, but you have authenticated yourself by an act of the will. But the difficulty is that authentication has no rational or logical content — all directions of an act of the will are equal. Therefore, similarly, if you are driving along and see the man in the rain, speed up your car, and knock him down, you have in an equal measure authenticated your will. Do you understand? If you do, cry for modern man in such a hopeless situation.

Second, Jaspers. He was basically a psychologist and spoke of a "final experience": that is, an experience so big that it gives you a certainty you are there and a hope of meaning—even though, rationally, you cannot have such hope. The problem with this "final experience" is that because it is totally separated from the rational, there is no way to communicate its content either to someone else *or to yourself.* A student from the Free University in Amsterdam had been trying to hang on to such an experience. He had gone to *Green Pastures* one night and felt such an experience that he thought there must be some sense to life. I met him some two years after this had happened. He was close to suicide. Think about it—hanging on to some meaning to life only on the basis of such an experience, an experience which you cannot communicate even to yourself except on the basis of repeating that it had occurred. The morning after, it might be strong, but two weeks later, two months, two years? How hopeless is hope based only on this final experience.

In addition, the final experience cannot be prepared for. There is no way to prepare for the final experience. The final experience is in the upper category—it just comes.

Third, you have what Heidegger called *Angst. Angst* is not just fear, for fear has an object. *Angst* is a vague feeling of dread—the uncomfortable feeling you have when you go into a house that might be haunted. Heidegger hung everything on this kind of basic anxiety. So the terms in which you express the upper story make no difference at all. The basis of this system lies in the leap. Hope is separated from the rational "downstairs."

Today there are almost no philosophies in the classical sense of philosophy—there are antiphilosophies. Men no longer think they can get rational answers to the big questions. The Anglo-Saxon linguistic philosophers shut themselves away from the great questions by limiting philosophy to a smaller area. They are concerned with the definition of words and have confined their operations to the lower story. The existentialists have hung on more to a classical concept of philosophy in that they are dealing with the big questions, but they do this by accepting completely the dichotomy between rationality and hope.

What makes modern man modern man is the existence of this dichotomy and not the multitude of types of things he places, as a leap, in the upper story. No matter what expression he places there, secular or religious, it still amounts to the same thing if it is rooted in this dichotomy. It is this that separates modern man from, on the one hand, Renaissance man, who had hope of a humanistic unity; and, on the other hand, from Reformation man, who actually possessed a rational unity above and below the line on the basis of the content of the biblical revelation.

Religious Existentialism

The same general picture that emerges from secular existentialism is present in Karl Barth's system and the new theologies which have extended his system. There is no rational interchange above and below the line. He held the higher critical theories until the day of his death — the Bible contains mistakes, but we are to believe it anyway. His position was that though the Bible contains mistakes, "a religious word" comes through anyway. "Religious truth" is separated from the historical truth of the Scriptures. Thus there is no place for reason and no point of verification. This constitutes the leap in religious terms. Aquinas opened the door to an independent man downstairs, a natural theology and a philosophy which were both autonomous from the Scriptures. This has led, in secular thinking, to the necessity of finally placing all hope in a nonrational upstairs. Similarly, in neo-orthodox theology, man is left with the need to leap because, as the whole man, he cannot do anything in the area of the rational to search for God. Man, in neo-orthodox theology, is less than biblical fallen man. The Reformation and the Scriptures say that man cannot do anything to save himself, but he can, with his reason, search the Scriptures which touch not only "religious truth," but also history and the cosmos. He not only is able to search the Scriptures as the whole man, including his reason, but he has the responsibility to do so.

The separation of what the Bible teaches in religious and spiritual matters — as being authoritative in these areas, while saying the Bible contains mistakes where it would be verifiable — is the crux of this form of irrationalism. This is so whether it is taught by those using radical theological terms or those using more conservative terms. In all such cases faith is isolated from reason. It is the religious expression of the prevailing thought-form of modern man.

The kind of words which are put in the upper story do not change the basic system. As far as the system is concerned, the use of religious or secular terms makes no difference to it. What is particularly important to notice in this system is the constant appearance in one form or another of the Kierkegaardian emphasis on the necessity of the leap. Because the rational and logical are totally separated from the nonrational and the nonlogical, the leap is total. Faith, whether expressed in secular or religious terms, becomes a leap without any verification because it is totally separated from the logical and the reasonable. We can now see, on this basis, how the new theologians can say that though the Bible, in the area of nature and history, is full of mistakes, this does not matter.

It does not matter what terms we adopt. The leap is common to every sphere of modern man's thought. Man is forced to the despair of such a leap because he cannot live merely as a machine. This, then, is modern man. It is modern man, whether expressed in his painting, his music, his novel, his drama or his religion.

The New Theology
In neo-orthodoxy, which grew out of the older strongly rationalistic liberal theology, the defined words are below the line:

NONRATIONAL — CONNOTATION WORDS

RATIONAL — DEFINED WORDS

Above the line the new theologian has undefined words. The "leap theology" centers everything in the undefined word. Tillich, for example, speaks of the "God behind God," with the first word "God" totally undefined. The defined words in the area of science and history are below the line; up above, there are only connotation words. Their value to him lies precisely in the fact that they *are* undefined.

Neo-orthodoxy seemed to have an advantage over secular existentialism because it uses words that have strong connotations, as they are rooted in the memory of the race — words like *resurrection, crucifixion, Christ, Jesus*. These words give an illusion of communication. The importance of these words to the new theologians lies in the illusion of communication, plus the highly motivated reaction men have on the basis of the connotation of the words. That is the advantage of the new theology over secular existentialism and the modern secular mysticisms. One hears the word *Jesus*, one acts upon it, but the word is never defined. The use of such words is always in the area of the irrational, the nonlogical. Being separated from history and the cosmos, they are divorced from possible verification by reason downstairs, and there is no certainty that there is anything upstairs. We need to understand, therefore, that it is an act of desperation to make this separation, in which all hope is removed from the realm of rationality. It is a real act of despair, which is not changed merely by using religious words.

Upper-Story Experiences

Man made in the image of God cannot live as though he is nothing; so he places in the upper story all sorts of desperate things. In order to illustrate that it does not matter what one places in the upper story, I shall try to show how wide-ranging these things are. We have considered already examples in Sartre's "existential experience," Jaspers's "final experience," and Heidegger's "*Angst*." In each case man is dead, as far as rationality and logic are concerned.

Aldous Huxley made a titanic addition to this way of thinking. We find him using the term "a first-order experience." In order to have such a first-order experience he advocated the use of drugs. I worked in the 1960s with many intelligent people taking LSD and found hardly any of them who did not realize that what they were doing was related to Aldous Huxley's teaching in regard to a "first-order experience." The point is that in the lower story — nature — life makes no sense; it is meaningless. In the 1960s drugs were taken to have a direct mystical experience that has no relation to the world of the rational. Jaspers, as we saw earlier, says you cannot prepare for this experience. Huxley, however, clung to the hope that you *can* prepare for it by taking drugs. So as people decided that our culture was, in the words of Timothy Leary, a "fake-prop-set society," they too turned to drugs.

The basic reason that drugs were seriously taken was not for escape or kicks, but because man is desperate. On the basis of rationality and logic man has no meaning, and culture is becoming meaningless. Man is therefore trying to find an answer in "first-order experiences." This is what lay behind the serious drug mania of the 1960s. It is related to a thousand years of pantheism, for Eastern mystics have taken hashish for centuries to achieve religious experience. So it is nothing new, even though it is new to us. In *The Humanist Frame*,[1] in which Aldous Huxley wrote the last chapter, he was still, right before his death, pleading for the use of drugs by "healthy people" for the "first-order experience." This was his hope.

Optimistic evolutionary humanism is yet another illustration of the fact that once one accepts a dichotomy of the upper and lower stories, it makes no difference what one then places in the upper story. Julian Huxley propagated this idea. Optimistic evolutionary humanism has no rational foundation. Its hope is always rooted in the leap of *mañana*. In looking for proof one is always diverted to tomorrow. This optimism is a leap, and we are foolish in our universities to be intimidated into thinking that the humanists have a rational basis for the "optimistic" part of their slogan. They have not — they are irrational. Julian Huxley himself has, in practice, accepted this, for he has put down the basic proposition that men function better if they think there is a god. There is no god, according to Huxley, but we will say there is a god. In other words, as Aldous Huxley looks to drugs, so Julian Huxley looks to a religious leap, even though to him it is a lie — there is no god. This is why it is not out of line for Julian Huxley to write the introduction to Teilhard de Chardin's *Phenomenon of Man*.[2] They were both involved in the leap. The mere use of religious words in contrast to nonreligious words changes nothing after the dichotomy and leap are accepted. Some positions seem further away from us and more shocking, some seem closer; but there is no essential difference.

In a BBC Third Programme broadcast, Anthony Flew addressed himself to the question "Must Morality Pay?"[3] He used the broadcast to show that on the basis of his own presuppositions, morality does not pay. And yet he himself could not stand this. At the very end he brings in out of thin air the concept that in spite of the fact that morality does not pay, a person is not a fool to be scrupulous — without a basis as to why a person is not a fool to be scrupulous and without any category even to give the word *scrupulous* meaning. This is a titanic leap.

The significant thing is that rationalistic, humanistic man began by saying that Christianity was not rational enough. Now he has come around in a wide circle and ended as a mystic — though a mystic of a special kind. He is a mystic with nobody there. The old mystics always said that there was somebody there, but the new mystic says that does not matter, because faith is the important thing. It is faith in faith, whether expressed in secular or religious terms. The leap is the thing and not the terms in which the leap is expressed. The verbalization — i.e., the symbol systems — can change; whether the systems are religious or nonreligious and whether more radical or more conservative religious terms are used, whether they use one word or another is incidental. Modern man is committed to finding his answer upstairs, by a leap away from rationality and away from reason.

Linguistic Analysis and the Leap

Some years ago I was leading a discussion in a particular British university where the linguistic philosophers were militant in their attack against the Christians. Some of them attended the discussion. As it went on, their position became obvious. They were building their academic prestige in the area below the line in reasonable definition of words. But to attack Christianity they leapt to an optimistic evolutionary humanism above the line, on the basis of the prestige which they had established below it in their own sphere. Some of them have quite properly established a reputation for rationality in the definition of words, but they then make a leap, changing their mask by attacking Christianity on the basis of a humanism which has no relationship whatsoever to the downstairs area of linguistic analysis. As we have said, linguistic analysis is an antiphilosophy in the sense that these men have limited themselves in their concept of philosophy. They no longer ask the big questions classical philosophy has always asked. Therefore, anything they say in the area of these questions has no relationship to their discipline and the prestige it entails.

The interesting thing today is that as existentialism and, in a different way, "defining philosophy" have become antiphilosophies, the real philosophic expressions have tended to pass over to those who do not occupy the chairs of philosophy — the novelists, the film producers, the jazz musicians, and even the teenage gangs in their violence. These are the people who are asking and struggling with the big questions in our day.

Five

Art as the Upper-Story Leap

We observed that from Rousseau's time the dichotomy was drawn between nature and freedom. Nature had come to represent determinism, the machine, with man in the hopeless situation of being caught in the machine. Then, in the upper story, we find man struggling for freedom. The freedom that was being sought was an absolute freedom with no limitations. There is no God, nor even a universal to limit him; so the individual seeks to express himself with total freedom, and yet, at the same time, he feels the damnation of being in the machine. This is the tension of modern man.

The field of art offers a variety of illustrations of this tension. Such tension affords a partial explanation of the intriguing fact that much of contemporary art, as a self-expression of what man is, is ugly. He does not know it, but he is expressing the nature of fallen man, which as created in the image of God is wonderful, yet now is fallen. As man strives to express his freedom in his autonomous fashion much, though certainly not all, of his art becomes meaningless and ugly. In contrast, much industrial design is becoming more orderly, with real beauty. I think the

245

explanation for the growing beauty of some industrial design is that it has to follow the curve of what is there — it follows the form of the universe.

This also illustrates how science as such is not autonomously free, but must follow what is there. Even if the scientist or philosopher says that all is random and meaningless, once he moves out into the universe he is limited, no matter what his philosophic system is, for he must follow what he finds there. If science does not do this, it is not science but science fiction. Industrial design, like science, is also bound up with the form of the universe and therefore is often more beautiful than an "Art" (with a capital *A*) which primarily expresses man's rebellion, ugliness and despair. We now come to some of the various expressions of art as the upper-story leap.

Poetry: The Later Heidegger

Heidegger could not accept his existentialism and changed his position — after he was seventy. In the book *What Is Philosophy?*[1] he ends with the admonition, "but listen to the poet." When he says, "listen to the poet," he does not mean that we are to listen to the content of what the poet says. Content is immaterial — one might have six poets all contradicting each other. It does not matter because the content is in the area of rationality, the lower story. What matters is that such a thing as poetry exists — and poetry is placed in the upper story.

Heidegger's position is as follows. A part of Being is the being, man, who verbalizes. Consequently, because there are words in the universe, one has the hope of some kind of meaning to Being — i.e., what is. One just notes that the poet exists and, in his mere existence, the poet becomes the prophet. Because poetry is with us, one hopes that there is more to life than merely what you know rationally and logically to be the case. Here then is another example of an irrational upstairs without any content.

Art: Andre Malraux

Malraux (1901-1976) was an intriguing man. He came through existentialism, fought in the Resistance, took drugs, led a very rough-and-tumble life at times, and finally turned out to be the Minister of Culture in France. In his book *The Voices of Silence*,[2] the last section is entitled "Aftermath of the Absolute." In it he showed that he understood very well the shift caused by the modern death of hope of an absolute.

A number of books tried to come to terms with his position. The 6 October 1966 issue of *The New York Review of Books* dealt with several. There we find the following comment. "All Malraux's works are torn . . . without help of resolution, between at least two positions: a basic antihumanism (which is represented, depending on the circumstances, by intellectual pride, the will to power, eroticism and so on), and an ultimately irrational aspiration towards charity, or rationally unjustifiable choice in favor of man."

In other words, there is a "torn-ness" in Malraux — in the upper story is placed something in art which has no rational basis whatsoever. It is the aspiration of a man separated from rationality. On the basis of rationality man has no hope; yet you look to art as art to provide it. It affords an integration point, a leap, a hope for freedom in the midst of what your mind knows is false. You are damned and you know it, and yet you look to art and try to find a hope that reasonably you know is not there. The review goes on to say, "Malraux is rising above such despair by eloquently summoning himself and others to see the identity of man in the timelessness of art." So Malraux's total work — his novels, his art history, his work as the French Minister of Culture — was a gigantic expression of this chasm and leap.

The system that surrounds us, of dichotomy and the leap, is a monolithic one. In England, Sir Herbert Read (1893-1968) was in the same category. In *The Philosophy of Modern Art*[3] he showed he understood when he said of Gauguin: "Gauguin substituted his love for beauty (as a painter) for man's love for his Creator." But in his understanding he also said that reason must give place to the mystique of art — not only theoretically, but as the starting-place of education for tomorrow.[4] In Sir Herbert Read, art is again put forth as the answer achieved by the leap.

Picasso
Picasso (1881-1973) furnishes another example. He had attempted to create a universal by means of abstraction. His abstract paintings had gone so far that it was no longer possible to distinguish a blonde from a brunette, or a man from a woman, or even a man from a chair. Abstraction had gone to such an extent that he had made his own universe on the canvas — in fact, he seemed at that

time to be successfully playing at being god on his canvas. But at the moment when he painted a universal and not a particular, he ran head-on into one of the dilemmas of modern man — the loss of communication. The person standing in front of the painting has lost communication with the painting — he does not know what the subject-matter is. What is the use of being god on a two-by-four surface when nobody knows what you are talking about.

However, it is instructive to see what happened when Picasso fell in love. He began writing across his canvas "*J'aime Eva.*" Suddenly there was now a communication between the people looking at the picture and Picasso. But it was an irrational communication. It was communication on the basis that he loved Eva, which we could understand, but not on the subject-matter of the painting. Here again is the leap. Because he is still a man he must leap, especially when he falls in love.

From that time on, it is possible to take Picasso's work and follow the curves of the paintings as he fell in and out of love. Later, for example, when he fell in love with Olga and married her, he painted her in a most human way. I am not saying the rest of his paintings are not great. He is a great painter, but he is a man who failed to do what he set out to do in his attempt to achieve a universal, and his whole life after this was a series of tensions. Later I saw some of his work when he fell in love again, with Jacqueline. I said at the time, "Picasso is in a new era — he loves this woman." True enough he later married her — his second marriage. Thus, in his paintings of Olga and Jacqueline, in a manner contrary to almost all of his other work, he expresses the irrational leap in the symbol system of the form of his paintings, but it is the same irrational leap which others express in words.

In passing, let us say that Salvador Dali (1901-) did the same thing by painting connotation Christian art symbols when he took the leap from his old surrealism to his new mysticism. In one period of his work the Christian symbols are painted using their connotative effect, rather than verbalized, as in the new theology. But this makes no difference. It is based on a leap, and an illusion of communication is given by using the connotative effect of the Christian symbols.

Bernstein
We are showing that we are faced with an almost monolithic concept today, of dichotomy and leap, and that once the leap is

accepted, it really makes no difference what you place upstairs, or in what terms or even symbol systems the upstairs is expressed. Leonard Bernstein (1918-) for example, in his *Kaddish*[5] indicated that music is the hope upstairs. The essence of modern man lies in his acceptance of a two-level situation, regardless of what words or symbols are used to express this. In the area of reason man is dead, and his only hope is some form of a leap that is not open to consideration by reason. Between these two levels there is no point of contact.

Pornography
Modern pornographic writing is explicable in these terms too. There have always been such writings, but the new ones are different. They are not just dirty writings of the kind that were always available — many of today's pornographic works are philosophic statements. If one takes the works of somebody like Henry Miller (1891-1980), one finds that they are a statement that rationally and logically even sex is dead; yet in later writing he leaps into a pantheism for a hope of meaning.

Another element in modern pornographic writing comes out in the works of Terry Southern (1924-). He is the author of *Candy* and *The Magic Christian*. Despite the dirt and destructiveness, he is making serious statements. But what does he put in its place? In the Introduction to a book called *Writers in Revolt*[6] he takes the following line. He calls the Introduction "Towards the Ethics of a Golden Age," and proceeds to show how Western modern man is falling to pieces. He shows how modern man is only psychologically orientated. He has in particular one clever sentence in this statement of our culture's psychological orientation: "Its implication in terms of any previously operative philosophy or cultural structure prior to this century, is shattering, for its ultimate meaning is that there is no such thing as crime: it destroys the idea of crime." He does not mean, of course, that we no longer have crime. He means that with psychological orientation "crime" does not exist. No matter what it is, it is not seen as crime, nor as morally wrong.

Evangelical Christians tend to write off such people and then get into trouble over understanding modern man, for in reality these people are the philosophers of the day. Our university chairs of philosophy are in effect largely vacant. The philosophy is being written by the Southerns of this modern world. When you come to the end of this Introduction I have quoted, you are left breathless at a terrific piece of writing. You feel like screaming and saying, "Well, then, what is there?" The fantastic thing is that the end of the Introduction says that they are writing pornographic material today in the hope that finally an ethic for the golden age will emerge. Thus pornographic writing is now put in the upper story. They conceive of pornography as the ultimate release — it is the leap to freedom. They are smashing away at the downstairs deadness, and say that they will not have its tyranny. And although there is of course much trash as well, there is in these serious pornographic writings, struggling with this problem, the hope that pornography will provide a new golden age. This is Rousseau and the autonomous freedom coming to a natural conclusion. Remember that in the Renaissance there was the dualistic separation like this:

LYRIC POETS — SPIRITUAL LOVE

NOVELISTS AND COMIC POETS (PORNOGRAPHIC)

But now rationalistic humanism has progressed logically to a total dichotomy between the upper and the lower, like this:

THE AUTONOMOUS PORNOGRAPHIC AS THE ONLY
HOPE OF FREEDOM AND OF MAN

RATIONALITY — MAN IS DEAD

This again is a mysticism with nobody there, a mysticism that flies in the face of rationality. There is nothing, and yet, driven by his aspirations — because he is made in the image of God — man tries all these overwhelming acts of desperation, even entertaining the hope that a golden age will emerge from Soho.

One such serious pornographic work has been written in which, because there is no God, a woman puts herself into a man's hands to be beaten. It states explicitly that since no God exists, she wants to be possessed by someone, and thus in her alienation is glad of the beatings and pain as a proof of possession by something, someone.

These people are in total desperation. We are fighting for our lives. If we love people, this is no age for a lack of comprehension, no age to play small-sized games, and no age to fall into the same thought-form of duality without realizing it.

In the 1980s there is much pornography just as pornography — just as there is in the 1980s mostly drug-takers for escape. However, it should be kept in mind that these things did go through a conscious philosophic period. Any idealism has largely been lost, and society has been influenced and changed — often with no realization as to why the change has come.

The Theatre of the Absurd

The note of desperation is reflected in the Theatre of the Absurd. The stress on the absurd recalls the whole structure of Sartre's thought. Man is a tragic joke in a context of total cosmic absurdity. He has been thrown up with aspirations which rationally have no fulfillment in the universe in which he lives. But this outlook as expressed in the Theatre of the Absurd goes beyond Sartre. Sartre says the universe is absurd, but uses words and syntax as they are normally used. The Theatre of the Absurd, however, deliberately uses abnormal syntax and a devaluation of words to shout the more loudly that all is absurd.

Martin Esslin (1918-), well-known for his work in the BBC, wrote a book on this subject which has a very interesting Introduction, "The Absurdity of the Absurd."[7] He says that there are three steps in the Theatre of the Absurd. The first step is that you say to the bourgeois: "Wake up! You have been asleep long enough." So you wake him — kick his bed and pour a bucket of water over him through the absurd theatre. Then as soon as he is awake, you look him in the eye and tell him there is nothing here. That is the second step. But there is a third step, once again an upper-story mysticism. This upper-story mysticism is an attempt to communicate "above" communication. As such, it is parallel to the happenings and environments following Marcel Duchamp (1887-1969). This is not the place to deal with this subject in detail, but it is my conclusion that this communication, "above" communication, which has no continuity with the rational, cannot communicate content, but must be taken seriously as a vehicle of manipulation. However, of the three steps in the Theatre of the Absurd, clearly two are towards pessimism, while the third is again a mystical leap without any roots at all in the first two steps.

Six

Madness

We still have not exhausted this subject of the leap. There are other areas where it shows itself. A book by Michel Foucault (1926-), called *Madness and Civilization*,[1] is important here. In a review of the book in *The New York Review of Books* (3 November 1966), entitled "In Praise of Folly," the reviewer, Stephen Marcus of Columbia University, comments, "What Foucault is finally against, however, is the authority of reason. . . . In this Foucault represents an important tendency in advanced contemporary thought. In his despair of the transcendent powers of rational intellect he embodies one abiding truth of our time — the failure of the nineteenth century to make good its promises." In other words, the heirs of the Enlightenment had promised that they would provide a unified answer on the basis of the rational. Foucault maintains correctly that this promise has not been fulfilled.

The reviewer continues: "This is partly why he turns at the end to the mad and half-mad artists and thinkers of the modern age. . . . Through their utterances the world is arraigned; mediated by their madness, the language of their art dramatizes the culpability of the world and forces it to recognize itself and reorder its consciousness. One cannot, in good conscience, deny the force and truth of these observations; they catch a reality of the intellectual situation of the present moment — a moment that is coming to think of itself as post-everything, post-modern, post-history, post-sociology, post-psychology. . . . We are in the position of having rejected the nineteenth and twentieth century systems of thought, of having outworn them without having transcended them with new truth, or discovered anything of comparable magnitude to take their place."

In other words, the rationalists have not found any kind of unity, or any other hope of a rational solution. So we find that Foucault follows Rousseau's thought to its conclusion: the ultimate in autonomous freedom is being crazy. It is a fine thing to be crazy, for then you are free.

THE NONRATIONAL — THE REAL FREEDOM
IS MADNESS

THE RATIONAL — MAN IS DEAD

It may be objected that this is a unique idea which Foucault and the reviewer have had, and it is therefore unimportant as totally extreme. And yet serious drug-taking was a self-imposed and, it was hoped, temporary mental illness. The results of drug-taking and schizophrenia are remarkably parallel, and this fact was understood by many in the 1960s. Foucault was not too far removed from Aldous Huxley. He is not to be thought of as too isolated to be of importance in understanding our era, and in understanding the end of duality and dichotomy. The logical end of the dichotomy, in which hope is separated from reason, is the giving up of all reason.

It must be said again, as in the shift from philosophic drug-taking to sheer escape, and as in the change from the philosophic pornographic to the pornographic for its own self, in this area we have been considering that the ideas of men like Foucault are rarely dealt with in the 1980s. But also once again it must be stressed that we do not understand the totality of the 1980s if we do not remember that the place where our society is was arrived at by these considerations being thought out in the 1960s. In the 1980s people may simply "join the system," but their attitudes are different, and the system as such is different than before these changes came.

The "Upstairs" in Film and Television

This almost monolithic concept can be felt in the cinema and television as well as in the other areas to which we have already referred. The gifted cinema producers of the classical philosophic films (Bergman, Fellini, Antonioni), the avant-garde cinema men in Paris, or the Double-Neos in Italy — all had basically the same message. People often ask which is better — American or BBC television. What do you want — to be entertained to death, or to be killed with wisely planted blows? That seems to be the alternative. BBC is better in the sense that it is more serious, but it is overwhelmingly on the side of the twentieth-century mentality. I happened to hear the program on BBC television when the famous four-letter word was first used. There was a tremendous outcry. Such usage was obviously a serious departure from old standards; yet I would say if we were given a choice *and had to choose*, let us have ten thousand four-letter words rather than the almost subliminal presentation on English television of twentieth-century thinking without the four-letter words. The really dangerous thing is that our people are being taught this twentieth-century mentality without being able to understand what is happening to them. That is why this mentality has penetrated into the lower cultural levels as well as among the intellectuals.

Bergman said that all the first films he made were intended to teach existentialism. He then came to the view, like Heidegger before him, that this was not adequate. He therefore made a film — *The Silence* — which showed the radical change. *The Silence* is a statement of the belief that man is really dead. It introduced a new kind of cinema — the camera eye simply looks at life and reports it as meaningless in nonhuman terms. The film is a series of pictures with no human statement connected with them.

This outlook appears too in the nihilistic "black" writers of our day. This was also the importance of Capote's *In Cold Blood*. One of the things almost all the reviewers noticed concerning Capote's book when it was published was that there is no moral judgment made. It simply reported — he picked up the murder weapon and did this — the same kind of statement a computer, hooked up to a camera eye, would be able to make about it.

However, the most startling cinema statement was not that man is dead downstairs, but the powerful expression of what man is above the line after the leap. The first of these films was *The Last Year at Marienbad*. This is not my guess. The film's director explained that this is what he wanted the film to show. That is the reason for the long, endless corridors and the unrelatedness in the film. If below the line man is dead, above the line, after the nonrational leap, man is left without categories. There are no categories because categories are related to rationality and logic. There is therefore no truth and no nontruth in antithesis, no right and wrong — you are adrift.

Juliet of the Spirits was another of several pictures of this kind. A student in Manchester, England told me that he was going to see *Juliet of the Spirits* for the third time to try to work out what was real and what was fantasy in the film. I had not seen it then, but I saw it later in a small art theatre in London. Had I seen it before I would have told him not to bother. One could go ten thousand times and never figure it out. It was deliberately made to prevent the viewer from distinguishing between objective reality and fantasy. There are no categories. One does not know what is real, or illusion, or psychological, or insanity.

Antonioni's *Blow-Up* was another statement of the same message, the portrayal of modern man upstairs without categories. It underlined the vital point here: since there are no categories once the dichotomy is accepted, it is immaterial what one places upstairs.

Upper-Story Mysticism

The mysticism with nobody there, as we have termed it earlier, is therefore a mysticism without categories; so it does not matter upstairs whether you use religious or nonreligious terms, art symbol systems, or pornography.

The same principle characterizes radical theology — not only is man dead below the line, but below the line God is dead also. The "God is dead" theologians said very clearly, "What is the use of talking about God in the upper story when we do not know anything about Him. Let us say quite honestly that God is dead." With the background we have traced in general culture, you can now see why these theologians were tired of the game. Why bother with all these god words? Why not just say it is all over, we accept the rational conclusion of the downstairs that God is dead.

So radical liberal theology can be set out like this:

NONRATIONAL	JUST THE CONNOTATION WORD GOD — NO CONTENT CONCERNING GOD — NO PERSONAL GOD
RATIONAL	GOD IS DEAD MAN IS DEAD

Upstairs with the vacuum we have been talking about, the radical liberal theologians have no idea that there is anything that really correlates with the connotation borne along by the *word* god. All they have is a semantic answer on the basis of a connotation word. Up above, the radical theology is left with the philosophic other — the infinite, impersonal everything. This brings us in Western thought into proximity with the East. The new theologian has lost the unique infinite-personal God of biblical revelation and of the Reformation. Much liberal theology of the current thinking has only god words as a substitute.

T. H. Huxley has proved to be a discerning prophet in all this. In 1890[2] he made the statement that there would come a time when men would remove all content from faith and especially from the pre-Abrahamic scriptural narrative. Then: "No longer in contact with fact of any kind, Faith stands now and forever proudly inaccessible to the attacks of the infidel." Because modern theology has accepted the dichotomy and removed the things of religion from the world of the verifiable, modern theology is now in the position grandfather Huxley prophesied. Modern theology now differs little from the agnosticism or even the atheism of 1980.

So then, in our day, the sphere of faith is placed in the nonrational and nonlogical as opposed to the rational and logical, the unverifiable as opposed to the verifiable. The new theologians use connotation words rather than defined words — words as symbols without any definition, in contrast to scientific symbols that are carefully defined. Faith is unchallengeable because it could be anything — there is no way to discuss it in normal categories.

Jesus the Undefined Banner
The "God is dead" school still used the word *Jesus*. For example, Paul Van Buren in *The Secular Meaning of the Gospel* said that

the present-day problem is that the *word* god is dead. He went on to point out, however, that we are no poorer by this loss, for all that we need we have in the man Jesus Christ. But Jesus here turns out to be a nondefined symbol. These theologians use the word because it is rooted in the memory of the race. It is humanism with a religious banner called "Jesus" to which they can give any content they wish. You find, therefore, that these men have made a sudden transference and slipped the word *Jesus* as a connotation word into the upper story. So notice once more that it does not matter what word you put up there — even biblical words — if your system is centered in the leap.

```
NONRATIONAL                          ⌐► JESUS
RATIONALITY      —      GOD IS DEAD⌐⌐
```

This emphasizes how careful the Christian needs to be. In the *Weekend Telegraph* of 16 December 1966, Marghanita Laski spoke of the new kinds of mysticisms which she saw developing and said, "In any case how could they be shown to be true or false?" What she meant is that men are removing religious things out of the world of the discussable and putting them into the nondiscussable, where you can say anything without fear of proof or disproof.

The evangelical Christian needs to be careful because some evangelicals have recently been asserting that what matters is not setting out to prove or disprove propositions; what matters is an encounter with Jesus. When a Christian has made such a statement he has, in an analyzed or unanalyzed form, moved upstairs.

```
NONRATIONAL — AN ENCOUNTER WITH JESUS
RATIONAL — ONE DOES NOT SET ABOUT PROVING
OR DISPROVING PROPOSITIONS
```

If we think that we are escaping some of the pressures of the modern debate by playing down propositional Scripture and simply putting the word *Jesus* or *experience* upstairs, we must face this question: What difference is there between doing this and doing what the secular world has done in its semantic mysticism, or what the radical theology has done? At the very least, the door has been opened for man to think it is the same thing.

If what is placed upstairs is separated from rationality, and the

Scriptures (especially where they touch on history and the cosmos) are not discussed as open to verification, why should one then accept the evangelical upstairs any more than the upstairs of the modern radical theology? On what basis is the choice to be made? Why should it not just as well be an encounter under the name Vishnu? Indeed, why should one not seek an experience, without the use of any such words, in a drug experience?

Our urgent need today is to understand the modern system as a whole, and to appreciate the significance of duality, dichotomy and the leap. The upstairs, we have seen, can take many forms — some religious, some secular, some dirty, some clean. However, the very essence of the system is that the type of words used upstairs does not matter — even such a well-loved word as *Jesus*.

I have come to the point where, when I hear the word *Jesus* — which means so much to me because of the Person of the historic Jesus and His work — I listen carefully because I have with sorrow become more afraid of the word *Jesus* than almost any other word in the modern world. The word is used as a contentless banner, and our generation is invited to follow it. But there is no rational, scriptural content by which to test it, and thus the word is being used to teach the very opposite things from those which Jesus taught. Men are called to follow the word with highly motivated fervency, and nowhere more than in the new morality which follows the radical theology. It is now Jesus-like to sleep with a girl or a man, if she or he needs you. As long as you are trying to be human, you are being Jesus-like to sleep with the other person — at the cost, be it noted, of breaking the specific morality which Jesus taught. But to these people this does not matter, because that is downstairs in the area of rational scriptural content.

We have come then to this fearsome place where the word *Jesus* has become the enemy of the Person Jesus, and the enemy of what Jesus taught. We must fear this contentless banner of the word *Jesus* not because we do not love Jesus, but because we do love Him. We must fight this contentless banner, with its deep motivations, rooted into the memories of the race, which is being used for the purpose of sociological form and control. We must teach our spiritual children to do the same.

This accelerating trend makes me wonder whether when Jesus said that towards the end-time there will be other Jesuses, He meant something like this. We must never forget that the great enemy who is coming is the Antichrist, he is not anti-non-Christ. He is anti-Christ. Increasingly over the last few years the word *Jesus*, separated from the content of the Scriptures, has become the enemy of the Jesus of history, the Jesus who died and rose and who is coming again and who is the eternal Son of God. So let us take care. If evangelical Christians begin to slip into a dichotomy, to separate an encounter with Jesus from the content of the Scriptures (including the discussable and the verifiable portions of Scripture), we shall, without intending to, be throwing ourselves and the next generation into the millstream of the modern system. This system surrounds us as an almost monolithic consensus.

Seven

Rationality and Faith

Some of the consequences of pitting faith against rationality in an unbiblical manner are as follows:

The first consequence of putting Christianity in an upper story concerns morality. The question arises, how can we establish a relationship from an upstairs Christianity down into the area of morals in daily life? The simple answer is that it can't be done. As we have seen, there are no categories upstairs, and so there is no way for the upstairs to provide categories! Consequently what really forms the "Christlike" act today is simply what the majority of the Church or the majority of society makes up its mind is desirable at the particular moment. You cannot have real morals in the real world after you have made this separation. What you have is merely a relative set of morals.

The second consequence of this separation is that you have no adequate basis for law. The whole Reformation system of law was built on the fact that God had revealed something real down into the common things of life. There is a beautiful painting by Paul Robert in Switzerland's old Supreme Court Building in Lausanne. It is called *Justice Instructing the Judges*. Down in the foreground of the large mural the artist depicts many sorts of litigation — the wife against the husband, the architect against the builder, and so on. How are the judges going to judge between them? This is the way we judge in a Reformation country, says Paul Robert. He has portrayed Justice pointing with her sword to a book upon which are the words, "The Law of God." For Reformation man there was a basis for law. Modern man has not only thrown away Christian theology; he has thrown away the possibility of what our forefathers had as a basis for morality and law.

Another consequence is that this throws away the answer to the problem of evil. Christianity's answer rests in the historic, space-time, real and complete Fall. The true Christian position is that in space and time and history, there was an unprogrammed man who made a choice, and actually rebelled against God. Once you remove this you have to face Baudelaire's profound statement, "If there is a God, He is the Devil," or Archibald MacLeish's statement in his play *J.B.*, "If he is God he cannot be good, if he is good he cannot be God." Without Christianity's answer that God made a significant man in a significant history, with evil being the result of Satan's and then man's historic space-time revolt, there is no answer but to accept Baudelaire's statement with tears. Once the historic Christian answer is put away, all we can do is to leap upstairs and say that against all reason God is good. Notice that if we accept a duality, thinking that we thus escape conflict with modern culture and the consensus of thinking, we are trapped in an illusion, for when we move on a few steps we will find that we come out at the same place where they are.

The fourth consequence of placing Christianity in the upper story is that we thus throw away our chance of evangelizing real twentieth-century people in the midst of their predicament. Modern man longs for a different answer than the answer of his damnation. He did not accept the line of despair and the dichotomy because he wanted to. He accepted it because, on the basis of the natural development of his rationalistic presuppositions, he had to. He may talk bravely at times, but in the end it *is* despair.

Christianity has the opportunity, therefore, to say clearly that its answer has the very thing modern man has despaired of — the unity of thought. It provides a unified answer for the whole of life. True, man has to renounce his rationalism; but then, on the basis of what can be discussed, he has the possibility of recovering his rationality. You can now see why I stressed so strongly, earlier, the difference between rationalism and rationality. Modern man has lost the latter. But he can have it again with a unified answer to life on the basis of what is open to verification and discussion.

Let Christians remember, then, that if we fall into the trap against which I have been warning, what we have done, among other things, is to put ourselves in the position where in reality we are only saying with evangelical words what the unbeliever is saying with his words. In order to confront modern man effectively, we must not have this dichotomy. You must have the Scriptures speaking truth both about God Himself and about the area where the Bible touches history and the cosmos. This is what our forefathers in the Reformation grasped so well.

As we said before, on the side of infinity we are separated from God entirely, but on the side of personality we are made in the image of God. So God can speak and tell us about Himself — not exhaustively, but truly. (We could not, after all, know anything exhaustively as finite creatures.) Then He has told us about things in the finite created realm, too. He has told us true things about the cosmos and history. Thus, we are not adrift.

But this answer exists only if we hold to the Reformation view of the Scriptures. It is not sufficient to say only that God reveals Himself in Jesus Christ, because there is not enough content in this if it is separated from the Scriptures. It then becomes only another contentless banner. All we know of what that revelation of Christ was, comes from the Scriptures. Jesus Himself did not make a distinction between His authority and the authority of the written Scriptures. He acted upon the unity of His authority and the content of the Scriptures.

There is the personal element involved in all this. Christ is Lord of all — over every aspect of life. It is no use saying He is the Alpha and Omega, the beginning and the end, the Lord of all things, if He is not the Lord of my whole unified intellectual life. I am false or confused if I sing about Christ's Lordship and contrive to retain areas of my own life that are autonomous. This is true if it is my sexual life that is autonomous, but it is at least equally true if it is my intellectual life that is autonomous — or even my intellectual life in a highly selective area. Any autonomy is wrong. Autonomous science or autonomous art is wrong, if by autonomous science or art we mean that it is free from the content of what God has told us. This does not mean that we have a static science or art—just the opposite. It gives us the form inside which, being finite, freedom is possible. Science and art cannot be placed in the framework of an autonomous downstairs without coming to the same tragic end that has occurred throughout history. We have seen that in every case in which the downstairs was made autonomous, no matter what name it was given, it was not long before the downstairs ate up the upstairs. Not only God disappeared, but freedom and man as well.

The Bible Can Stand on Its Own

Often people say to me, "How is it that you seem to be able to communicate with these far-out people? You seem to be able to talk in such a way that they understand what you're saying, even if they do not accept it." There may be a number of reasons why this is so, but one is that I try to get them to consider the biblical system and its truth without an appeal to blind authority—that is, as though believing meant believing just because one's family did, or as though the intellect had no part in the matter.

This is the way I became a Christian. I had gone to a "liberal" church for many years. I decided that the only answer, on the basis of what I was hearing, was agnosticism or atheism. On the basis of liberal theology I do not think I have ever made a more logical decision in my life. I became an agnostic, and then I began to read the Bible for the first time in order to place it against some Greek philosophy I was reading. I did this as an act of honesty insofar as I had given up what I thought was Christianity, but had never read the Bible through. Over a period of about six months I became a Christian because I was convinced that the full answer which the Bible presented was alone sufficient to the problems I then knew, and sufficient in a very exciting way.

I have always tended to think visually, so I thought of my problems as balloons floating in the sky. I did not know then as many of the basic problems of men's thoughts as I know now. But what was exciting to me (and *is* exciting) was that when I came to the Bible, I found it did not simply shoot down the problems, as an antiaircraft gun would, knocking down the individual balloons—it did something far more exciting. It answered the problems in the sense that I, limited though I was, could stand as though having a cable in my hand with all the problems and answers linked together as a system, in the framework of what the

Bible says truth is. Over and over again I have found my personal experience repeated. It is possible to take the system the Bible teaches, put it down in the marketplace of the ideas of men, and let it stand there and speak for itself.

Let us notice that the system of the Bible is excitingly different from any other, because it is the only system in religion or philosophy that tells us why a person may do what every man must do — that is, begin with himself. There is, in fact, no other way to begin apart from ourselves — each man sees through his own eyes — and yet this involves a real problem. What right have I to begin here? No other system explains my right to do so. But the Bible gives me an answer as to why I can do what I must do — that is, to begin with myself.

The Bible says, first of all, that in the beginning all things were created by a personal-infinite God who had always existed. So what is, therefore, is intrinsically personal rather than impersonal. Then the Bible says that He created all things outside of Himself. The term "outside of Himself" is, I think, the best way to express creation to twentieth-century people. We do not mean to use the phrase in a spatial sense, but to deny that creation is any kind of pantheistic extension of God's essence. God exists — a personal God who has always existed — and He has created all other things outside of Himself. Thus, because the universe begins with a truly personal beginning, love and communication (which are a burden of twentieth-century men's hearts) are not contrary to that which intrinsically is. The universe began in a personal as against an impersonal beginning, and, as such, those longings of love and communication which man has are not contrary to that which intrinsically is. And the world is a real world, because God has created it truly outside of Himself. What He has created is objectively real; thus there is true historic cause and effect. There is a true history and there is a true me.

In this setting of a significant history, the Bible says that God made man in a special way, in His own image. If I do not understand that man's basic relationship is upward, I must try to find it downward. In relating it downward, a person is very old-fashioned today if he finally relates himself to the animals. Today modern man seeks to relate himself to the machine.

But the Bible says that my life of reference need not lead downward. It is upward because I have been made in God's image. Man is not a machine.

If the intrinsically personal origin of the universe is rejected, what alternative outlook can anyone have? It must be said emphatically that there is no final answer except that man is a product of the impersonal, plus time, plus chance. No one has ever succeeded in finding personality on this basis, though many, like the late Teilhard de Chardin, have tried. It cannot be done. The conclusion that we are the natural products of the impersonal, plus time and chance, is the only one, unless we begin with personality. And no one has shown how time plus chance can produce a qualitative change from impersonal to personal.

If this were true, we would be hopelessly caught. But when the Bible says that man is created in the image of a personal God, it gives us a starting-point. No humanistic system has provided a justification for man to begin with himself. The Bible's answer is totally unique. At one and the same time it provides the reason why a man may do what he must do (start with himself), and it tells him the adequate reference point, the infinite-personal God. This is in complete contrast to other systems in which man begins with himself, neither knowing why he has a right to begin from himself, nor in what direction to begin inching along.

Beginning from Myself and Yet . . .
When we talk about the possibility of men beginning from themselves to understand the meaning of life and the universe, we must be careful to define clearly what we mean. There are two concepts or ideas of knowing which must be kept separate. The first is the rationalistic or humanistic concept — namely, that man, beginning totally independently and autonomously, can build a bridge towards ultimate truth — as if attempting to build a cantilever bridge out from himself across an infinite gorge. This is not possible, because man is finite and, as such, he has nothing toward which he can point with certainty. He has no way, beginning from himself, to set up sufficient universals. Sartre saw this very clearly when, as a result of finding no infinite reference point, he came to the conclusion that everything must be absurd.

The second concept is the Christian one. That is, as man has been created in God's image, he can begin with himself — not as infinite but as personal; plus the important fact (as we shall see below) that God has given to fallen man contentful knowledge which he desperately needs.

The fact that man has fallen does not mean that he has ceased to bear God's image. He has not ceased to be man because he is fallen. He can love, though he is fallen. It would be a mistake to say that only a Christian can love. Moreover, a non-Christian painter can still paint beauty. And it is because they can still do these things that they manifest that they are God's image-bearers or, to put it another way, they assert their unique "mannishness" as men.

So it is a truly wonderful thing that although man is twisted and corrupted and lost as a result of the Fall, yet he is still man. He has become neither a machine nor an animal nor a plant. The marks of "mannishness" are still upon him — love, rationality, longing for significance, fear of nonbeing, and so on. This is the case even when his non-Christian system leads him to say these things do not exist. It is these things which distinguish him from the animal and plant world and from the machine. On the other hand, beginning only from himself autonomously it is quite obvious that being finite, he can never reach any absolute answer. This would be true if only on the basis of the fact that he is finite, but to this must be added, since the Fall, the fact of his rebellion. He rebels against, and perverts, the testimony of what exists — the external universe and its form, and the "mannishness" of man.

The Source of the Knowledge We Need
In this setting the Bible sets forth its own statement of what the Bible itself is. It presents itself as God's communication of propositional truth, written in verbalized form, to those who are made in God's image. Functioning on the presupposition of the uniformity of natural causes in a closed system, both the secular and the unbiblical theological thinking of today would say that this is impossible. But that is precisely what the Bible says it does set forth. We may take, for example, what occurred at Sinai.[1] Moses says to the people, "You saw; you heard." What they heard (along with other things) was a verbalized propositional communication from God to man, in a definite, historic, space-time situation. It was not some kind of contentless, existential experience, nor an anti-intellectual leap. We find exactly the same kind of communication occurring in the New Testament, as for example when Christ spoke to Paul in Hebrew on the Damascus road. Therefore, on one hand we have the kind of propositional communication God gives in the Scriptures. On the other hand, we see to whom this propositional communication is directed.

The Bible teaches that though man is hopelessly lost, he is not nothing. Man is lost because he is separated from God, his true reference point, by true moral guilt. But he will never be nothing. Therein lies the horror of his lostness. For man to be lost, in all his uniqueness and wonder, is tragic.

We must not belittle man's achievements. In science, for instance, man's achievements demonstrate that he is not junk, though the ends to which he often puts them show how lost he is. Our forefathers, though they believed man was lost, had no problem concerning man's significance. Man can influence history, including his own eternity and that of others. This view sees man, as man, as something wonderful.

In contrast to this there is the rationalist who has determinedly put himself at the center of the universe and insists on beginning autonomously with only the knowledge he can gather, and has ended up finding himself quite meaningless. It comes to the same thing as Zen-Buddhism, which expresses so accurately the view of modern man: "Man enters the water and causes no ripple." The Bible says he causes ripples that *never* end. As a sinner, man cannot be selective in his significance, so he leaves behind bad as well as good marks in history; but he certainly he is not a zero.

Christianity is a system which is composed of a set of ideas which can be discussed. By *system* we do not mean a scholastic abstraction; nevertheless we do not shrink from using the word. The Bible does not set out unrelated thoughts. The system it sets forth has a beginning and moves from that beginning in a noncontradictory way. The beginning is the existence of the infinite-personal God as Creator of all else. Christianity is not just a vague set of incommunicable experiences, based on a totally unverifiable "leap in the dark." Neither conversion (the beginning of the Christian life), nor spirituality (the growth) should be such a leap. Both are firmly related to the God who is there and the knowledge He has given us — and both involve the whole man.

The "Leap in the Dark" Mentality

Modern man has come to his position because he has accepted a new attitude in regard to truth. Nowhere is this more clearly and yet tragically seen than in modern theology.

In order to see this new attitude to truth in perspective, let us consider two other concepts of truth: first that of the Greeks, and then that of the Jews. Often the Greek concept of truth was a nicely balanced metaphysical system brought into harmony with itself at all points. The Jewish and biblical concept of truth is different. It is not that the rational concept which the Greeks held to was unimportant to the Jews, for both the Old and the New Testaments function on the basis of that which can be reasonably discussed; but to the Jewish mind, something firmer was needed. And the firmer base was an appeal to real history — history in space and in time which could be written down and discussed as history.

The modern view of truth drives a wedge between the Greek and Jewish views, but it does so at the wrong point. Those who hold the modern view would picture the Greeks as holding to rational truth and the Jews as being existentialists. In this way they would seek to claim the Bible for themselves. This is ingenious, but a complete mistake. The Jewish concept is separated from the Greek in that the Jewish was rooted in space-time history and not just a balanced system. But the Jewish and biblical concept of truth is much closer to the Greek than to the modern, in the sense that it does not deny that which is a part of the "mannishness" of man — the longing for rationality, that which can be reasonably thought about and discussed in terms of antithesis.

The Unchanging in a Changing World

There are two things we need to grasp firmly as we seek to communicate the gospel today, whether we are speaking to ourselves, to other Christians, or to those totally outside.

The first is that there are certain unchangeable facts which are true. These have no relationship to the shifting tides. They make the Christian system what it is, and if they are altered, Christianity becomes something else. This must be emphasized because there are evangelical Christians today who, in all sincerity, being concerned with their lack of communication and in order to bridge the gap in communication, are tending to change what must remain unchangeable. If we do this we are no longer communicating Christianity, and what we have left is no different than the surrounding consensus.

But we cannot present a balanced picture if we stop here. We must realize that we are facing a rapidly changing historical situation, and if we are going to talk to people about the gospel we need to know what is the present ebb and flow of thought-forms. Unless we do this, the unchangeable principles of Christianity will fall on deaf ears. And if we are going to reach the intellectuals and the workers, both groups right outside our generally middle-class churches, then we shall need to do a great deal of heart-searching as to how we can speak what is eternal into a changing historical situation.

It is much more comfortable, of course, to go on speaking the gospel only in familiar phrases to the middle classes. But that would be as wrong as, for example, if Hudson Taylor had sent missionaries to China and then told them to learn only one of three separate dialects that the people spoke. In such a case, only one group out of three could hear the gospel. We cannot imagine Hudson Taylor being so hard-hearted. Of course he knew men do not believe without a work of the Holy Spirit, and his life was a life of prayer for this to happen; but he also knew that men cannot believe without hearing the gospel. Each generation of the Church in each setting has the responsibility of communicating the gospel in understandable terms, considering the language and thought-forms of that setting.

In a parallel way we are being as overwhelmingly unfair, even selfish, towards our own generation as if the missionaries had deliberately spoken in only one dialect. The reason often we cannot speak to our children, let alone other people's, is because we have never taken the time to understand how different their thought-forms are from ours. Through reading and education and the whole modern cultural bombardment of the mass media, even today's middle-class children have become thoroughly twentieth-century in outlook. In crucial areas many Christian parents, ministers and teachers are as out of touch with many of the children of the Church, and the majority of those outside, as though they were speaking a foreign language.

So what is said in this book is not merely a matter of intellectual debate. It is not of interest only to academics. It is utterly crucial for those of us who are serious about communicating the Christian gospel in the twentieth century.

BOOK THREE

HE IS THERE AND HE IS NOT SILENT

Introduction

This book (*He Is There and He Is Not Silent*) makes a unified base along with [the other two books in this volume]. Without these three books as the foundation, the various applications in the later books are really a few feet off the ground. This book deals with one of the most fundamental of all questions: how we know, and how we know we know. Unless our epistemology is right, everything is going to be wrong. That is why I say this book goes with *The God Who Is There* — a link emphasized by its title. The infinite-personal God is there, but also He is not silent; that changes the whole world. Wittgenstein, in his *Tractatus*, can find only silence in the area of values and meaning. Bergman made the same point in his film *The Silence*. This book challenges their pessimism. He is there. He is not silent.

These three books constitute a conscious unity — a unity which I believe reflects the unity of Scripture itself.

It will be clear that this book, dealing as it does with a primary area, forms a vital part of our case in speaking historic Christianity into the twentieth century. He is there and is not a silent, nor far-off God.

— Francis A. Schaeffer, 1982
[From the *Introduction* in the Complete Works]

275

CHAPTER ONE

The Metaphysical Necessity

This book deals with the philosophic necessity of God's being there and not being silent — in the areas of metaphysics, morals, and epistemology.

We should understand first of all what the three basic areas of philosophic thought are. The first is in the area of metaphysics, of *Being.* This is the area of what is — the problem of existence. This includes the existence of man, and we must realize that the existence of man is no greater problem as such than is the fact that anything exists at all. No one said it better than Jean-Paul Sartre, who said that the basic philosophic question is that something is there rather than nothing being there. Nothing that is worth calling a philosophy can sidestep the fact that things do exist and that they exist in their present form and complexity. This is what I mean, then, by the problem of metaphysics — the existence of Being.

The second area of philosophical thought is that of man and the dilemma of man. Man is personal, and yet he is finite; so he is not a sufficient integration point for himself. We might remember another profound statement from Sartre: that no finite point has any meaning unless it has an infinite reference point. The Christian would agree that he is right in this statement.

Man is finite; so he is not a sufficient integration point for himself. Yet man is different from non-man. Man is personal in contrast to that which is impersonal; or, to use a phrase which I have used in my books, man has his "mannishness."

Behaviorism, and all forms of determinism, say that man is not personal — that he is not intrinsically different from the impersonal. But the difficulty with this is first that it denies the observation man has made of himself for at least 40,000 years (if we accept the modern dating system); and second, there is no determinist or behaviorist who can really live consistently on the basis of his determinism or his behavioristic psychology — saying, that is, that man is only a machine. This is true of Francis Crick, who reduces man to the mere chemical and physical properties of the DNA template. The interesting thing, however, is that Crick clearly shows that he cannot live with his own determinism. In one of his books, *Of Molecules and Men*, he soon begins to speak of nature as "her," and in a smaller, more profound book, *The Origin of the Genetic Code*, he begins to spell nature with a capital *N*. B. F. Skinner, author of *Beyond Freedom and Dignity*, shows the same tension.

So there are these two difficulties with the acceptance of modern determinism and behaviorism, which say there is no intrinsic difference between man and non-man: first, one has to deny man's own observation of himself through all the years, back to the cave paintings and beyond; and second, no chemical determinist or psychological determinist is ever able to live as though he is the same as non-man.

Another question in the dilemma of man is man's nobility. Perhaps you do not like the word *nobility*, but whatever word you choose, there is something great about man. I want to add here that evangelicals have often made a serious mistake by equating the fact that man is lost and under God's judgment with the idea that man is nothing — a zero. This is not what the Bible says. There is something great about man, and we have lost perhaps our greatest opportunity of evangelism in our generation by not insisting that it is the Bible which explains *why* man is great.

However, man is not only noble (or whatever word you want to substitute), but man is also cruel. So we have a dilemma. The first dilemma is that man is finite and yet he is personal; the second dilemma is the contrast between man's nobility and man's cruelty.

Or one can express it in a modern way: the alienation of man from himself and from all other men in the area of morals.

So now we have two areas of philosophic thought: first, metaphysics, dealing with Being, with existence; second, the area of morals. The third area of this study is that of epistemology — the problem of knowing.

Now let me make two general observations. First, philosophy and religion deal with the same basic questions. Christians, and especially evangelical Christians, have tended to forget this. Philosophy and religion do not deal with different questions, though they give different answers and use different terms. The basic questions of both philosophy and religion (and I mean religion here in the wide sense, including Christianity) are the questions of Being (that is, what exists), of man and his dilemma (that is, morals), and of epistemology (that is, how man knows). Philosophy deals with these points, but so does religion, including evangelical, orthodox Christianity.

The second general observation concerns the two meanings of the word *philosophy*, which must be kept completely separate if we are to avoid confusion. The first meaning is a discipline, an academic subject. That is what we usually think of as philosophy: a highly technical study which few people pursue. In this sense, few people are philosophers. But there is a second meaning that we must not miss if we are going to understand the problem of preaching the gospel in the twentieth-century world. For philosophy also means a person's *worldview*. In this sense, all people are philosophers, for all people have a worldview. This is as true of the man digging a ditch as it is of the philosopher in the university.

Christians have tended to despise the concept of philosophy. This has been one of the weaknesses of evangelical, orthodox Christianity — we have been proud in despising philosophy, and we have been exceedingly proud in despising the intellect. Our theological seminaries hardly ever relate their theology to philosophy, and specifically to the current philosophy. Thus, students go out from the theological seminaries not knowing how to relate Christianity to the surrounding worldview. It is not that they do not know the answers. My observation is that most students graduating from our theological seminaries do not know the questions.

In fact, philosophy is universal in scope. No man can live without a worldview; therefore, there is no man who is not a philosopher.

There are not many possible answers to the three basic areas of philosophic thought, even though there is a great deal of possible detail surrounding the basic answers. It will help us tremendously — whether we are studying philosophy at university and feel buffeted to death, or whether we are trying to be ministers of the gospel, speaking to ordinary people — if we realize that although there are many details which can be discussed, the possible answers — in their basic concepts — are exceedingly few.

There are two classes of answers given to these questions.

1. The first class of answer is that there is no logical rational answer. This is rather a phenomenon of our own generation — under "the line of despair." I am not saying that nobody in the past had these views, but they were not the dominant view. Today it is much more dominant than it has ever been previously. This is true not only of philosophers in their discussions, but it is equally true of discussion on the street corner, at the cafe, at the university dining room, or at the filling station. The solution commonly proposed is that there is no logical, rational answer — all is finally chaotic, irrational, and absurd. This view is expressed with great finesse in the existential world of thinking, and in the Theatre of the Absurd. This is the philosophy, or worldview, of many people today. It is part of the warp and woof of the thinking of our day: that there are no answers, that everything is irrational and absurd.

If a man held that everything is meaningless, nothing has answers and there is no cause-and-effect relationship, and if he really held this position with any consistency, it would be very hard to refute. But in fact, no one can hold consistently that everything is chaotic and irrational and that there are no basic answers. It can be held theoretically, but it cannot be held in practice that everything is absolute chaos.

The first reason the irrational position cannot be held consistently in practice is the fact that the external world is there and it has form and order. It is not a chaotic world. If it were true that all is chaotic, unrelated, and absurd, science as well as general life would come to an end. To live at all is not possible except in the understanding that the universe that is there — the external universe — has a certain form, a certain order, and that man conforms to that order and so can live within it.

Perhaps you remember one of Godard's movies, *Pierrot le Fou*, in which he has people going out through the windows, instead of through the doors. But the interesting thing is that they do not go out through the solid wall. Godard is really saying that although he has no answer, yet at the same time he cannot go out through that solid wall. This is merely his expression of the difficulty of holding that there is a totally chaotic universe while the external world has form and order.

Sometimes people try to bring in a little bit of order; but as soon as you bring in a little bit of order, the first class of answer—that everything is meaningless, everything is irrational—is no longer self-consistent and falls to the ground.

The view that everything is chaotic and there are no ultimate answers is held by many thinking people today, but in my experience they always hold it very selectively. Almost without exception (actually, I have never found an exception), they discuss rationally until they are losing the discussion, and then they try to slip over into the answer of irrationality. But as soon as the one we are discussing with does that, we must point out to him that as soon as he becomes selective in his argument of irrationality, he makes his whole argument suspect. Theoretically the position of irrationalism can be held, but no one lives with it in regard either to the external world or the categories of his own thought-world and discussion. As a matter of fact, if this position were argued properly, all discussion would come to an end. Communication would end. We would have only a series of meaningless sounds—blah, blah, blah. The Theatre of the Absurd has said this, but it fails, because if you read and listen carefully to the Theatre of the Absurd, it is always trying to communicate its view that one cannot communicate. There is always a communication about the statement that there is no communication. It is always selective, with pockets of order brought in somewhere along the line. Thus we see that this class of answer—that all things are irrational—is not an answer.

2. The second class of answer is that there is an answer which can be rationally and logically considered, and communicated with others externally. In this chapter we will deal with metaphysics in the area of answers that can be discussed; later we will deal with man in his dilemma, the area of morals, in relation to answers that can be discussed. So now we are to consider such answers in the area of Being, of existence.

I have already said that there are not many basic answers, although there are varieties of details within the answers. Now curiously enough, there are only three possible basic answers to this question which would be open to rational consideration. The basic answers are very, very few indeed.

We are considering existence, the fact that something is there. Remember Jean-Paul Sartre's statement that the basic philosophic question is that something is there rather than nothing being there. The first basic answer is that everything that exists has come out of absolutely nothing. In other words, you begin with nothing. Now, to hold this view, it must be *absolutely* nothing. It must be what I call *nothing* nothing. It cannot be nothing something or something nothing. If one is to accept this answer, it must be nothing nothing, which means there must be no energy, no mass, no motion, and no personality.

My description of nothing nothing runs like this. Suppose we had a very black blackboard which had never been used. On this blackboard we drew a circle, and inside that circle there was everything that was — and there was nothing within the circle. Then we erase the circle. This is nothing nothing. You must not let anybody say he is giving an answer beginning with nothing and then really begin with something: energy, mass, motion, or personality. That would be something, and something is not nothing.

The truth is, I have never heard this argument sustained, for it is unthinkable that all that now is has come out of utter nothing. But theoretically, that is the first possible answer.

The second possible answer in the area of existence is that all that now is had an impersonal beginning. This impersonality may be mass, energy, or motion, but they are all impersonal, and all equally impersonal. So it makes no basic philosophic difference which of them you begin with. Many modern men have implied that because they are beginning with energy particles rather than old-fashioned mass, they have a better answer. Salvador Dali did this as he moved from his surrealistic period into his new mysticism. But such men do not have a better answer. It is still impersonal. Energy is just as impersonal as mass or motion. As soon as you accept the impersonal beginning of all things, you are faced with some form of reductionism. Reductionism argues that everything which exists, from the stars to man himself, is finally to be understood by reducing it to the original, impersonal factor or factors.

The great problem with beginning with the impersonal is to find any meaning for the particulars. A particular is any individual factor, any individual thing — the separate parts of the whole. A drop of water is a particular, and so is a man. If we begin with the impersonal, then how do any of the particulars that now exist — including man — have any meaning, any significance? Nobody has given us an answer to that. In all the history of philosophical thought, whether from the East or the West, no one has given us an adequate answer.

Beginning with the impersonal, everything, including man, must be explained in terms of the impersonal plus time plus chance. Do not let anyone divert your mind at this point. There are no other factors in the formula, because there are no other factors that exist. If we begin with an impersonal, we cannot then have some form of teleological concept. No one has ever demonstrated how time plus chance, beginning with an impersonal, can produce the needed complexity of the universe, let alone the personality of man. No one has given us a clue to this.

Often this answer — of beginning with the impersonal — is called pantheism. The new mystical thought is almost always some form of pantheism — and almost all the modern liberal theology is pantheistic as well. Often this beginning with the impersonal is *called* pantheism, but really this is a semantic trick, because by using the root *theism* a connotation of the personal is brought in, when by definition the impersonal is meant. In my discussions I never let anybody talk unthinkingly about pantheism. Somewhere along the way I try to make the point that it is not really pan*theism*, with its semantic illusion of personality, but pan-*everythingism*. The ancient religions of Hinduism and Buddhism, as well as the modern mysticism, the new "pantheistic" theology, are not truly pan*theism*. A semantic solution is being offered. Theism is being used as a connotation word. In *The God Who Is There* I have emphasized the fact that the modern solutions are usually semantic mysticisms, and this is one of them.

But whatever form pan-everythingism takes, including the modern scientific form which reduces everything to energy particles, it always has the same problem: in all of them the end is the impersonal.

There are two problems which always exist — the need for unity and the need for diversity. Pan-everythingism gives an answer for the need of unity, but none for the needed diversity. Beginning with the impersonal, there is no meaning or significance to diversity. We can think of the old Hindu pantheism, which begins everything with *om*. In reality, everything ought to have ended with *om* on a single note, with no variance, because there is no reason for significance or variance. And even if pan-every-thingism gave an answer for form, it gives no meaning for freedom. Cycles are usually introduced as though waves were being tossed up out of the sea, but this gives no final solution to any of these problems. Morals, under every form of pantheism, have no meaning as morals, for everything in pan-everythingism is finally equal. Modern theology must move towards situational ethics because there is no such thing as morals in this setting. The word *morals* is used, but it is really only a word.

This is the dilemma of the second answer, which is the one that most people hold today. Naturalistic science holds it, beginning everything with energy particles. Many university students hold some form of pan-everythingism. Liberal theological books today are almost uniformly pantheistic. But beginning with an impersonal, as the pantheist must do, there are no true answers in regard to existence with its complexity, or the personality — the "mannishness" of man.[1]

The third possible answer is to begin with a personal beginning. With this we have exhausted the possible basic answers in regard to existence. It may sound simplistic, but it is true. That is not to say there are no details that one can discuss, no variations, subheadings, or subschools — but these are the only basic schools of thought which are possible. Somebody once brilliantly said that when you get done with any basic question there are not many people in the room. By this he meant that the farther you go in depth in any basic question, finally the choices to be made are rather simple and clear. There are not many basic answers to any of the great questions of life.

So now let us think what it means to begin with that which is personal. This is the very opposite of beginning with the impersonal. That which is personal began everything else. In this case man, being personal, does have meaning. This is not abstract. Many of the people who come to L'Abri would not become Christians if we did not discuss in this area. Many would have turned away, saying, "You don't know the questions." These things are not abstract, but have to do with communicating the Christian gospel in the midst of the twentieth century.

At times I get tired of being asked why I don't just preach the "simple gospel." You have to preach the simple gospel so that it is simple to the person to whom you are talking, or it is no longer simple. The dilemma of modern man is simple: he does not know why man has any meaning. He is lost. Man remains a zero. This is the damnation of our generation, the heart of modern man's problem. But if we begin with a personal and this is the origin of all else, then the personal *does* have meaning, and man and his aspirations are not meaningless. Man's aspirations to the reality of personality are in line with what was originally there and what has always intrinsically been.

It is the Christian who has the answer at this point — a titanic answer! So why have we as Christians gone on saying the great truths in ways that nobody understands? Why do we keep talking to ourselves, if men are lost and we say we love them? Man's damnation today is that he can find no meaning for man, but if we begin with the personal beginning we have an absolutely opposite situation. We have the reality of the fact that personality does have meaning because it is not alienated from what has always been, and what is, and what always will be. This is our answer, and with this we have a solution not only to the problem of existence of bare being and its complexity — but also for man's being different, with a personality which distinguishes him from non-man.

We may use an illustration of two valleys. Often in the Swiss Alps there is a valley filled with water and an adjacent valley without water. Surprisingly enough, sometimes the mountains spring leaks, and suddenly the second valley begins to fill up with water. As long as the level of water in the second valley does not rise higher than the level of the water in the first valley, everyone concludes that there is a real possibility that the second lake came from the first. However, if the water in the second valley goes thirty feet higher than the water in the first valley, nobody gives that answer. If we begin with a personal beginning to all things, then we can understand that man's aspiration for personality has a possible answer.

If we begin with less than personality, we must finally reduce personality to the impersonal. The modern scientific world does this in its reductionism, in which the word *personality* is only the impersonal plus complexity. In the naturalistic scientific world, whether in sociology, psychology or in the natural sciences, a man is reduced to the impersonal plus complexity.

But once we consider a personal beginning, we have yet

another choice to make. This is the next step: are we going to choose the answer of God or gods? The difficulty with gods instead of God is that limited gods are not big enough. To have an adequate answer of a personal beginning, we need two things. We need a personal-infinite God (or an infinite-personal God), and we need a personal unity and diversity in God.

Let us consider the first choice — a personal-infinite God. Only a personal-infinite God is big enough. Plato understood that you have to have absolutes, or nothing has meaning. But the difficulty facing Plato was the fact that his gods were not big enough to meet the need. So although he knew the need, the need fell to the ground because his gods were not big enough to be the point of reference or place of residence for his absolutes, for his ideals. In Greek literature the Fates sometimes seem to be behind and controlling the gods, and sometimes the gods seem to be controlling the Fates. Why the confusion? Because everything fails in their thinking at this point — because their limited gods are not big enough. That is why we need a personal-infinite God. That is first.

Second, we need a personal unity and diversity in God — not just an abstract concept of unity and diversity, because we have seen we need a personal God. We need a personal unity and diversity. Without this we have no answer. Christianity has this in the Trinity.

What we are talking about is the philosophic necessity, in the area of Being and existence, of the fact that God is there. That is what it is all about: *He is there.*

There is no other sufficient philosophical answer than the one I have outlined. You can search through university philosophy, underground philosophy, filling-station philosophy — it does not matter — there is no other sufficient philosophical answer to existence, to Being, than the one I have outlined. There is only one philosophy, one religion, that fills this need in all the world's thought, whether the East, the West, the ancient, the modern, the new, the old. Only one fills the philosophical need of existence, of Being, and it is the Judeo-Christian God — not just an abstract concept, but rather that this God is really there. He exists. There is no other answer, and orthodox Christians ought to be ashamed of having been defensive for so long. It is not a time to be defensive. There is no other answer.

Let us notice that no word is as meaningless as is the word *god.*

Of itself it means nothing. Like any other word, it is only a linguistic symbol — g-o-d — until content is put into it. This is especially so for the word *god*, because no other word has been used to convey such absolutely opposite meanings. The mere use of the word *god* proves nothing. You must put content into it. The word *god* as such is no answer to the philosophic problem of existence, but the Judeo-Christian content to the word *God* as given in the Old and New Testaments does meet the need of what exists — the existence of the universe in its complexity and of man as man. And what is that content? It relates to an infinite-personal God, who is personal unity and diversity on the high order of Trinity.

Every once in a while in my discussions someone asks how I can believe in the Trinity. My answer is always the same. I would still be an agnostic if there was no Trinity, because there would be no answers. Without the high order of personal unity and diversity as given in the Trinity, *there are no answers.*

Let us return again to the personal-infinite. On the side of God's infinity, there is a complete chasm between God on one side and man, the animal, the flower, and the machine on the other. On the side of God's infinity, He stands alone. He is the absolute other. He is, in His infinity, contrary to all else. He is differentiated from all else because only He is infinite. He is the Creator; all else was created. He is infinite; all else is finite. All else is brought forth by creation; so all else is dependent and only He is independent. This is absolute on the side of His infinity. Therefore, concerning God's infinity, man is as separated from God as is the atom or any other machine-portion of the universe.

But on the side of God being personal, the chasm is between man and the animal, the plant, and the machine. Why? Because man was made in the image of God. This is not just "doctrine." It is not dogma that needs just to be repeated as a proper doctrinal statement. This is really down in the warp and woof of the whole problem. Man is made in the image of God; therefore, on the side of the fact that God is a personal God the chasm stands not between God and man, but between man and all else. But on the side of God's infinity, man is as separated from God as the atom or any other finite of the universe. So we have the answer to man's being finite and yet personal.

It is not that this is the best answer to existence; it is the only answer. That is why we may hold our Christianity with intellectual integrity. The only answer for what exists is that He, the infinite-personal God, really is there.

Now we must develop the second part a bit farther—personal unity and diversity on the high order of Trinity. Einstein taught that the whole material world may be reduced to electromagnetism and gravity. At the end of his life he was seeking a unity above these two, something that would unite electromagnetism and gravity, but he never found it. But what if he had found it? It would only have been unity in diversity in relationship to the material world, and as such it would only be child's play. Nothing would really have been settled because the needed unity and diversity in regard to personality would not have been touched. If he had been able to bring electromagnetism and gravity together, he would not have explained the need of personal unity and diversity.

In contrast, let us think of the Nicene Creed—three Persons, one God. Rejoice that they chose the word "person." Whether you realize it or not, that catapulted the Nicene Creed right into our century and its discussions: three Persons in existence, loving each other, and in communication with each other, before all else was.

If this were not so, we would have had a God who needed to create in order to love and communicate. In such a case, God would have needed the universe as much as the universe needed God. But God did not need to create; God does not need the universe as the universe needs Him. Why? Because we have a full and true Trinity. The Persons of the Trinity communicated with each other and loved each other before the creation of the world.

This is not only an answer to the acute philosophic need of unity in diversity, but of *personal* unity and diversity. The unity and diversity cannot exist before God or be behind God, because whatever is farthest back *is* God. But with the doctrine of the Trinity, the unity and diversity is God Himself—three Persons, yet one God. That is what the Trinity is, and nothing less than this.

We must appreciate that our Christian forefathers understood this very well in A.D. 325, when they stressed the three Persons in the Trinity, as the Bible had clearly set this forth. Let us notice that it is not that they invented the Trinity in order to give an answer to the philosophical questions which the Greeks of that time understood. It is quite the contrary. The unity and diversity problem was there, and the Christians realized that in the Trinity, as it had been taught in the Bible, they had an answer that no one else had. They did not invent the Trinity to meet the need; the Trinity was already there and it *met* the need. They realized that in the Trinity we have what all these people are arguing about and defining, but for which they have no answer.

Let us notice again that this is not the *best* answer; it is the *only* answer. Nobody else, no philosophy, has ever given us an answer for unity and diversity. So when people ask whether we are embarrassed intellectually by the Trinity, I always switch it over into their own terminology — unity and diversity. Every philosophy has this problem, and no philosophy has an answer. Christianity does have an answer in the existence of the Trinity. The only answer to what exists is that He, the starting-place, is there.

So we have said two things. The only answer to the metaphysical problem of existence is that the infinite-personal God is there; and the only answer to the metaphysical problem of existence is that the Trinity is there.

Now surely by this time we will have become convinced that philosophy and religion are indeed dealing with the same questions. Notice that in the basic concept of existence, of Being, it is the Christian answer or nothing. No matter how evangelical and orthodox you are, it will change your life if you understand this.

Let me add something, in passing. I find that many people who are evangelical and orthodox see truth just as true to the dogmas, or to be true to what the Bible says. Nobody stands more for the full inspiration of Scripture than I, but this is not the end of truth as Christianity is presented, as the Bible presents itself. The truth of Christianity is that it is true to what is there. You can go to the end of the world and you never need be afraid, like the ancients, that you will fall off the end and the dragons will eat you up. You can carry out your intellectual discussion to the end of the discussion because Christianity is not only true to the dogmas, it is not only true to what God has said in the Bible, but it is also true to what is there, and you will never fall off the end of the world! It is not just an approximate model; it is true to what is there. When the evangelical catches that — when evangelicalism catches that — we may have our revolution. We will begin to have something beautiful and alive, something which will have force in our poor, lost world. This is what truth is from the Christian viewpoint and as God sets it forth in the Scripture. But if we are going to have this answer, notice that we must have the *full biblical answer*. Christianity must not be reduced to the pan-every-thingism of the East, or the pan-everythingism of modern, liberal theology (whether Protestant or Roman Catholic), and the Bible must not be weakened. We must not allow a theological pantheism to begin to creep in, and we must not reduce Christianity to the modern existential, upper-story theology. If we are going to have these great, titanic answers, Christianity must be the full biblical answer. We need the full biblical position to have the answer to the basic philosophical problem of the existence of what is. We need the full biblical content concerning God: that He is the infinite-personal God, and the starting-place.

Now let me express this in a couple of other ways. One way to say it is that without the infinite-personal God, the God of personal unity and diversity, there is no answer to the existence of what exists. We can say it in another way, however, and that is that the infinite-personal God, the God who is Trinity, has spoken. He is there, and He is not silent. There is no use having a silent God. We would not know anything about Him. He has spoken and told us what He is and that He existed before all else, and so we have the answer to the existence of what is.

He is not silent. The reason we have the answer is because the infinite-personal God, the full Trinitarian God, has not been silent. He has told us who He is. Couch your concept of inspiration and revelation in these terms, and you will see how it cuts down into the warp and woof of modern thinking. He is not silent. That is the reason we know. It is because He has spoken. What has He told us? Has He told us only about other things? No, He has told us truth about Himself — and because He has told us truth about Himself — that He is the infinite-personal, triune God — we have the answer to existence. Or we may put it this way: at the point of metaphysics — of Being, of existence — general and special revelation speak with one voice. All these ways of saying it are really expressing the same thing from slightly different viewpoints.

In conclusion, man, beginning with himself, can define the philosophical problem of existence, but he cannot generate from himself the answer to the problem. The answer to the problem of existence is that the infinite-personal, triune God is there, and that the infinite-personal, triune God is not silent.

CHAPTER TWO

The Moral Necessity

We now turn to the second area of philosophic thought, which is man and the dilemma of man. There are, as we have seen, two problems concerning man and his dilemma. The first of them is the fact that man is personal, different from non-man, and yet finite. Because he is finite, he has no sufficient integration point in himself. Again, as Jean-Paul Sartre put it, if a finite point does not have an infinite reference point, it is meaningless and absurd.

Yet despite this, man is different from non-man; he is personal; he has the "mannishness" of man which distinguishes him from non-man. This is the first problem: he is different because of his "mannishness" and yet he is finite. He does not have a sufficient integration point within himself.

The second point concerning man and the dilemma of man is what I call the nobility of man. We might not like this term, because of its romantic ties with the past, but still there is the wonder of man; but contrasted with this there is his cruelty. So man stands with all his wonder and nobility, and yet also with his horrible cruelty that runs throughout the warp and woof of man's history.

Or we could express it in yet another way — man's estrangement from himself and other men in the area of morals. And this brings us to the word *morals*. Up to this point we have concerned ourselves with the problem of metaphysics, but now we enter the area of morals.

Leaving aside the "answer" that says there are no answers in the area of reason, the first answer given to this dilemma of morals is (as in the area of metaphysics) the impersonal beginning. As we consider man's finiteness and his cruelty, it would certainly seem that these things are not one, but two. Mankind has always thought of these things as being different. Man's finiteness is his smallness; he is not a sufficient reference point to himself. But his cruelty has always been considered as distinct from his finiteness. Yet we must notice something. If we accept the impersonal beginning, finally we will come to the place where man's finiteness and his cruelty become the same thing. This is an absolute rule. No matter what kind of impersonality we begin with, whether it is the modern scientist with his energy particles, or the pan-everythingism of the East, or neo-orthodox theology, eventually these two things merge into one problem rather than two. With an impersonal beginning, morals really do not exist as morals. If one starts with an impersonal beginning, the answer to morals eventually turns out to be the assertion that there are no morals (in however sophisticated a way this may be expressed). This is true whether one begins with the Eastern pantheism or the new theology's pantheism, or with the energy particle. With an impersonal beginning, everything is finally equal in the area of morals. With an impersonal beginning, eventually morals is just another form of metaphysics, of Being. Morals disappear, and there is only one philosophic area rather than two.

Left in this position, we can talk about what is antisocial, or what society does not like, or even what I do not like, but we cannot talk about what is really right and what is really wrong. If we begin with the impersonal, man's alienation as he is now is only because of chance; he has become that which is out of line with what the universe has always been — that is, the impersonal. So man's dilemma, man's tension, if you begin with the impersonal is never in the area of morals. Rather, man has been kicked out of line with the universe as it always has been and is intrinsically.

Assuming the beginning was impersonal, man has, by chance, become a being with aspirations, including moral motions for which there is no ultimate fulfillment in the universe as it is. Man has been "kicked up" in that he has developed a feeling of moral motions, when in reality these have no meaning in the universe as it is. Here is the ultimate cosmic alienation, the dilemma of our generation — Giacometti, with his figures standing there always alienated from everybody else and from the spectator as he observes them in the museum. The problem of our generation is a feeling of cosmic alienation, including the area of morals. Man has a feeling of moral motions; yet in the universe as it is, his feeling is completely out of line with what is there.

You may ask why I use the term "moral motions." I choose the term simply because I am not talking about specific norms. I am talking about the fact that men have always felt that there is a difference between right and wrong. All men have this sense of moral motions. You do not find man without this anywhere back in antiquity. You do not find the little girl prostitute upon the street without some feeling of moral motions. You do not find the determinist, the behaviorist in psychology, without the feeling of moral motions, even if he says morals as morals do not exist. So we find man cast up with a feeling of moral motions which in reality leads only to a complete cosmic alienation, because if you begin with the impersonal, in the universe as it is, there is no place for morals as morals. There is no standard in the universe which gives final meaning to such words as *right* and *wrong*. If you begin with the impersonal, the universe is totally silent concerning any such words.

Thus, to the pantheist, the final wrong or tension is the failure to accept your impersonality. If you look at those places in the East where pantheism has worked itself out consistently you will find that the final wrong in man, the final Karma, if you will, is the fact that he will not accept his impersonality. In other words, he will not accept who he is.

In the Hindu pan-everythingism there is a high development of the concept that there is no ultimate difference between cruelty and noncruelty. This can be seen clearly in the person of Kali. In the Hindu representations of God, there is always a feminine figure. Sometimes people say there is a trinity in Hinduism because there are three different faces shown in a bas-relief. But this is only because they do not understand that it is only a bas-relief. There are really five faces in a Hindu presentation — four around, if you have a free-standing figure, and one on top, looking upward, even if you cannot see it or even if it is not actually carved. There is no trinity in Hinduism. Not only is it not three but five, but even more important, these are not persons, they are only manifestations of the final, impersonal god. But one of the manifestations is always feminine, because the feminine must be there as well as the masculine. But interestingly enough, the feminine Kali is also always the destroyer. She is often pictured as having great fangs, with skulls hanging around her neck. Why? Because finally, cruelty is just as much a part of what is as noncruelty. So you have Vishnu taking his three constructive steps, but on the other hand you must always see Kali, the one who tears down, the one who destroys, the one who is ready to devour your flesh and tear to pieces. Cruelty is as much a part of all that is as noncruelty.

Why is the cruel part always feminine? Nobody knows, but I would hazard a guess that it is a perverted memory concerning Eve. Myth usually goes back to something — but it has also usually become perverted.

But eventually, as you examine the new theology as well as the pantheism of the East, you come to the place where you cannot rightly speak of right or wrong. In Western religious pan-every-thingism, we find men trying to avoid this conclusion, and to retain a distinction between cruelty and noncruelty. They try to hold off the acknowledgment that there is no basic meaning to the words *right* and *wrong*. But it cannot be done. It is like starting a stone downhill. Beginning with the impersonal, though one may use religious terms and even Christian terms, there is no final absolute and there are no final categories concerning right and wrong. Hence, what is left may be worded in many different ways in different cultures, but it is only the relative — that which is sociological, statistical, situational — nothing else. You have situational, statistical ethics — the standard of averages — but you cannot have morality.

Finally, we must understand that in this setting, to be right is just as meaningless as to be wrong. Morals as morals disappear, and what we are left with is just metaphysics. We are just the little against the big; nothing has meaning in terms of right and wrong.

We are rapidly coming to this in our modern culture. Consider Marshall McLuhan's concept that democracy is finished. What will we have in place of democracy or morals? He says there is coming a time in the global village (not far ahead, in the area of electronics) when we will be able to wire everybody up to a giant computer, and what the computer strikes as the average at a given moment will be what is right and wrong. You may say that is far-fetched and there may never be such a worldwide computer system. But the concept of morals only being the average of what people are thinking and doing at a given time is a present reality. You must understand that that is exactly what Kinsey set forth in *Sexual Behavior of the Human Male* (1948) as statistical sexual ethics. This is not theoretical. We have come to this place in our Western culture because man sees himself as beginning from the impersonal, the energy particle and nothing else. We are left with only statistical ethics, and in that setting there is simply no such thing as morals as morals.

If we use religious language instead of secular language, it may seem to remove the strain somewhat. But when we get behind the religious words, they have no more real meaning than the natural-istic, psychological reduction of morals to conditioning and reflexes. Behind the religious connotation words, we find only the same problem as we find in the secular world. The concept of morals as morals eventually disappears. The man who has expressed this better than anyone else is the Marquis de Sade, with his chemical determinism, who simply made this statement: "What is, is right." No one can argue against this if we begin with an impersonal beginning.

Let us summarize: Beginning with the impersonal, there is no explanation for the complexity of the universe or the personality of man. As I said in the previous chapter, it is not that Christianity is a better answer, but that if you begin with the impersonal, in reality you do not have any answer at all to the metaphysical questions. And the same thing is true in the area of morals. If you begin with the impersonal, no matter how you phrase that imper-sonal, there is no final meaning for morals.

Look now at the opposite answer—the personal beginning. With this answer, there is a possibility of keeping morals and metaphysics separate. This is a profound thing, though it may sound simple. Whereas the impersonal beginning leads us to a merging of morals and metaphysics, the personal beginning pro-vides the possibility of keeping them separate. In other words, man's finiteness may be separated from his cruelty.

However, as soon as we say this we are faced with a serious question. If we begin with a personal beginning and look at man as he now is, how do we explain the dilemma of man's cruelty? In what perspective do we regard this?

There are two possibilities. The first is that man as he is now in his cruelty is what he has always *intrinsically* been: that is what man is. The symbol m-a-n equals that which is cruel, and the two cannot be separated. But if it is true that man has always been cruel, we are faced with two problems.

I want to deal with the first of these at length. If man was created by a personal-infinite God, how can we escape the conclusion that the personal God who made man cruel is himself also bad and cruel? This is where the French thinkers Charles Baudelaire and Albert Camus come on the scene. Baudelaire, who was a famous art historian, poet, and great thinker, had a famous sentence: "If there is a God, He is the Devil." At first, Bible-believing Christians may react negatively to this sentence. But after thought, a real Christian would agree with Baudelaire that if there is an unbroken line between what man is now and what he has always intrinsically been, then if there is a God, He must be the Devil. Although as Christians, we would definitely differ from Baudelaire, we would agree with this conclusion *if* we begin with his premise.

Now Camus dealt with the same problem from a slightly different viewpoint. He argued that if there is a God, then we cannot fight social evil, for if we do, we are fighting God who made the world as it is. What these two men say is irrefutable if we accept the basic premise that man stands where he has always stood—that there has been a continuity of intrinsic cruelty.

At this point, there are those who offer a selective answer in the area of irrationality. The first class of answer we dealt with in Chapter One was the one which says there are no answers—everything is finally chaotic and irrational. Much that is religious, and specifically Western liberal theology, moves over into the field of irrationality and says, "We have no answer for this, but let us take a step of faith against all reason and all reasonableness and say that God is good." That is the position of modern liberal theology, whether it is the old-line rational liberalism or whether it is the Barthian thinking. But this should be seen for what it is: a part of the answer of chaos and irrationality.

I have said that people who argue irrationality to be the answer are always selective about where they will become irrational. That is certainly true of this area. Suddenly men who have been saying that they are arguing with great emphasis on reason become irrationalists at this point, and say that there is only an irrational answer for the question of how God is good. Liberal modern theology is firmly fixed in this point of view.

Let us look at this more carefully. As soon as irrationality is brought in at this point, it will lead to tension in two directions simultaneously. First, there will be a motion back toward reason. As people argue that God is a good God against all reason and rationality, there is something in them that is in tension. Consequently, liberals who offer this answer frequently split off back into reason; and every time they do, they lose this blindly optimistic answer. As soon as they reintroduce reason, the optimistic answer is gone, because all the optimism concerning God's goodness rests upon irrationality. If they step back into the area of reason, they are back into pessimism — if there is a God, He is a bad God. In Baudelaire's words, He is the Devil. As one flees into irrationality at this point, there is the tendency to spin off back into pessimism.

The other tension that is immediately set up when people give this answer is to spin off in the opposite direction — towards making everything irrational. As they do so, they ask, where do we stop? They tend to say that perhaps one should just accept the whole irrational chaotic situation, and decide there is no meaning in the use of religious "god words" at all. Irrationalism cannot be shut up to the single area of saying God is good against all reason. These are the two tensions that are set up as soon as one tries to bring in the answer of irrationality at this crucial point.

The second problem inherent in this situation is this: if we say that man in his present cruelty is what man has always been, and what man intrinsically is, how can there be any hope of a qualitative change in man? There may be a quantitative change — that is, he may become just a little less cruel — but there can never be a qualitative change. If God has made man as man now is, then this is what man, as man, is. So we are left with pessimism concerning man and his actions. These are the two problems that arise if one takes the position that man is made by a personal God (has a personal beginning rather than an impersonal beginning) and that man has always been what he now is.

However, if there was a personal beginning for man, man created by a personal God, there is a second possibility. That is, that man as he is now is not what he was; that man is discontinuous with what he has been, rather than continuous with what he has always been. Or, to put it another way, man is now abnormal — he has changed.

This involves yet another question and choice: If God changed him, or made him abnormal, then He is still a bad God, and we have solved nothing. But there is another possibility at this point: that man created by God as personal has changed himself — that he stands at the point of discontinuity rather than continuity not because God changed him, but because he changed himself. Man, by his own choice, is not what he intrinsically was. In this case we can understand that man is now cruel, but that God is not a bad God. This is precisely the Judeo-Christian position.

We have taken the other philosophical possibilities, and we have seen where they lead in each case. Now we have come to the other possibility, the Judeo-Christian position. There was a space-time, historic change in man. There is a discontinuity and not a continuity in man. Man, made in the image of God and not programmed, turned by choice from his proper integration point at a certain time in history. When he did this, he became something that he previously was not, and the dilemma of man becomes a true moral problem rather than merely a metaphysical one. Man, at a certain point of history, changed himself, and hence stands, in his cruelty, in discontinuity with what he was, and we have a true moral situation: morals do exist. Everything hangs upon the fact that man is abnormal now, in contrast to what he originally was.

The difference between Christian thinking and the non-Christian philosopher has been sharp at this point. The non-Christian philosopher has said that man is normal now, but biblical Christianity says he is abnormal now. It is interesting in this regard that the "later Heidegger" saw that you could not come up with final answers if you say that man has always been as he is now; he in his own way says man is abnormal. But he proposed a very different kind of abnormality, an epistemological one, at the point of Aristotle. This did not give any real answer to the problem, but it is intriguing that Heidegger, perhaps the greatest of the modern non-Christian philosophers, did see that the position that man is normal leads to a dead-end.

When you come to the Christian answer, however — that is, that man is abnormal now because at a point of space-time history he changed himself (not epistemologically but morally) — four things immediately emerge.

1. We can explain that man is now cruel, without God being a bad God.

2. There is a hope of a solution for this moral problem which is not intrinsic to the "mannishness" of man. If this cruelty is intrinsic to the "mannishness" of man — if that is what man always has been — then there is no hope of a solution. But if it is an abnormality, there is a hope of a solution. It is in this setting that the substitutionary, propitiatory death of Christ ceases to be an incomprehensible concept. In liberal theology, the death of Christ is always an incomprehensible god word. But in this setting to which we have come, the substitutionary death of Christ now has meaning. It is not merely god words or an upper-story, existential thing. It has solid meaning. We can have the hope of a solution concerning man if man is abnormal now.

3. On this basis we can have an adequate ground for fighting evil, including social evil and social injustice. Modern man has no real basis for fighting evil, because he sees man as normal — whether he comes out of the pan-everythingism of the East or modern liberal theology, or out of the pan-everythingism of everything's being reduced (including man) to only the energy particle. But the Christian has — he can fight evil without fighting God. He has the solution for Camus' problem: we can fight evil without fighting God, because God did not make things as they are now — as man in his cruelty has made them. God did not make man cruel, and He did not make the results of man's cruelty. These are abnormal, contrary to what God made, and so we can fight the evil *without fighting God.*

In another of my books, I have used the account of Jesus before the tomb of Lazarus. To me, what Jesus did at the tomb of Lazarus sets the world on fire — it becomes a great shout into the morass of the twentieth century. Jesus came to the tomb of Lazarus. The One who claims to be God stood before the tomb, and the Greek language makes it very plain that he had two emotions. The first was tears for Lazarus, but the second emotion was anger. He was furious; and he could be furious at the abnormality of death without being furious with Himself as God. This is tremendous in the context of the twentieth century. When I look at evil — the cruelty which is abnormal to that which God made — my reaction should be the same. I am able not only to cry over the evil, but I can be angry at the evil — as long as I am careful that egoism does not enter into my reaction. I have a basis to fight the thing which is abnormal to what God originally made.

The Christian should be in the front line, fighting the results of man's cruelty, for we know that it is not what God has made. We are able to be angry at the results of man's cruelty without being angry at God or being angry at what is normal.

4. We can have real morals and moral absolutes, for now God is absolutely good. There is the total exclusion of evil from God. God's character is the moral absolute of the universe. Plato was entirely right when he held that unless you have absolutes, morals do not exist. Here is the complete answer to Plato's dilemma; he spent his time trying to find a place to root his absolutes, but he was never able to do so because his gods were not enough. But here is the infinite-personal God who has a character from which all evil is excluded, and His character is the moral absolute of the universe.

It is not that there is a moral absolute *behind* God that binds man and God, because that which is farthest back is always finally God. Rather, it is God Himself and His character who is the moral absolute of the universe.

Again, as in the area of metaphysics, we must understand that this is not simply the best answer—it is the only answer in morals. The only answer in the area of morals, as true morals (including the problem of social evil), turns upon the fact of God's being there. If God is not there (not just the word *God*, but God Himself being there objectively—the God of the Judeo-Christian Scriptures), there is no answer at all to the problem of evil and morals. Again, it is not only necessary that He be there, but that He is not silent. There is a philosophic necessity in both metaphysics and morals that He is there and that He is not silent. He has spoken, in verbalized, propositional form, and He has told us what His character is.

Evangelicals often make a mistake today. Without knowing it, they slip over into a weak position. They often thank God in their prayers for the revelation we have of God in Christ. This is good as far as it goes, and it is wonderful that we do have a factual revelation of God in Christ. But I hear very little thanks from the lips of evangelicals today for the propositional revelation in verbalized form which we have in the Scriptures. He must indeed not only be there, but He must have spoken. And He must have spoken in a way which is more than simply a quarry for emotional, upper-story experiences. We need propositional facts. We need to know who He is, and what His character is, because His character is the law of the universe. He has told us what His character is, and this becomes our moral law, our moral standard. It is not arbitrary, for it is fixed in God Himself, in what has always been. It is the very opposite of what is relativistic. It is either this, or morals are not morals. They become simply sociological averages or arbitrary standards imposed by society, the state or an elite. It is one or the other.

It is important to remember that it is not improper for men to ask these questions concerning metaphysics and morals. And Christians should point out that there is no answer to these questions except that God is there and He is not silent. Students and other young people should not be told to keep quiet when they ask these questions. They are right to ask them, but we should make it plain to them that these are not probability answers; the Christian answers are the only answers. It is this or nothing.

But if this is true, then man is not just metaphysically small, but really morally guilty. He has true moral guilt, and he needs a solution for it. As I have said, it is here that the substitutionary, propitiatory death of Christ is needed and fits in. And His death must be substitutionary and propitiatory, or the whole thing has no meaning. There is nothing wrong with man's being metaphysically small, in being finite. This is the way God made him in the first place. But we need a solution for our true moral guilt before the absolutely good God who is there. That is our need.[1]

Finally, as in the area of metaphysics, we must stress that the answer can never lie in the *word* God; that will never do. Modern men are trying to find answers just in the word *God*, in god words. This is true of the new theology, the hippie cult, and some of the "Jesus people" of a few years ago. But the answer is not in the use of the word, but in its *content*: what God has told us concerning Himself as being the infinite-personal God and the true Trinity.

In the area of morals, we have none of these answers except on the basis of a true, space-time, historic Fall. There was a time before the Fall, and then man turned from his proper integration point by choice; and in so doing, there was a moral discontinuity — man became abnormal. Remove that and the Christian answer in the area of morals is gone. Often I find evangelicals playing games with the first half of Genesis. But if you remove a true, historic, space-time Fall, the answers do not exist. It is not only that historic, biblical Christianity as it stands in the stream of history is gone, but every answer we possess in the area of man and his moral dilemma is also gone.

CHAPTER THREE

The Epistemological Necessity:
The Problem

Epistemology is the theory of the method or grounds of knowledge — the theory of knowledge, or how we know, or how we can be certain that we know. Epistemology is the central problem of our generation; indeed, the so-called "generation gap" is really an epistemological gap, simply because the modern generation looks at knowledge in a way radically different from previous ones. I have dealt with the reasons for this at some length in two earlier books,[1] so will now only touch upon what I covered in those books concerning Thomas Aquinas and the dilemma brought about by the gradual development and extension of his assumptions. Here I want to start farther back in the time of the great Greek philosophers.

The Greek philosophers spent much time grappling with this problem of knowledge, and the one who wrestled with it most, and with the greatest sensitivity, was Plato. He understood the basic problem, and that is that in the area of knowledge, as in the area of morals, there must be more than particulars if there is to be meaning. In the area of knowledge we have *particulars*, by which we mean the individual "things" which we see in the world. At any given moment, I am faced with thousands, indeed

303

literally millions of particulars, just in what I see with a glance of my eyes. What are the universals which give these particulars meaning, and bind them into a unity? This is the heart of the problem of epistemology and the problem of knowing.

A related problem arises in our learning. For example, in considering apples, we could list the different varieties every time we spoke of apples, and name two or three hundred kinds. But in practice we draw these all together under the word *apple* and so have a greater comprehension of what we are looking at and what we are talking about. So we are all involved in the progression from particulars to universals.

It is much the same with science. Science is looking at particulars and trying to make laws which cover sufficient numbers of them for us to see the associations and understand them properly. "Super" laws (for example, electromagnetism and gravity) are laws which go further than that, and reduce all the particulars in the material universe to as few universals as possible. So whether we are talking about apples or about science, in learning we are constantly moving from particulars to universals.

This is not only a linguistic thing; it is the *way we know*. It is not just an abstract theory, or some kind of scholasticism, but the very substance of how we actually know, and how we know that we know. The Greek philosophers, and especially Plato, were seeking for universals which would make the particulars meaningful.

We can understand this very easily in the area of morals. In the previous chapter, I dealt with the fact that in the area of morals we need universals (absolutes) if we are to determine what is right and what is wrong. Not having universals, the modern concept is finally sociological: one assesses the statistics of public opinion of right and wrong, and a majority determines moral questions. Or we can think of an elite emerging to tell us what is right and what is wrong. But both these approaches are merely matters of *averages*. The Greeks understood that if we were really to know what was right and what was wrong, we must have a universal to cover all the particulars.

Now while we can see this more easily in the area of morals, in reality it is even more important in the area of knowledge. How can we find universals which are large enough to cover the particulars so that we can know we know? Plato, for example, put forward the concept of ideals which would provide the needed universal. For example, let us think of chairs: let us say that there is somewhere an ideal chair, and that this ideal chair has meaning in reference to the ideal chair and not to the particular one. So when we use the word *chair* there is a meaning that is beyond our mere gathering up of the particulars about chairs. This is Plato's solution: an "ideal" somewhere that covers all the possible particulars that anybody could ever possibly find about chairs. There would be no chairs outside this universal or beyond the concept which was covered by the "ideal" chair. Anything outside of it is not a chair.

From the parallel in the area of morals, we can comprehend the problem of knowledge, of knowing, of being sure. The Greeks thought of two ways to try to come to this. One was the sense of the *polis*. The word *polis* simply means "city," but in Greek thinking the *polis* had meaning beyond merely the geographic city. It had to do with the structure of society. Some Greeks had an idea that the *polis*, the society, could supply the universal. But the Greeks were wise enough to see that this was unsatisfactory, because then one is right back to the 51 percent vote or the concept of a small elite. So one would end with Plato's philosopher kings, for example. But this, too, was limited. Even if one only chose the philosopher kings in the *polis*, eventually they would not be able to give a universal which would cover all the particulars.

So the next step was to move back to the gods, on the grounds that the gods can give something more than the *polis* can give. But the difficulty is that the Greek gods (and this includes Plato's gods) simply were inadequate. They were personal gods — in contrast to the Eastern gods, who include everything and are impersonal — but they were not big enough. Consequently, because their gods were not big enough, the problem remained unsolved for the Greeks.

Just as society did not solve the problem because it was not big enough, so also the gods did not settle it because they were not big enough. The gods fought among themselves and had differences over all kinds of petty things. All the classical gods put together were not really enough, which is why, as we saw in a previous chapter, in the concept of fate in Greek literature, one never knows for sure whether the Fates are controlled by the gods, or whether the Fates control the gods. Are the Fates simply the vehicle of the action of the gods, or are the Fates the universal behind the gods and do they manipulate the gods? There is a constant confusion between the Fates and the gods as the final control. This expresses the Greeks' deep comprehension that their gods simply were not adequate: they were not big enough with regard to the Fates, and they were not big enough with regard to *knowledge.* So though Plato and the Greeks understood the necessity of finding a universal, and saw that unless there was a universal nothing was going to turn out satisfactorily, they never found a place from which the universal could come either for the *polis* or for the gods.

Thomas Aquinas picked up the dilemma of the Greek philosophers. Before his time, the Byzantine world had no real interest in particulars. They lived in the midst of them, but they had an entirely different thought-form. They were not interested in nature, or in the particulars. We can thank Thomas Aquinas for the fact that because of his view, nature was again brought into importance in man's thinking.

Gradually, as Thomas Aquinas's emphasis spread (as I pointed out in *Escape from Reason*), it began to be understood and disseminated in the area of the arts. Cimabue (1240-1302), for example, began to paint in a different way. Then Dante (1265-1321) began to write in a different way. Nature had its emphasis. But there was also arising growing tension between nature and grace. In nature you have men, and natural cause and effect influencing the world; in grace you have the heavenly forces, and how these unseen forces can effect the world. In nature you have the body; in grace you have the soul. But eventually we always come down to the problem of particulars and universals. In nature you have the particulars; in grace you have the universal. These men, Cimabue and Dante and others, like Giotto (1267-1337), who followed them, began to emphasize nature. This is to the good, as we have said, but there was the problem. There is that which is good, because nature was being reestablished and reemphasized in men's thinking; there is that which was destructive. They were making the particulars autonomous and thus losing the universal that gave the particulars meaning.

As I have emphasized in my previous books, there is a principle here; that is, if nature or the particulars are autonomous from God, then nature begins to eat up grace. Or we could put it in this way: all we are left with are particulars, and universals are lost, not only in the area of morals (which would be bad enough), but in the area of knowing. Here you can see the drift toward modern man and his cynicism. It was born back there. We are left with masses of particulars but no way to get them together. So we find that by this time nature is eating up grace in the area of morals, and even more basically, in the area of epistemology as well.

This is where Leonardo da Vinci is so important. He was the first modern mathematician, and he really understood this dilemma. It is not that I am reading back into him our dilemma of modern cynicism. He really understood it. He understood where rationalistic man would end up in the passage of all these hundreds of years between himself and modern man, if man failed to find a solution. This is what real genius is — understanding before your time; and Leonardo da Vinci did understand. He understood that if you began on the basis of rationalism — that is, man beginning only from himself, and not having any outside knowledge — you would have only mathematics and particulars and would end up with only mechanics. In other words, he was so far ahead of his time that he really understood that everything was going to end up only as a machine, and there were not going to be any universals or meaning at all. The universals were going to be crossed out. So Leonardo really became very much like the modern man. He said we should try to paint the universals. This is really very close to the modern concept of the upper-story experience. So he painted and painted and painted, trying to paint the universals. He tried to paint the universal just as Plato had had the idea that if we were really to have a knowledge of chairs, there would have to be an ideal chair somewhere that would cover all kinds of chairs. Leonardo, who was a Neoplatonist, understood this, and he said, "Let man produce the universals." But what kind of men? The mathematical men? No, not the mathematical men but the painters. The sensitive men. So Leonardo is a very crucial thinker in the area of humanistic epistemology.

At this point in *Escape from Reason* I developed the difference between what I call "modern science" and "modern modern science."

In my earlier books I referred to Whitehead and Oppenheimer, two scientists — neither one a Christian — who insisted that modern science could not have been born except in the Christian milieu. Bear with me as I repeat this, for I want in this book to carry it a step further, into the area of knowing. As Whitehead so beautifully points out, the early scientists all believed that the universe was created by a reasonable God and therefore the universe could be investigated by reason. This was their base. In the birth of modern science, the scientists were men who believed in the uniformity of natural causes in a *limited* or *open* system, a system which could be reordered by God and by man made in the image of God. This is a cause-and-effect system in a limited time span. But from the time of Newton (not with Newton himself, but with the Newtonians who followed him), we have the concept of the "machine" extended until we are left with only the machine. At that point we move into "modern modern science," in which we have the uniformity of natural causes in a *closed* system, including sociology and psychology. Man is included in the machine. This is the world in which we live in the area of science today. No longer believing that they can be sure the universe is reasonable because created by a reasonable God, the question is raised which Leonardo da Vinci already understood and which the Greeks understood before that: "How does the scientist know? On what basis can he know that what he knows he really knows?"

So rationalism put forth at this point the epistemological concept of *positivism*. Positivism is a theory of knowledge which assumes that we know facts and objects with total objectivity. Modern "scientism" is built on it.

It is a truly romantic concept, and while it held sway rationalistic man stood ten feet tall in his pride. It was based on the notion that without any universals to begin with, finite man could reach out and grasp with finite reason sufficient true knowledge to make universals out of the particulars.

Jean-Jacques Rousseau is crucial at this point, because he changed the formulation from "nature and grace" to "nature and freedom," absolute freedom. Rousseau and the men around him saw that in the area of "nature," everything had become the machine. "Upstairs" they added the other thing — that is, absolute freedom. In the sense of absolute freedom upstairs, not only is man not to be bound by revelation, but he is not to be bound by society, the *polis*, either. This concept of autonomous freedom is clearly seen in Gauguin, the painter. He was getting rid of all the restraints — not just the restraint of God, but also the restraint of the *polis*, which for Gauguin was epitomized by the highly-developed culture of France. He left France and went to Tahiti to be rid of the culture. In doing this, he practiced the concept of the noble savage which Jean-Jacques Rousseau had previously set forth. You get rid of the restraints, you get rid of the *polis*, you get rid of God or the gods; and then you are free. Unhappily, though not surprisingly, this did not turn out as he expected.

So what we have is a destructive freedom not only in morals (though it shows itself very quickly in morals, especially quickly perhaps in sexual anarchy), but in the area of knowledge as well. In metaphysics, in the area of Being, as well as morals, we are supposed to have absolute freedom. But then the dilemma comes; how do you know and how do you know you know?

We may imagine the Greeks and Leonardo da Vinci and all the Neoplatonists at the time of the High Renaissance coming in and asking Rousseau and his followers, "Don't you see what you have done? Where are the universals? How are you going to know? How are you going to build enough universals out of particulars even for society to run, let alone build true knowledge, knowledge that you really know, and are sure that you know?"

It is only a step, really, from men like Gauguin to the hippie culture of the 1960s, and as a matter of fact, to the whole modern culture. In a certain sense there is a parenthesis in time from Rousseau until the birth of the hippie culture and the whole modern culture which is founded on the view that there are no universals anywhere — that man is totally, hedonistically free, that the individual is totally, hedonistically free, not only morally but also in the area of knowledge. We can easily see the moral confusion that has resulted from this, but the epistemological confusion is worse. If there are no universals, how do we know reality from nonreality? At this point, we are right in the lap of modern man's problem, as I will explain later.

Now let us go back to the period immediately after Rousseau, to Immanuel Kant, and Hegel, who changed the whole concept of epistemology. Before this, in epistemology, man always thought in terms of antithesis: That is, you learn by saying "A is A" and "A is not non-A." These are the first steps of classical logic. In other words, in antithesis if this is true, then its opposite is not true. You can make an antithesis. That is the classical methodology of epistemology, of knowing. But Hegel saw that antithesis has never turned out well on a rationalistic basis; so he proposed to change the methodology. In his position all things are relativized. Instead of dealing with antithesis, we are left with synthesis. This sets up a triangle: each thing is a thesis, it sets up an antithesis, and the answer is always synthesis. The whole world changed in the area of morals and political science, but it changed more profoundly, though less obviously, in the area of knowing itself. This changed the whole theory of how we know.

In my books I move to Kierkegaard, whose thinking took this a step further. Those who followed him set up an absolute dichotomy between reason and nonreason. The Kierkegaardianism which was extended from his teaching teaches that that which would give meaning is always separated from reason. Reason only leads to knowledge downstairs, which is mathematical knowledge without meaning, but upstairs you hope to find a nonrational meaning for the particulars.

All of this flows from the teaching of four men — Rousseau, Kant, Hegel, and Kierkegaard — and their thinking in the area of epistemology. From Hegel onward, this kind of thinking has replaced antithesis with synthesis, so turning the whole theory of knowledge upside down.

The teaching of Kierkegaard was extended in secular and religious existentialism. Secular existentialism took three forms: the French, Jean-Paul Sartre and Camus; the German, Heidegger; and Karl Jaspers, who is also a German but lived in Switzerland. The distinctions between the forms of existentialism do not change the fact that it is the same system even though it has different expressions with these different men: namely, that rationality only leads to something absurd in every area, including knowledge. Indeed, not *including* knowledge, but *first of all* knowledge — *principally* knowledge. To these men as rationalists the knowledge we can know with our reason is only a mathematical formula in which man is only a machine. Instead of reason they hope to find some sort of mystical experience "upstairs," apart from reason, to provide a universal.

Here we can feel the whole drift of the hippie movement and the drug culture of the 1960s. And it is very much with us in the 1980s. Man hopes to find something in his head because he cannot know certainly that anything is "out there." I am convinced that the generation gap is basically in the area of epistemology. Before man had a romantic hope that on the basis of rationalism he was going to be able to find a meaning to life, and put universals over the particulars. But on this side of Rousseau, Kant, Hegel, and Kierkegaard, this hope no longer exists; the hope is given up. People today live in a generation that no longer believes in the hope of truth as truth. That is why I use the term "true truth" in my books, to emphasize real truth. This is not just a tautology. It is an admission that the word *truth* now means something that before these four men would not have been considered truth at all. So I coined the expression "true truth" to make the point, but it is hard to make it sharp enough for people to understand how large the problem is.

Rationality is seen as leading to pessimism. We can have mathematical knowledge, but man is only a machine, and any kind of optimism one could have concerning meaning would have to be in the area of the nonrational, the "upstairs." So rationality, including modern science, will lead only to pessimism. Man is only the machine; man is only a zero, and nothing has any final meaning. I am nothing — one particular among thousands of particulars. No particulars have meaning, and specifically man has no meaning — specifically the particular of myself. I have no meaning; I die; man is dead. If people wonder why they are treated like computer data, it is for no less reason than this.

So man makes his leap "upstairs" into all sorts of mysticisms in the area of knowledge — and they *are* mysticisms, because they are totally separated from all rationality. This is a mysticism like no previous mysticism. Previous mysticisms always assumed something was there. But modern man's mysticisms are semantic mysticisms that deal only with words; they have nothing to do with anything being there, but are simply concerned with something in one's own head, or in language in one form or another. The idealistic taking of drugs in the 1960s began as one way to try to find meaning within one's head.

The present situation is one where we have in the area of the rational that which leads to mathematical formulae and man as a machine, and in the nonrational area all kinds of nonrational mysticisms.

Now we must turn our attention again to the "downstairs" *positivism*. This was the great hope of rationalistic man, but gradually positivism has died. I remember when I first lectured at Oxford and Cambridge, one had to change gears between the two great universities because in Oxford they were still teaching logical positivism, but in Cambridge it was all linguistic analysis. Gradually positivism has died. For a careful study as to why this has happened, I would recommend Michael Polanyi's book *Personal Knowledge, an Introduction to Post-critical Philosophy*. Polanyi is a name that hardly ever appears in the popular press and he is unknown by many, but he was one of the dominant thinkers in the intellectual world. His book shows why positivism is not a sufficient epistemology, and why the hope of modern science to have any certain knowledge is doomed to failure. And truly there is probably not a chair of philosophy of importance in the world today that teaches positivism. It is still held by the naive scientist who, with a happy smile on his face, is building on a foundation that no longer exists.

Now we must notice where we have come. The first of the modern scientists, Copernicus, Galileo, up to Newton and Faraday (as Whitehead pointed out), had the courage to begin to formulate modern science because they believed the universe had been created by a reasonable God, and therefore it was possible to find out what was true about the universe by reason. But when we come to naturalistic science, that is all destroyed; positivism was put in the place of the basis for knowing which was held by the early modern scientists. But now positivism itself is destroyed.

Polanyi argues that positivism is inadequate because it does not consider the *knower* of what is known. It acts as though the knower may be overlooked — as though the knower knew without actually being there. Or you might say positivism does not take into account the knower's theories or presuppositions. That is, positivism assumes that the knower approaches everything without any presuppositions, without any grid through which he feeds his knowledge.

But here is the dilemma, as Polanyi shows, because this simply is not true. There is no scientist who holds to the positivistic position who does not feed knowledge through a grid — a theory or worldview through which he sees and finds. The concept of the totally innocent, objective observer is utterly naive. And science cannot exist without an observer.

When I was younger, people would always say that science is completely objective. Then, some years ago in Oxford, it began to be insisted that this is not true; there is no such thing as science without the observer. The observer sets up the experiment, the observer observes it, and then the observer makes the conclusions. Polanyi says the observer is never neutral; he has a grid, he has presuppositions through which he feeds the things which he finds.

I would go a step further. I have always insisted that positivism has an even more basic problem. One must always judge a system in its own total structure. Within positivism as a total structure there is no way of saying with certainty that anything exists. Within the system of positivism itself, by the very nature of the case, you simply begin nakedly with nothing there. You have no reason within the system to know that the data is data, or that what is reaching you is data. Within the system there is no universal to give you the right to be sure that what is reaching you is data. The system of positivism itself gives you no certainty that anything is there, or that there is really, in the first move, any difference between reality and fantasy.

There is a further problem. Not only does the positivist not know with certainty that anything is there, but even if it is there he can have no reason to think he knows anything truly, nor even anywhere near truly. There is no reason within the system to be sure that there is a correlation between the observer — that is, the subject — and the thing — that is, the object.

To bring it further up to date, Karl Popper, who is another of the well-known thinkers of our day, has argued that a thing is meaningless unless it is open to verification and falsification. But in a later book he took a step backwards. He said there is *no possibility of verification*. You cannot verify anything — only falsify. That is, you cannot say what a thing is; you can only say certain things that it is not.

In science the same problem is involved with much of the "model" concept. One often finds that the objective reality is getting dim and that which remains is the model in the scientist's thinking.

We are left then with this: Positivism did not leave one with knowledge but only with a set of statistical averages and approximations — with no certainty that anything was there finally and no certainty of continuity in the things that were there.

One can relate this to Alfred Korzybski's and D. David Bourland's "general semantics," which would not allow the verb "to be" ever to be used. All their books are written without the use of the verb "to be." Why? Because they say there is no certainty of continuity.

I should like to turn to the philosopher Ludwig Wittgenstein, who is in many ways the key to this whole matter. There is an early Wittgenstein and there is a later Wittgenstein, but in his *Tractatus*, to which we refer here, we are concerned with the early Wittgenstein. Later he moved into linguistic analysis, but in this early stage he argued that down here in the world (in the area of reason) you have facts: you have the propositions of natural science. This is all that can be said; it is all that you can put into language. This is the limit of language and the limit of logic. "Downstairs" we can speak, but all that can be spoken is the mathematical propositions of natural science. Language is limited to the "downstairs" of reason, and that ends up with mathematical formulations.

But, as Bertrand Russell emphasizes, Wittgenstein was a mystic. Even in his early days, there were already the elements of mysticism. In the "upper story" he put silence, because you could not talk about anything outside of the known world of natural science. But man desperately needs values, ethics, meanings to it all. Man needs these desperately, but there is only silence there. It was at this point that the title of this present book was born. It is Wittgenstein's word "silence" that gave me the title for this book.

Wittgenstein said that there is only silence in the area of the things man desperately needs most—values, ethics, and meanings. Man knows it needs to be there, he argues, but he cannot even talk or think about it. Wittgenstein as a mystic greatly valued "the silence," but no matter how much we need values, ethics, meanings, there is only silence.

From this he plunged into linguistic analysis, which became the dominant philosophy all over the world. It was born at this place in the desperation that followed when positivism was seen to be inadequate. The "old" Wittgenstein and the existentialist really are very, very close at this particular point, though if you move from England to the Continent in the study of philosophy you find that people usually assume that they are completely at variance. Yet there is a way of looking at them in which they are very close at the moment when Wittgenstein says there is no real value or meaning in all these things, only silence.

For those who know Bergman's film *The Silence* this will ring a very familiar bell. Bergman is a philosopher who came to the place where he decided that there would never be anything spoken from this upper level, that God (even as the existentialist would use that word) was meaningless. At that point he made the film *The Silence*, and Bergman himself changed from that point onward. In other words, he agreed with what Wittgenstein, the brilliant philosopher, had said many years before. So really

Bergman and Wittgenstein must be seen together, and the film *The Silence* was a demonstration of this particular point.

What we are left with, let us notice, is an antiphilosophy, because everything that makes life worthwhile, or gives meaning to life, or binds it together beyond isolated particulars is in an "upstairs" of total silence.

Thus we are left with two antiphilosophies in the world today. One is existentialism, which is an antiphilosophy because it deals with the big questions but with no rationality. But if we follow the later Wittgenstein's development, we move into linguistic analysis, and find that this also is an antiphilosophy. Although it defines words using reason, finally language leads to neither values nor facts. Language leads to language, and that is all. It is not only the certainty of values that is gone, but the certainty of knowing.

Speaking of Wittgenstein and his moving into the area of language, it is well to mention at this point the later Heidegger, who also dealt with language, though in a very different way. Heidegger was originally an existentialist who believed that there was only the *Angst* toward the universe that gave the hope that something was there. But later he moved on into the view that because there was language in the universe, we may hope that there is something there, a nonrational hope of an ultimate meaning to it all. So Heidegger says, "Just listen to the poet" — not the *content* of the poet, but listen just because there is a being (that, is the poet) who speaks; so we can hope that Being — that is, existence — has meaning. He adds a different note in an attempt to make his position empirical and not just abstract. What he did was to claim that there was, in the far past, in the pre-Socratic age before Aristotle, a great, golden language embodying a direct "first-order experience" from the universe. This was purely hypothetical. It has no base historically, but he proposed it as an act of desperation in an attempt to lay an historical foundation on or under an otherwise purely hypothetical and nebulous concept.

We must understand that these things are not just theoretical in their effects. The later Heidegger is crucially important in certain forms of modern liberal theology. These things have their effect in the student world as well. They are not abstract. They are changing our world.

Let us at this point note an important factor. Whether we are dealing with Heidegger saying, "Listen to the poet" (and offering an upper-story semantic mysticism which seems to give hope), or with Wittgenstein (who moves in the opposite direction and is more honest in saying that there is only silence upstairs and therefore all we can do is define words which will never deal finally with meanings or values), the interesting thing is that modern man has come to conclude that the secret of the whole thing lies somehow in language. This is the age of semantics at this very basic point.

Notice what this means to us. The whole question with Heidegger and Wittgenstein — and with Bergman — is whether there is anyone adequately there in the universe to *speak*. We are surrounded by a sea of antiphilosophy. Positivism, which was an optimistic rationalism and the base of naturalistic science, has died. It has proved to be an insufficient epistemology. But the alternatives — existentialism on the one hand, linguistic analysis on the other — are antiphilosophies which cause man to be hopeless concerning ethics, values, meaning, and the certainty of knowledge. So in epistemology we are surrounded by a sea of antiphilosophy.

Polanyi was so magnificent in destroying logical positivism, and also in insisting that the subject-object relationship is real and that the subject can know the object. He is also known for championing truth; yet he developed no adequate base as to why these things are true. At the end of his life he at times gave religious motifs. For example, he said he repeated the Apostles' Creed, but when questioned further said that he did not believe the propositional content of the phrases of the Creed — rather, that for him they represented something, as the flag stands for patriotism. We truly can be thankful for his coming out for "truth," but he failed to give us a base and method as to how "the truth" can epistemologically be known to be truth.

Positivism is dead, and what is left is cynicism or some mystical leap as to knowing. That is where modern man is, whether the individual man knows it or not.

Those who have been raised in the last couple of decades stand right here in the area of epistemology. The really great problem is not, for example, drugs or amorality. The problem is knowing. This is a generation of antiphilosophy people caught in an uncertainty of knowing. In the downstairs area, which modern man ascribes to rationality and concerning which he talks with meaningful language, he can see himself only as a machine, a totally determined machine, and so has no way to be sure of knowing even the natural world. But in the area of the upstairs, which he ascribes to nonrationality, modern man is without categories, for categories are related to reason and antithesis. In the upstairs he has no reason to say that this is right as opposed to that being wrong (or nonright, perhaps, to use the more modern idiom). In the area of morals, in the upstairs he has no way to say one thing is right as opposed to another thing being nonright. But notice it is more profound and more horrible. Equally, living upstairs he has no way to say that this is true as opposed to that which is non-true.

We see this vividly in the cinema. I have dealt with this already at some length in *Escape from Reason* and elsewhere, but it is a necessary part of the picture here, too, and so I must repeat myself. Antonioni's film *Blow-up* was an example of this problem. The main character is the photographer. He is a perfect choice because what he is dealing with is not a set of human values but an impersonal photographic lens. The camera could be just as easily hooked up to an impersonal computer as to this photographer. The photographer runs around taking his snapshots, a finite human being dealing only with particulars and totally unable to put any meaning into them, and the cold camera lens offers no judgment, no control in anything it sees. The posters advertising Antonioni's film read: "Murder without guilt, love without meaning." In other words, there are no categories in the area of morals — murder is without guilt; but equally there are no categories in the human realm — love is without meaning. So Antonioni pictures the death of categories.

In the area of morality, there is no universal above; we are left only with particulars. The camera can click, click, click, and we are left with a series of particulars and no universals. That is all that rationalistic man can do for himself

But the modern cinema and other art forms go beyond the loss of human and moral categories. They point out quite properly that if you have no place for categories, you not only lose categories where moral and human values are concerned, but you also lose any categories which would distinguish between reality and fantasy.

All the way back to the Greeks, we have for 2,000 years the cleverest men who have ever lived trying to find a way to have meaning and certainty of knowledge; but man, beginning with himself with no other knowledge outside of himself, has totally failed, and Antonioni pointed it out powerfully in his film.

Modern man has no categories once he has moved out of the lower area of reason. Downstairs he is already dead; he is only a machine, and none of these things have any meaning. But as soon as he moves upstairs into the area of the upper-story mysticism, all that is left is a place with no categories with which to distinguish the inner world from the outer world with any certainty. Modern man has no categories to enable him to be at all sure of the difference between what is real and what is illusion.

There are four groups of categories involved here. We have considered three of these: first, the moral category; second, the human; third, the categories of reality and fantasy. The fourth, which we examine now, concerns our knowing other people.

The third group of categories was concerned with moving from inside the head to outside the head with certainty, and being sure that there is any difference between reality and fantasy. The fourth group is the reverse. How can two people meeting ever know each other — moving from outside their heads into each other's heads? How do we have any categories to enable us to move into the other person's thought world? This is a part of the modern man's alienation; this is the blackness which so many modern people face, the feeling of being totally alienated. A couple can sleep together for ten or fifteen years, but how are they going to get inside each other's heads to know anything about the other person as a person, in contrast to a language machine? It is easy to know the facade of a language machine, but how can you get in behind the language and know the person in this kind of setting? This is a very special modern form of lostness.

I had this brought strongly to my attention a number of years ago when a very modern couple came to L'Abri. We put them in one of the chalets. They kept everyone awake night after night because they would talk all the way through the night, until morning — talk, talk, talk. They were driving everyone crazy. Naturally, I became intrigued. I wondered what they were talking about. These people had been together for a long time; what did they talk about all the time? When I got to know them I found out, and it opened a new dimension for me as it dawned on me what the dilemma really is. I found out that they talked because they were trying desperately to know each other. They were really in love, and they were talking and talking in order to try to find one sentence or one phrase which they could know *exhaustively* together so that they could begin to know each other and to move inside each other's heads. They had no universals in their world, and thus they had to make a universal by a totally exhaustive point of contact. Being finite, they could not reach this.

In such a case, how do you begin? You are left with only particulars. Moving outward, you have no certainty that there is anything there, outside. Moving inside, inward, you are trying to move into somebody else's head. How do you know you are touching him? In this setting, human beings are the only ones who are there. There is no one else there to speak — only silence. So if you do not have the exhaustive phrase, how do you begin? You just cannot begin by knowing something partially; it must be exhaustive because there is no one else anywhere to provide any universals. The universal, the certainty, must be in your own conversation, in one exhaustive sentence or one exhaustive phrase to begin with. The problem is in the area of epistemology, and it centers on language.

Modern man is left either downstairs as a machine with words that do not lead either to values or facts but only to words, or he is left upstairs in a world without categories in regard to human values, moral values, or the difference between reality and fantasy. Weep for our generation! Man, made in the image of God and intended to be in vertical communication with the One who is there and who is not silent, and meant to have horizontal communication with his own kind, has, because of his proud rationalism, making himself autonomous, come to this place.

I would end this chapter with a quotation from *Satyricon* by Fellini. Toward the end of the film a man looks down at his friend who is dying a ridiculous death, an absolutely absurd death. With all his hopes, he has come to a completely absurd end. Modern man, made in the image of God and meant to be in communication with God and then with his kind, has come to this place of horrible silence. In the film Fellini has the voice say, "O God, how far he lies from his destination now." There was never a truer word.

CHAPTER FOUR

The Epistemological Necessity: The Answer

There is a Christian answer to the epistemological problem. Let us begin by remembering that the High Renaissance had a problem of nature and grace: their rationalism and humanism had no way to bind nature and grace together. They never achieved an answer to the problem, and the dilemma of the twentieth century really springs from this. Rationalistic and humanistic men, brilliant as they were, could never find the way to bind nature and grace together. However, at about the same time, as I have emphasized in my other books, the Reformation was taking place, and the Reformation had no such problem of nature and grace. This is really a tremendous distinction. Nature and grace arose as a problem out of the rationalistic, humanistic Renaissance, and it has never been solved. It is not that Christianity had a tremendous problem at the Reformation, and that the reformers wrestled with all this and then came up with an answer. No, there simply was *no problem of nature and grace* to the Reformation, because the Reformation had verbal, propositional revelation, and there was no dichotomy between nature and grace. The historic Christian position had no nature and grace problem because of propositional revelation, and revelation deals with language.

In our own generation, we have reached the core of the problem of language. We have already discussed the later Heidegger's use of language, and also Wittgenstein's use of language and linguistic analysis. But the difference is that Heidegger and Wittgenstein realized that there must be something spoken if we are going to know anything, but they had no one there to speak. It is as simple and as profound as that. Is there anyone there to speak? Or do we, being finite, just gather enough facts, enough particulars, to try to make our own universals as we listen to ourselves speaking?

In the Reformation and the Judeo-Christian position in general, we find that there is someone there to speak, and that He has given us information in two areas. He has spoken first about Himself, not exhaustively but truly; and second, He has spoken about history and about the cosmos, not exhaustively but truly. This being the case, and as He has told us about both things on the basis of propositional, verbalized revelation, the Reformation had no nature and grace problem. The reformers had a unity, for the simple reason that revelation spoke concerning both areas; thus the problem simply did not exist. Rationalism could not find an answer, but God speaking gives the unity needed for the nature and grace dilemma.

This brings us to a very basic question. Is the biblical position intellectually possible? Is it possible to have intellectual integrity while holding to the position of verbalized, propositional revelation? I would say the answer is this: It is not possible if you hold the presupposition of the uniformity of natural causes in a closed system. If you do, any idea of revelation becomes nonsense. It is not only that there are detailed problems in such a case, but that it becomes absolute nonsense if you really believe in the uniformity of natural causes in a closed system — namely, that *everything* is a machine. Whether you begin with a naturalistic view in philosophy or a naturalistic view in theology makes no difference. For the liberal theologian, it is quite impossible to think of real propositional revelation. Discussion only about some detail is not going to solve the problem. The big thing has to be faced, the question of the presuppositions. If I am completely committed without question to the uniformity of natural causes in a closed system, then whether I express myself in philosophical or religious terms is irrelevant. Propositional, verbalized revelation — knowledge that man has from God — is a totally unthinkable concept. This is because by definition everything is a machine, so naturally there is no knowledge from outside, from God. If this is your world-view, and you refuse to consider the possibility of any other, even though your naturalistic worldview leads to the dehumanization of man and is against the facts that we know about man and things, you are at a dead-end. You must remember you can only hold the uniformity of natural causes in the closed system, which is the almost monolithic consensus today, by denying what man knows about man. But if you insist upon holding this view, even though it dehumanizes man, and even though it is opposed to the evidence of what man knows about man, then there is no place for revelation. Not only that, but if you are going to hold to the uniformity of natural causes in the closed system, against all the evidence (and I do insist it is against the evidence), then you will never, never be able to consider the other presupposition which was the basis for modern science in the first place: the uniformity of natural causes in a *limited* system, open to reordering by God and by man.

There is an interesting factor here, and that is that in modern, secular anthropology (and I stress secular), the distinction between man and non-man is made in the area of language. It was not always so. The distinction used to be made in the area of man as the tool maker, so that wherever you found the tool maker it was man as against non-man. This is no longer true. The distinction is now language. The secular anthropologists agree that if we are to determine what is man in contrast to what is non-man this lies not in the area of tool making, but in the area of verbalization. If it is a verbalizer, it is man. If it is a nonverbalizer, it is not man.

We communicate propositional communication to each other in spoken or written form in language. Indeed, it is deeper than this because the way we think inside of our own heads is in language. We can have other things in our heads besides language, but it always must be linked to language. A book, for example, can be written with much figure of speech, but the figure of speech must have a continuity with the normal use of syntax and a defined use of terms, or nobody knows what the book is about. So whether we are talking about outward communication or inward thought, man is a verbalizer.

Now let us look at this argument from a non-Christian view, from the modern man's view of the uniformity of natural causes in a closed system. Here all concept of propositional revelation, and especially verbalized propositional revelation, is totally nonsense. The question I have often tried to raise in connection with this presupposition of the uniformity of natural causes in a closed system is whether this presupposition is viable in the light of what we know. I would insist it is not. It fails to explain man. It fails to explain the universe and its form. It fails to stand up in the area of epistemology.

It is obvious that propositional, verbalized revelation is not possible on the basis of the uniformity of natural causes. But the argument stands or falls upon the question: Is the presupposition of the uniformity of natural causes really acceptable? In my earlier books and in the previous chapters of this book we have considered whether this presupposition is in fact acceptable, or even reasonable, not upon the basis of Christian faith, but upon the basis of what we know concerning man and the universe as it is.

Christianity offers an entirely different set of presuppositions. The other presuppositions simply do not meet the need. Let us say, by the way, that one must be careful of words. In Britain, for instance, *presupposition* is sometimes a difficult word. A presupposition is something you do not know you have. But that is not the way I use the word. I use "presupposition" as a base, and we can choose it. Many people do get their presuppositions from their family or from society without knowing it, but it does not need to be this way. What I urge people to do is to consider the two great presuppositions — the uniformity of natural causes in a closed system and the uniformity of natural causes in an open system, in a limited time span — and to consider which of these fits the facts of what is.

Christianity's presupposition begins with a God who is there, who is the infinite-personal God, who has made man in His image. He has made man to be a verbalizer in the area of propositions in his horizontal communication to other men. Even secular anthropologists say that somehow or other, they do not know why, man is a verbalizer. You have something different in man. The Bible says, and the Christian position says, I can tell you why: God is a personal-infinite God. There has always been communication, before the creation of all else, in the Trinity. And God has made man in His own image, and part of making man in His own image is that man is a verbalizer. That stands in the unity of the Christian structure.

Now let us ask ourselves this question: In the Christian structure, would it be unlikely that this personal God who is there and made man in His own image as a verbalizer, in such a way that he can communicate horizontally to other men on the basis of propositions and languages — is it unthinkable or even surprising that this personal God could or would communicate to man on the basis of propositions? The answer is, no. I have never met an atheist who thought that this would be regarded as surprising within the Christian structure. Indeed, it is what one would expect. If God has made us to be communicators on the basis of verbalization, and given the possibility of propositional, factual communication with each other, why should we think He would not communicate to us on the basis of verbalization and propositions? In the light of the total Christian structure, it is totally reasonable. Propositional revelation is not even surprising, let alone unthinkable, within the Christian framework.

The personal God has made us to speak to each other in language. So if a personal God has made us to be language communicators — and that is obviously what man is — why then should it be surprising to think of Him speaking to Paul in Hebrew on the Damascus road? Why should it be a surprise? Do we think God does not know Hebrew? Equally, if the personal God is a good God, why should it be surprising, in communicating to man in a verbalized, propositional, factual way that He should tell us the true truth in all areas concerning which he communicates?[1] It is only surprising if you have been infiltrated by the presuppositions of the uniformity of natural causes in a closed system. Then, of course, it is impossible. But as I have said, it is a question of which of these two sets of presuppositions really and empirically meets the facts as we look about us in the world.

What we now find is that the answer rests upon language in revelation. Christianity has no nature and grace problem, and the reason for this rests upon language in revelation. The amazing thing is that Heidegger and Wittgenstein, two of the great names in the area of modern epistemology, both understood that the answer must be in the area of language, but they had no one there to speak.

Christianity has no problem of nature and grace. But let me add, very gently, Christianity has no problem of epistemology either. Remember Chapter Three and the absolute agony of modern man in the area of knowing, in epistemology — the utter, utter blackness of what is involved. To the Christian, there is no problem in the area of epistemology, just as there is no problem in the area of nature and grace. It is not that we happen to have an answer, but rather that *there is no problem* in the Christian structure.

Let us be clear as to why there is no problem of epistemology in the Christian structure. From the Christian viewpoint, we must come back and grasp really deeply what Oppenheimer and Whitehead have said about the birth of modern science.

May I remind you of a point I made in an earlier chapter. Whitehead and Oppenheimer said modern science could not have been born except in the milieu of Christianity. Why? In the area of biblical Christianity, Galileo, Copernicus, Kepler, Francis Bacon — all these men, up to Newton, Faraday and Maxwell — understood that there was a universe because God had made it. And they believed, as Whitehead has so beautifully said, that because God was a reasonable God one could discover the truth of the universe by reason. So modern science was born. The Greeks had almost all the facts that the early scientists had, but it never turned into a science like modern science. This came, as Whitehead said, out of the fact that these men really were sure that the truth of the universe could be pursued with reason because it had been made by a reasonable God.

I do not believe for a moment that if the men back at that point of history had had the philosophy, the epistemology of modern man, there would ever have been modern science. I also think science as we have known it is going to die. I think it is going to be reduced to two things: mere technology, and another form of sociological manipulation.[2] I do not believe for a moment that science is going to be able to continue with its objectivity once the base that brought forth science has been totally destroyed, and since the hope of positivism as a base has also been destroyed. But one thing I am sure of, and that is that science never would have begun if men had had the uncertainty that modern man has in the area of epistemology. There would have been no way to take with certainty the first steps which the early modern scientists were able to take.

Now notice that when we carry this over into epistemology, the position is exactly the same. It was because the infinite-personal God who exists — not just an abstraction — made things in correlation that the early scientists had courage to expect to find out the explanation of the universe. The God who is there made the universe, with things together, *in relationships*. Indeed, the whole area of science turns upon the fact that He has made a world in which things are made to stand together, that there are relationships between things. So God made the external universe, which makes true science possible, but He also made man and made him to live in that universe. He did not make man to live somewhere else. So we have three things coming together: God, the infinite-personal God, who made the universe; and man, whom He made to live in that universe; and the Bible, which He has given us to tell us about that universe. Are we surprised that there is a unity between them? Why should we be surprised?

So God made the universe, He made man to live in that universe, and He gives us the Bible, the verbalized, propositional, factual revelation, to tell us what we need to know. In the Bible He not only tells us about morals, which makes possible real morals instead of merely sociological averages, but He gives us comprehension to correlate our knowledge. The reason the Christian has no problem of epistemology is exactly the same as the reason why there is for the Christian no problem of nature and grace. The same reasonable God made both things—namely, the known and the knower, the subject and the object—and He put them together. So it is not surprising if there is a correlation between these things. Is that not what you would expect?

If modern science could be born on the basis of there being a reasonable God, which makes it possible to find out the order of the universe by reason, should we be taken by surprise that the knower who is to know and the object which is to be known should have a correlation? It is exactly what we should expect. Because we have a reasonable God who made them in the first place, there is a reasonable correlation between the subject and the object.

In the previous chapter we saw that the really basic horror of great darkness for modern man is that he cannot have any certainty of the relationship of the subject and the object. But the Christian position starts from another set of presuppositions altogether, that there is a reason for a correlation between the subject and the object. Now, interestingly, this is not against human experience. This is the experience of all men. If it were some mystical, religious thing that somebody offers as a leap completely out of reality and with no way to test it objectively, it would indeed be just one more piece of pie in the sky. But it does not matter how thoroughly a man in his philosophy holds a concept of unrelatedness; in reality he lives as though there is correlation between the subject and the object. Remember Godard's film, where you may perhaps go out through the windows instead of the doors, but you do not go out through the solid walls.

The fact is that if we are going to live in this world at all, we must live in it acting on a correlation of ourselves and the thing that is there, even if we have a philosophy that says there is no correlation. There is no other way to live in this world. Even the person who holds theoretically the most consistent concept of unrelatedness (for example, Hume) lives in this world on the basis of his experience that there is a correlation between the subject and the object and cause and effect. He not only lives that way, he *has* to live that way. There is no other way to live in this world. That is the way the world is made. So just as all men love even if they say love does not exist, and all men have moral motions, even though they say moral motions do not exist, so all men act as though there is a correlation between the external and the internal world, even if they have no basis for that correlation.

What I am saying is that the Christian view is exactly in line with the experience of every man. But no other system except the Judeo-Christian one — that which is given in the Old and New Testaments together — tells us why there is a subject-object correlation. Everybody does act on it, everybody must act on it, but no other system tells you *why* there is a correlation between the subject and object. In other words, all men constantly and consistently act as though Christianity is true.

Let me draw the parallel again. Modern men say there is no love, there is only sex, but they fall in love. Men say there are no moral motions, everything is behavioristic, but they all have moral motions. Even in the more profound area of epistemology, no matter what a man says he believes, actually — every moment of his life — he is acting as though Christianity were true, and it is only the Christian system that tells him why he can, must, and does act the way he does.

Though man is different from other things, in that man is made in the image of God and other things are not (he has personality, "mannishness"), yet nevertheless he is as much a creature as the other things. They and he are equally created. At this level they are equal, on the level of creaturehood. It follows, therefore, that though we are separated from other created things by personality, nevertheless we are fellow creatures in a common world because God made it that way.

If you have read my application of this argument to the subject of ecology, *Pollution and the Death of Man, The Christian View of Ecology*, you will remember how I developed this point. In the area of ecology, I argue that because we are fellow creatures, we are to treat the tree, the animal, and the air properly. That, I believe, is the Christian basis of ecology. Now, in epistemology, do you not feel that it is just a step further? In epistemology, this fellow creature is the object and I am the subject. We are both made by the same reasonable God, and hence I can know my fellow creature truly. In ecology, I am to treat it well, according to the way God made it. I am not to exploit it. But it is deeper than this. I am not only to treat it well, but I can *know* it truly as a fellow creature.

In epistemology we know the thing is there because God made it to be there. It is not an extension of his essence, it is not a dream of God, as much Eastern thinking says things are. It is really there. It has a true objective reality, and we are not surprised to find that there is a correlation between the observer and the observed because God made them to go together. They are made by the same God in the same frame of reference. God made them together, the subject and the object, the knower and the known, and He made them in the same frame of reference. The Christian does not have a problem with epistemology. And every man lives as though it is true, regardless of what he says in his epistemological theories. The Christian is not surprised that the tree is there, and he is not surprised that he cannot walk through it, because he knows the tree is really there.

Now everybody has to face this truth, whether it is a very intellectual man who might fight the Christian view, or whether it is the very simple one who lives as though the Christian view is true simply because he acts that way without asking any questions. To both of these the Christian says, what do you expect? Naturally this is the way it is, because the reasonable God made both the subject and object. He makes the subject and He makes the object, and He gives us the Bible to give us knowledge we need about the universe.

When Michael Polanyi destroyed positivism so magnificently, as we pointed out in an earlier chapter, modern man was left with only cynicism or some mystical leap. But the Christian is not left with cynicism or a mystical leap in regard to the subject-object relationship because the same God made them both. Therefore, the correlation between them is not a surprise to the Christian.

However, there is a question raised that we must deal with. That is, how do we approach the problem of the accuracy of knowledge? These things relate to language, which introduces the modern subject of semantics and linguistic analysis, not as a philosophy but as a tool. Linguistic analysis can be at certain points a helpful tool if one consciously rejects it as a rationalistic philosophy. Indeed, the subject-object relationship and the problem of language are related in a very real way.

Now, we must realize that there are three possible views of language. The first is that because we bring our own backgrounds to every word we ever use, every sentence we ever say, it means that we cannot communicate at all. Our own backgrounds so mark our words and our phrases that they do not touch the person spoken to.

The opposite is that as soon as we use any term in a symbol system of language, everybody has an exhaustive, absolute, and common meaning of that term because we are all using the same words.

So here we have these two extreme views, neither adequate: Your terms are so marked by your past experience that they do not touch at all, or else every term automatically has an exhaustive meaning, common to the speaker and hearer. But obviously neither of these two views, these extreme views, is an adequate explanation of what really happens in language. In reality, how do we find that language operates in the world? Surely we find it is like this: Though we do bring our own backgrounds to language, which gives the words a special cast out of our own backgrounds, yet there is also, with reasonable care, enough overlapping on the basis of the external world and the human experience to ensure that we can communicate even though we fall short of an exhaustive meaning of the same word — our words overlap, even while they do not fit completely. And that is the way we all operate in the area of language.

The illustration I like to use here concerns the word *tea*. *Tea* is a symbol in our English linguistic symbol system representing a real, identifiable object. But my wife was born in China and her first experience of the thing which t-e-a represents (in our linguistic symbol system) was in Chinese homes. There the Chinese taught her something that she remembers to this day, that the way to drink tea is to drink it from a bowl with a mouthful of rice which you pack into one cheek. In fact, you learn to drink the tea around the rice without touching or disturbing it. To her, that is all bound up in her word *tea*.

But for me *tea* begins with my mother and me in Germantown, Philadelphia, making tea in a way I would not make it today, with an aluminum tea caddy that you put into the water. These things mark the word *tea* to both of us, but do you think for a moment that because we have these different connotations, these different shadows of the word *tea*, that I cannot say to my wife, "Dear, will you please bring me a pot of tea?" and I do not get a pot of tea? Do you understand what I have said? If you are wrestling with semantics and linguistic analysis, you need to understand this. Keep away from the two extremes; recognize that there are overlaps in our external world and in our common, human experience.

This is true with language, and we must also realize it is true with knowing. We do not have to choose between the two extremes, either in language or epistemology. We can know truly without knowing exhaustively. As long as the thing is there, and I am there in correlation with that other thing, I do not have to know it exhaustively. After all, this does not surprise us because we come down to the fact that nobody knows anything exhaustively except God; *nobody*.

We notice that (just as in the area of language) we do not need to have exhaustive knowledge of a thing in order to know truly — as long as it is there, I am there, and we have sufficient correlation together. In the Christian background we are all creatures of God and we live in His world. When we use words, we do not exhaust them, even words like *house* or *dog*. These are not exhausted between one person and another, and yet though they have personal overtones we can communicate in an accurate if not an exhaustive way.

We should not be surprised if the same thing is true in our knowing, not in hearing a spoken word, but in the subject-object relationship. We are not surprised if we do not know the object exhaustively, but neither are we surprised if we find that we can know it truly. If the same reasonable God made both the subject and the object, we are not surprised that there is a correlation between them.

So we have seen why Christianity has no problem of epistemology. In past ages, when people were working on a Christian base, epistemology was never discussed with the awful tension which surrounds it today. Men studied many of these questions and the details of them, but there was none of the dilemma that is so common today. The reason for the modern dilemma is that men have moved from uniformity of natural causes in an open system — open to reordering by God and man — into the uniformity of natural causes in a closed system. With that, epistemology dies. But on a Christian basis, there is no problem.

What follows from this? Three things: First of all, here am I, looking outward. Although that is a very simple way to put it, it nevertheless represents the basic problem of epistemology. How can I have any certain knowledge, or knowledge in general, or knowledge of knowledge in general; and secondly, how can I distinguish between knowledge of what is there objectively in contrast to hallucination and illusion?

Clearly, there are borderline cases. Brain injury, schizophrenia, and other forms of mental illness may blur the distinction between objective reality and fantasy. Of course, the taking of drugs can produce a similar condition. Whether it is a psychological illness or an artificially imposed mental schizophrenia caused by drugs, the Christian sees it as a symptom of the Fall. Things are not completely the way God made them in the first place. There are alienations between man and God, between man and himself, and between man and nature. All this is a result of the Fall; so it is not surprising that there are borderline cases in the realm of true knowledge and fantasy.

Nevertheless, the Christian is in an entirely different situation from modern man — for instance, different from the thinking behind Antonioni's *Blow-up* as we considered it earlier. The Christian has a certainty right from the start that there is an external world that is there, created by God as an objective reality. He is not like the man who has nowhere to begin, who is not sure that there is anything there. The dilemma of positivism, as I have shown, is that, within its own system, it must start without any knowledge that there is anything there. The Christian is not in this position. He knows it is going to be there because God has made it there. The reason why the East never produced a science of its own is that Eastern thinking has never had a certainty of the objective existence of reality. Without the certainty of an external world there is no subject for scientific study, no basis for experiment or deduction. But the Christian, being sure of the reality of the external world, has a basis for true knowledge. Even though we must acknowledge that we live in a fallen world, and there are abnormalities and borderline cases, yet the Christian is not caught in the dilemma with which Antonioni wrestles in *Blow-up*.

Not only that, but the Christian can live in the world that God has made. This must be the test, after all. That is the difference between science and science fiction. Science must fit into the world that is there; it cannot be isolated from it.

It is not surprising that if a reasonable God created the universe and put me in it, He should also correlate the *categories of my mind* to fit that universe, simply because I have to live in it. This is a logical extension of my previous points. If this world is made the way the Judeo-Christian system says it is made, we should not be surprised that man should have categories of the mind to fit the universe in which he lives.

There has been a great deal of work done on the subject of uniform categories in the human mind, by men like Claude Levi Strauss, for example, or Noam Chomsky in his idea of basic grammar. These men found that somehow or other there are uniform categories of the human mind. But the Christian says, What do you expect? The personal-infinite God who has made the world and has put me into it is naturally going to make the categories of mind to fit the place where He put me.

Let us bring this over into the physical world. I have a lung system, and the lung system conforms to the earth atmosphere in which I live. It would not fit Venus or Mars and it does not fit the moon, but it fits my own environment. Why does it fit the world in which I live? It is not surprising that my lung system is in correlation to the world's atmosphere, for the same reasonable God made both my lung system and the atmosphere and He put me in this world. So we should expect a correlation between my lung system and the atmosphere in which I live. Going back to the area of epistemology, there is no surprise that God has given me a correlation between the categories of my mind and the world in which I live. Thus in the matter of knowledge, if a reasonable God made the world and has also made me, we are not surprised if He made the categories of the human mind to fit into the categories of the external world. Both are His creation. There are categories in the external world, and there are categories of my mind. Should I be surprised if they fit?

This, of course, is very different from positivism, which has nothing in its system to explain why anything is there. As I said previously, positivism of all forms died because the word *data* can only be a faith word to positivism. There is nothing inherent in the system to explain why data would be there. It is exactly opposite to the Christian position.

Let us notice another element in the biblical position in this matter of categories. The Bible teaches in two different ways: first, it teaches certain things in didactic statements, in verbalizations, in propositions. For example, it teaches me the principles we have been dealing with in this book. Second, the Bible teaches by showing how God works in the world that He Himself made. We should read the Bible for various reasons. It should be read for facts, and it should also be read devotionally. But reading the Bible every day of one's life does something else — it gives one a different mentality. In the modern world we are surrounded by the mentality of the uniformity of natural causes in a closed system, but as we read the Bible it gives us a different mentality. Do not minimize the fact that in reading the Bible we are living in a mentality which is the right one, opposed to the great wall of this other mentality which is forced upon us on every side — in education, in literature, in the arts, and in the mass media.

When I read the Bible, I find that when the infinite-personal God Himself works in history and in the cosmos, He works in a way which confirms what He has said about the external world. That is what I call the covenant of creation. What He does never violates what He tells us. When God works in the flow of history, He works consistently with the way He says the external world is. The universal working into the particulars defines and confirms what He says the particulars are.

So in the Bible we have two things — we have the didactic teaching of the Scripture, and we also have that which makes us say, "Yes, God works that way." This is a profound concept indeed. There are miracles in the Bible, but the great stretch of the Bible is not made up of miracles. They are unusual happenings, and that is why we call them miracles. Usually we find God working in the world within the natural laws of the world as He made it. The Red Sea is pushed back; He uses the east wind. Jesus cooked a fish, and there was a fire to cook it on. Certainly these are miracles, but for the most part God acts in the world in a way that confirms both my observations of the world, and also the way God says it is in the didactic portions of the Bible.

These two eyes which the Bible gives us to look through always agree perfectly — the eye of didactic teaching and the eye of God working into history and in the cosmos. This is parallel to that profound statement in the Westminster Confession of Faith, that when God reveals His attributes to man, they are true not only to man but to God. God is not just telling a story; He is telling us what is really true to Himself. What He tells us is not exhaustive, because we are finite and we know nothing in an exhaustive way. We cannot even communicate with each other exhaustively, because we are finite. But He tells us truly — even the great truth about Himself. He is not playing games with us.

On the same basis we find that science need not be a game. At times today it seems science is becoming a game. As I have said, I do not believe for a moment that science, which has given up the base which began it, and now has lost its positivism as well, can continue in a really objective way. Science becomes a game in two different ways. With many a scientist, science becomes a kind of gamesmanship. He is playing a complicated game within a very limited area so that he never has to think of the real problems or of meaning. There is many a scientist in his laboratory who has shut himself up to the reading on the dials, and the specimen all but disappears. This is another bourgeois gamesmanship, like a rich playboy skiing downhill watching only the second hand on his watch. But for the Christian the world has meaning; it has objective reality. Science is not a game.

The second and more terrifying way, I think, is the headlong rush towards sociological science.[3] Because men have lost the objective basis for certainty of knowledge in the areas in which they are working, more and more we are going to find them manipulating science according to their own sociological or political desires rather than standing upon concrete objectivity. We are going to find increasingly what I would call sociological science, where men manipulate the scientific facts. Carl Sagan (1934-), professor of astronomy and space science at Cornell University, demonstrates that the concept of a manipulated science is not far-fetched. He mixes science and science fiction constantly. He is a true follower of Edgar Rice Burroughs (1875-1950). The media gives him much TV prime time and much space in the press and magazine coverage, and the United States Government spent millions of dollars in the special equipment which was included in the equipment of the Mars probe — at his instigation, to give support to his obsessive certainty that life would be found on Mars, or that even large-sized life would be found there. With Carl Sagan the line concerning objective science is blurred, and the media spreads his mixture of science and science fiction out to the public as exciting fact.

The loss of the certainty of objectivity is a serious thing to the scientist just as it is for the drug addict. We can see it in the drug addict — he has often lost the distinction between reality and fantasy, the objectivity is gone. But the scientist can be in the same place. If he loses the epistemological base, he, too, is in a serious position. What does science mean once you are no longer sure of the objectivity of the thing, or you are no longer on an epistemological base which gives the certainty of a correlation between the subject and the object, or a clear base for the difference between reality and fantasy?

But the Christian has a reason as to why he expects to touch the real, to find out about it, and distinguish the real from the nonreal, just as the early scientists did. This is where we stand. When the Christian does reach out without cynicism in the area of knowing, the external world really is there. Why? Because God made it to be there, and He made a correlation between the subject and the object.

The above concerns me, looking outward.

The second result of the Christian view of epistemology concerns others looking at me: what I am, the inward reality of my thought world, in contrast to what I seem to be from the viewpoint of others. This is a serious problem for many modern people. They are always trying to know each other, and all they find is a facade. How do you get behind this? How do you get behind, to the real person who is there?

The Christian does not have to choose between knowing the external *or* inward worlds totally, or not knowing them at all. I must not expect to know this other man perfectly, because I am finite. But I may expect what I do know to fit together because, after all, the same One has made it all. The strength of the Christian system — the acid test of it — is that everything fits under the apex of the existing, infinite-personal God, and it is the only system in the world where this is true. No other system has an apex under which everything fits. That is why I am a Christian and no longer an agnostic. In all the other systems something "sticks out," something cannot be included; and it has to be mutilated or ignored. But without losing his own integrity, the Christian can see everything fitting into place beneath the Christian apex of the existence of the infinite-personal God who is there.

This is true when I am looking out at the world, but it is also true as I look inward to other people in this desperately important area that occupies so much of the thinking of modern people. How can they know other people? How are they going to get beyond this wooden facade? How does one know there is anything back there? What about the contrast between what I may be inside, what I am inside, and what I appear outwardly? How can I know anyone else?

The biblical revelation, according to God's teachings, binds not only the outward man but the inward man as well. The norms of Scripture are not just for the outward man, but also for the inward man. In the Old Testament, what is the last commandment? It is internal: "You shall not covet." This concerns the inward man. Without this all the rest falls to the ground.

God's revelation binds not only the outward man in regard to *morals*, but the inward man too; and similarly God's giving of *knowledge* where it touches history and the cosmos binds not only the outward man, but the inward man. Thus, two people who are living under God's revelation have in their thought worlds a common framework, a common reality.

We find, therefore, that the Bible gives a propositional, factual revelation of God which promotes norms both for the inward and the outward man. The inward man, according to the Bible, is not autonomous, any more than the outward man is autonomous. Every time the inward man becomes autonomous, it is just as much a revolution as when the outward man becomes autonomous. Every human problem, as I have stressed in *Escape from Reason*, arises from man's trying to stake out something as autonomous from God, and as I have emphasized, as soon as anything is made autonomous from God, then "nature eats up grace."

We have this same thing in the area of knowing other people. Nothing is to be autonomous from God. The inward areas of knowledge, meaning, and values, and the inward areas of morals, are bound by God as much as is the outward world. As the Christian grows spiritually he should be a man who consciously, more and more, brings his thought world as well as his outward world under the norms of the Bible. But what about the non-Christian? As a Christian approaches the non-Christian, he still has a starting-place from which to know the person in a way that the non-Christian does not have, because he knows who the person is. One of the most brilliant men I have ever worked with sat in my room in Switzerland crying, simply because he was a real humanist and existentialist. He had gone from his home in a South American country to Paris, because this was the center of all this great humanistic thought. But he found it was so ugly. The professors cared about nothing. It was inhuman in its humanism. He was ready to commit suicide when he came to us. He said, "How do you love me, how do you start?" "I know who you are," I told him, "because you are made in the image of God." We went on from there. Even with a non-Christian, the Christian has some way to begin: to go from the facade of the outward to the reality of the inward, because no matter what a man says he is, we know who he *really* is. He is made in the image of God; that's who he is. And we know that down there somewhere — no matter how wooden he is on the outside, or how much he has died on the outside, or even if he believes he is only a machine — we know that beyond that facade there is the person who is a verbalizer and who loves and wants to be loved. And no matter how often he says he is amoral, in reality he has moral motions. We know this because he has been made in the image of God. Hence, even with a non-Christian, the Christian has a way to start, from the outside to the inside, in a way that non-Christians simply do not have.

But among Christians there should be a more profound way to know each other. Let us say we want to have communication, we are sick of this horrible mechanical inhumanity that we find around us. We are sick of being simply IBM cards. The Christian boy and girl who want to be open with each other, the Christian husband and wife who want to be open with each other, the pastor and the people who want to be open with each other — how can they really do it, moving from the outside inward? The problem of knowing each other is the discrepancy between what a man seems to be and what he is inside. That is always the problem with getting inside and getting to know each other. So, how do you get through?

Can you see that to the extent to which people accept biblical teaching for the inward man as well as the outward man, there is an increasing integration of the inward and the outward man — because they see both the inward and the outward man under the unity of the same norms, in regard to both values and knowing? It is possible to move from the outward man to the inward man because there is an increasing alignment as both are bound by the same universal. We must allow the norms of God in values and knowing to bind the inward man as well as the outward man, so that there is less and less discrepancy between the two.

Unhappily, we will not keep God's norm perfectly in the internal world of thought any more than we do externally, and (in a fallen world) perhaps not as much. But with God's norms of truth, morals, values, and knowing, we have tracks (or to use a better analogy, a North Star) which give unity to the internal and external world. God's norms not only give unity, but they provide a bridge between these two worlds. This applies both for ourselves and then to get down inside each other. When we step from the external to the internal world of thought, we are not on a sea without a shore either in regard to ourselves or in regard to the woman or the man who stands before us.

For those who are walking through the swamps of this present generation, this is beauty. As this is understood, suddenly the inward man is no longer autonomous and there is a bringing together of the particulars about the inward man and the outward man under the same universal; and with this unity, thank God, we can really begin to get inside each other.

This, too, ought to be part of salvation, of the continuing work of Christ in the Christian's life. It is the loss of this that has deprived this poor generation of real human communication. Men and women who sleep together for years are shut off from each other, because there is no universal that binds the inward particulars and the outward particulars. But to the Christian there is: As we grow spiritually and bring the inward particulars of the thought world — meaning values, knowledge, and morals — under the norms of God, to that extent what we seem to be outwardly increasingly conforms to what we are inwardly, so that we can really know each other.

I have spoken of myself looking outward and of other people looking at me. Now, the third result of the Christian view of epistemology concerns reality and imagination. In a way, this is the most important of the three. We were considering in an earlier chapter the modern view of epistemology, where modern man has no distinction between reality and fantasy. Now I am talking about the reverse side of that for the Christian. I live in a thought world which is filled with creativity; inside my head there is creative imagination. Why? Because God, who is the Creator, has made me in His own image, I can go out in imagination beyond the stars. This is true not only for the Christian, but for every person. Every person is made in the image of God; therefore, no person in his or her imagination is confined to his or her own body. Going out in our imagination, we can change something of the form of the universe as a result of our thought world — in our painting, in our poetry, or as an engineer, or a gardener. Is that not wonderful? I am there, and I am able to impose the results of my imagination on the external world.

But notice this: Being a Christian and knowing God has made the external world, I know that there is an objective external reality and that there is that which is imaginary. I am not uncertain that there is an external reality which is distinct from my imagination. The Christian is free; free to fly, because he has a base upon which he need not be confused between his fantasy and the reality which God has made. We are free to say, "This is imagination." Is it not marvelous to be a painter and make things a little different from nature — not just to "photograph" nature, but to make things a little different? Is it not wonderful to be made in the image of God and be able to use our creativity in this way? As a Christian I have the epistemology that enables me not to get confused between what I think and what is objectively real. The modern generation does not have this, and this is the reason why some young people are all torn up in these areas. But Christians should not be torn up here.

Thus the Christian may have fantasy and imagination without being threatened. Modern man cannot have daydreams and fantasy without being threatened. The Christian should be the person who is alive, whose imagination absolutely boils, which moves, which produces something a bit different from God's world because God made us to be creative.

In conclusion, we see three interrelated results of the Christian's view of epistemology: first, as I look out to the external world, to the world of relationships, in the subject-object relationship; second, as other people look to me and I look to other people — as I want to know and understand another person; and third, to the internal world of my thoughts, fantasies, and imaginations. I look outward and I understand why there is a subject-object relationship. I look at another man, a non-Christian, and I know he is made in the image of God. As Christians allow the norms of Scripture more and more to bring together the inward and the outward man, we can know each other in greater and greater beauty and greater and greater depth. And because he is not threatened by the difference between reality and fantasy, the Christian should be the man with the flaming imagination and the beauty of creativity. All of these things are ours. The modern alienation in the area of epistemology can make each of these three areas literally into a thing of black horror. The loss of the reality of the subject-object relationship; the difficulty of people getting to know each other; and the awful nightmare of the confusion between reality and fantasy: modern epistemology leads to these three terrors. But under the unity of the apex of the infinite-personal God, in all of these areas we can have meaning, we can have reality, and we can have beauty. It is truth, but also beauty.

Because man revolted against God and tried to stand autonomous, the great alienation is in the area of man's separation from God. When that happened, then everything else went too. This autonomy is carried over into the very basic area of epistemology, of knowing, so that man is not only divided from other men in the area of knowing, he is divided from himself. If there are no common categories between the internal fantasy and the external world, man is divided and feels alienated from himself. He has no universals to cover the particulars in his own life. He is one thing inside and another thing outside. Then he begins to scream, "Who am I?" Does that sound familiar to any of you who do Christian work today? At L'Abri we have youngsters come from the ends of the earth and say, "I have come to try to find out who I am." It is not just some psychological thing, as we usually think of psychological. It is basically epistemological. Man's attempted autonomy has robbed him of reality. He has nothing to be sure of when his imagination soars beyond the stars, if there is nothing to guarantee a distinction between reality and fantasy. But on the basis of the Christian epistemology, this confusion is ended, the alienation is healed. This is the heart of the problem of knowing, and it is not solved until our knowledge fits under the apex of the infinite-personal, triune God who is there and who is not silent. When it does, and only when it does, there simply is no problem in the area of epistemology.

Is Propositional Revelation Nonsense?

There are two ways to consider the question of propositional revelation and infallibility. The first is through consideration of the presuppositions involved; the second is through consideration of the detailed problems. This appendix will deal with the first. However, until the first is in place, the second cannot be sensibly pursued.

To modern man, and much modern theology, the concept of propositional revelation and the historic Christian view of infallibility is not so much mistaken as meaningless. It is so in the same way, and for the same basic reasons, that for most modern men and most modern theology the concept of sin ,and guilt, in any real moral sense, is meaningless. But, of course, one must ask if their presupposition is the proper and adequate one.

The Christian presupposition is that there was a personal beginning to all things — someone has been there and made all the rest. This someone would have to be big enough, and this means being infinite. One still has the question of the personal-infinite someone always having been there; but if this were the case, the other problems would no longer exist. *And everyone has to explain the fact that the universe and he, the individual, does exist; thus, something has "been there."*

Now if this personal-infinite someone always having been there is the case, everything else would be limited in contrast to his own enough-ness, or infiniteness. But just suppose that he made something limited, but on his own wavelength — let's say in his own image — then one would have both an infinite, noncreated Personal and a limited created personal. On this presupposition, the personality of the limited, created personal would be explained. On this same presupposition, why could not the non-created Personal communicate to the created personal if He wished? Of course, if the infinite, uncreated Personal communicated to the finite, created personal, He would not exhaust Himself in His communication; but two things are clear here:

1. Even communication between one created person and another is not exhaustive; but that does not mean that for that reason it is not true. Thus, the problem of communication from the uncreated Personal to the created personal would not have to be of a qualitatively different order from the communication between one created personal being and another. It would not be exhaustive, but that would not make it untrue, any more than the created-person to created-person communication would be untrue, unless the uncreated Personal were a liar or capricious.

2. If the uncreated Personal really cared for the created personal, it could not be thought unthinkable for Him to tell the created personal things of a propositional nature; otherwise, as a finite being, the created personal would have numerous things he could not know if he just began with himself as a limited, finite reference point.

In such a case, there is no intrinsic reason why the uncreated Personal could only communicate some vaguely true things, but could not communicate clear propositional truth concerning the world surrounding the created personal — let's say, truth about the cosmos. Or why He could not communicate propositional truth concerning the sequence that followed the uncreated Personal's original creation — let's call that history. There is no reason why He could not communicate these two types of propositions. The communication would not be exhaustive, but can we think of any reason why it would not be true?

The above is, of course, what the Bible claims for itself concerning propositional revelation.

If the uncreated Personal wished to give these communications through individual created personalities in such a way that they would write (in their own individual style, etc.) the exact things the uncreated Personal wanted them to write in the areas of religious truth and things of the cosmos and history — then by this time it is impossible to make an absolute and say that He could not or would not. And this, of course, is the Bible's claim concerning inspiration.

Within this framework, why would it be unthinkable that the noncreated Personal should communicate with the created personal in verbalized form, if the noncreated Personal made the created personal a language-communicating being? And we are (even if we do not know why) language-communicating beings. There is only one reason to rule out as unthinkable the fact that Jesus gave a propositional communication to Saul in verbalized form in the Hebrew language, using normal words and syntax (Acts 26:14), or that God did so to the Jews at Sinai: that is, to have accepted the other set of presuppositions — even if, by using religious terminology, one obscures that one has accepted the naturalistic presuppositions. Now one may obscure what one has done in accepting naturalistic presuppositions by using religious terminology and saying or implying, "Jesus (without in this case having any way to know what or who that really is) gave to Saul some form of a first-order, noncontentful experience, in which the words used in the biblical text to express this inexpressible are just words which reflect views of life, history, and the cosmos which were then current." If one does this, however, one is left with a faith which is equivalent to saying, "I believe . . ." without ever finishing, or being able to finish, the sentence — or even knowing if a definite or an indefinite article comes next in the sentence.

Further, if the noncreated Personal placed the communication He gave man in a book of history, why would it then be unlikely that the noncreated Personal would communicate truly concerning the space-time history in that book? How strange if the noncreated Personal is not a liar or capricious, that He should give "religious truth" in a book in which the whole structural framework, implicitly and explicitly, is historic, and yet that history be false or confused. Surely, except on the preconceived presupposition that that book can only be "man feeling upward" within the framework of the uniformity of natural causes, such an idea would be peculiar beyond measure. This is especially so as the book itself gives no indication of two levels; it gives no indication of a "religious truth" out of contact with the history in the book. It repeatedly appeals to the history open to verification as a proof of the truth of what is given; and it gives no indication of the enveloping space-time history being only so much error-conditioned incrustration.

Why could not the noncreated Personal teach the created personal truly on the level of knowledge which is the basis of so much of what we know on the created personal level: namely, one who knows, telling one who does not know — not exhaustively, yet truly? Surely this is how we have our knowledge from other created personal sources. Further, why could not the noncreated Personal also tell about Himself truly (though not exhaustively) — unless we have already accepted the presupposition that that which is the "noncreated" must be the "philosophic other." If we begin with a noncreated Personal creating man in His own image, what rules out the statement of the Westminster Larger Catechism that God made known to us, through the Scripture, what God is? Is there any reason why the noncreated Personal could not so tell us truly about Himself, though not exhaustively?

By this stage, two things should be obvious: first, that from the presupposition that all things started from mass or energy, the idea of either revelation or infallibility is unthinkable; and second, that from the presupposition of a personal beginning, these ideas are not unthinkable or nonsense at all. The reasonableness of the matter thus rests totally on which way one begins — that is, on which presupposition one adopts at the outset.

If one starts with the impersonal everything, then the question naturally has nothing to do with even the possibility of an uncreated Personal communicating to a created personal; that, from the premise, is nonsense. Yet if one does begin with a nonpersonal everything, there is a question that now really shouts: Is not man-to-man communication equally nonsense?

With this presupposition no one has discovered a way to find meaning either in man's speaking to man or in man's hearing, except through an act of faith against his whole basic presuppositional structure. Worse yet, for those who hold this other presupposition, the little men (I and the others) are not content to think that they do not speak meaningfully; and furthermore everything in experience convinces us that the others hear truly, though not exhaustively.

By this time, is this not something like a Francis Bacon

painting? One must scream, but the whole situation is a lostness and a damnation, including the scream.

Well now, in the light of this total confusion to which the other presupposition (the impersonal + time + chance) leads us, the presupposition of a personal beginning is worth another very careful look. If everything did begin with that uncreated Personal beginning, then neither communication from the created personal to the created personal, nor from the noncreated Personal to the created personal is unthinkable. Nor is it even intrinsically unlikely.

The importance of all this is that most people today (including some who still call themselves evangelical) who have given up the historical and biblical concept of revelation and infallibility have not done so because of the consideration of detailed problems objectively approached, but because they have accepted, either in analyzed fashion or blindly, the other set of presuppositions. Often this has taken place by means of cultural injection, without their realizing what has happened to them.

Having accepted the other presupposition against the evidence of true, though not exhaustive, man-to-man communication, I wonder what would make them listen? It is strange to communicate the concept that one rejects the concept of a noncreated Personal "being there," when there is no way then to know the how, why, or what of communication with my own kind. And the strangeness continues if one says that it is unreasonable per se to consider the fact of the noncreated Personal being there, when that would explain the how, why, and what of the communication I do have with my own kind!

Having come to this point, we are in a position to consider the detailed problems — the so-called "critical problems." But the historic view of the Bible and of the Church about revelation and infallibility is no longer nonsense per se; and even most of the detailed problems look very different once the nonsense connotation is dealt with.

"Faith" versus Faith

One must analyze the word *faith* and see that it can mean two completely opposite things.

Suppose we are climbing in the Alps and are very high on the bare rock, and suddenly the fog shuts down. The guide turns to us and says that the ice is forming and that there is no hope; before morning we will all freeze to death here on the shoulder of the mountain. Simply to keep warm the guide keeps us moving in the dense fog further out on the shoulder until none of us have any idea where we are. After an hour or so, someone says to the guide, "Suppose I dropped and hit a ledge ten feet down in the fog. What would happen then?" The guide would say that you might make it until the morning and thus live. So, with absolutely no knowledge or any reason to support his action, one of the group hangs and drops into the fog. This would be one kind of faith, a leap of faith.

Suppose, however, after we have worked out on the shoulder in the midst of the fog and the growing ice on the rock, we had stopped and we heard a voice which said, "You cannot see me, but I know exactly where you are from your voices. I am on another ridge. I have lived in these mountains, man and boy, for over sixty years and I know every foot of them. I assure you that ten feet below you there is a ledge. If you hang and drop, you can make it through the night and I will get you in the morning."

I would not hang and drop at once, but would ask questions to try to ascertain if the man knew what he was talking about and if he was not my enemy. In the Alps, for example, I would ask him his name. If the name he gave me was the name of a family from that part of the mountains, it would count a great deal to me. In the Swiss Alps there are certain family names that indicate mountain families of that area. In my desperate situation, even though time would be running out, I would ask him what to me would be the adequate and sufficient questions, and when I became convinced by his answers, then I would hang and drop.

This is faith, but obviously it has no relationship to the other use of the word. As a matter of fact, if one of these is called faith, the other should not be designated by the same word. The historic Christian faith is not a leap of faith in the post-Kierkegaardian sense because *He is not silent*, and I am invited to ask the adequate and sufficient questions, not only in regard to details, but also in regard to the existence of the universe and its complexity and in regard to the existence of man. I am invited to ask adequate and sufficient questions and then believe Him and bow before Him metaphysically in knowing that I exist because He made man, and bow before Him morally as needing His provision for me in the substitutionary, propitiatory death of Christ.

Notes

The God Who Is There

SECTION I

Chapter 1: The Gulf Is Fixed
1. The consideration of classical and presuppositional apologetics is continued in Section III, Chapter 5. Also see Appendix A.
2. (London: Allen and Unwin, 1961).
3. James 1:27.

Chapter 2: The First Step in the Line of Despair: Philosophy
1. Cf., e.g., Professor A. J. Ayer in *What I Believe*, ed. Unwin (London: Allen and Unwin, 1966), and Professor Anthony Flew, "Must Morality Pay?," *The Listener*, October 13, 1966.
2. *The Humanist Frame*, ed. Sir Julian Huxley, p. 46.
3. *Ibid.*, p. 409.
4. (New York: University Books, 1964).

Chapter 3: The Second Step: Art
1. See Chapter 2, Section II.
2. This is the translation suggested by Dr. H. R. Rookmaaker in *Synthetist Art Theories* (Amsterdam: 1959), p. 23 and note w to Chapter IX.
3. A letter written in February 1898.
4. Dr. Rookmaaker, *op. cit.*, notes n, p, aa, af to Chapter 9.
5. Two works with Eva's name written on them were exhibited in the Picasso and Man Exhibition at the Toronto Art Gallery, January 1964.
6. *Fur Theo van Doesburg*, DE STIJL, January 1932.

Chapter 4: The Third and Fourth Steps: Music and the General Culture
1. See paragraph on the Beatles in Chapter 4, Section I.
2. Ducretet-Thomson, Paris, No. 320 c. 100.
3. *Collected Poems, 1934-52* (London: J. M. Dent and Sons, 1959), pp. 179, 180.
4. S.M.O. Records, 81.045.
5. E.M.I. Records, R5570.
6. E.M.I. Records, P.M.C. 7027.

Chapter 5: The Unifying Factor in the Steps of Despair
1. (New York: Frederick A. Praeger, 1964).
2. Leopold Sedar Senghor, *Selected Poems* (Oxford University Press, 1964).
3. French Jesuit paleontologist who wrote *The Phenomenon of Man* (London: Collins, 1959; New York: Harper & Row) and other books.
4. Sir Julian Huxley wrote the Introduction to the British edition of *The Phenomenon*

351

of Man in 1958. In this he agrees both with the methodology and broad conclusions of Teilhard de Chardin regarding the evolutionary future of man. Later, in 1961, he develops his general agreement with these conclusions in the direction of the use of religion in his Introduction to *The Humanist Frame*. What Senghor does in his book in applying Teilhard de Chardin's principles to the State of Senegal, Huxley seeks to do on a global scale.

5. Cf. 1 Corinthians 15:13, 14, 32.

SECTION II

Chapter 1: The Fifth Step: Theology

1. In regard to Kierkegaard, it is important to keep in mind what is stated in Chapter 2, Section IV.

Chapter 2: Modern Mysticism: Despair Beyond Despair

1. My thinking has led me to believe that there is a collective cultural consciousness or memory which is related to words. I would suggest there are two parts to it: a collective memory of a specific race, and a collective memory of all men as to what man is and what reality is.

   Thus man, in his *language*, "remembers" (regardless of his personal belief) that God does exist. For example, when the Russian leaders curse, they curse by God, and not by something less; and atheistic artists often use "god" symbols. This, I believe, is a deeper yet simpler explanation than Jung's view of god as the supreme archetype arising (according to him) out of the evolution of the race. Moreover, in man's language, man also remembers that humanity is unique (created in the image of God), and therefore words like *purpose, love, morals* carry with them in connotation their real meaning. This is the case regardless of the individual's personal worldview and despite what the dictionary or scientific textbook definition has become.

   At times the connotation of the word is deeper and more "unconscious" than its definition. The use of such words trigger responses to a greater degree in line with what the specific race has thought they mean and how it has acted on their meaning, and to a lesser degree in line with what really is and what man is. I would further suggest that after the worldview and experiences of the race form the definition and connotation of the words of any specific language, then that language as a symbol system becomes the vehicle for keeping alive and teaching this worldview and experience.

   It would therefore seem to me that the whole matter is primarily one of language, as man thinks and communicates in language. I would say that in this context the division of languages at the tower of Babel is an overwhelmingly profound moment of history.

2. *Leonardo da Vinci* (New York: Raynal and Company, 1956), p. 174.

3. I am consciously omitting here the intermediate and important change in the formulation at the time of Kant (1724-1804) and Rousseau (1712-1778). That formulation was:

$$\frac{\text{FREEDOM}}{\text{NATURE}}$$

See *Escape from Reason*, pages 32-36.

Chapter 3: Modern Mysticism in Action: Art and Language

1. Sylvia Sprigge, *Berenson, A Biography* (Boston: Houghton Mifflin, 1960).

2. Cf. 1 Corinthians 15:6.

3. Published in 1920.
4. In the same way you have a parallel situation with the two women Picasso married. One is a very human picture of Olga, painted in 1917-1918, the other is a lovely painting of Jacqueline done on October 5, 1954. There is a further parallel in that Jacqueline keeps this drawing in her sitting room. In these paintings, it is not only that the painting speaks of the love of the artist for his wife, but the woman has meaning as a human being.
5. Since his painting of *The Basket of Bread*, he has painted many pictures in which a Mary-like figure is the focus-point of the painting. The Gallery of Modern Art in New York has some of these paintings in which the figure appears several times in one painting. However, on inspection, one sees that these Mary-like figures are portraits of Dali's wife.
6. (London: Vision Press Ltd., 1956).

Chapter 4: Modern Mysticism in Action: Music and Literature
1. Columbia KL 6005 or KS 6005.
2. November 28, 1964, by Calvin Tomkins.
3. Because his theories have produced in music noise or total silence, which is therefore monotonous, most modern music has not followed him. But through Merce Cunningham and others, John Cage has become the central force in some modern dance, against Martha Graham who put much emphasis on form and meaning.
4. The translation of this Preface is that which appeared in *Vogue*, December 1964.

Chapter 5: The Next Phase of Modern Theology
1. In recent years it has often been said that Karl Barth changed his views toward the end of his life. If this was so, then all could have been easily cared for by his writing one more book amongst his many books and, while he was yet living, making it known that his views of Scripture, his lack of a space-time Fall, and his implicit universalism had been publicly repudiated. In the light of his crucial influence as the originator of the new theology and his wide publication, it would seem difficult to think that anything less would have met his responsibility before God and men. If he had done this, many of us would have truly rejoiced. Note Chapter 3, Section III for a consideration of the deficient concept of justification and the place of universalism in the new theology.
2. The italics are mine.
3. As an example, see Dr. Alan Richardson, "When Is a Word an Event?," in *The Listener*, June 3, 1965.
4. *The Unknown Christ of Hinduism* (London: Darton, Longman and Todd, 1964).
5. *Jubilee*, November 1963.
6. Loyola University ecumenical forum as reported in the Chicago *Daily News-Post Dispatch*, December 14, 1963.

Section III

Chapter 1: Personality or a Devilish Din
1. In John 17:24 Jesus, in His prayer to His Father, speaks of the love with which "thou lovedst me before the foundation of the world." In Genesis 1:26 there is reported communication within the Trinity.
2. *The Wild Duck.*

Chapter 2: Verifiable Facts and Knowing
1. (London: Constable and Co. Ltd.), pp. 90, 91.

2. Exodus 24:12.
3. Acts 26:14.
4. John 17:24.

Chapter 3: The Dilemma of Man

1. *La Peste*, 1947, translated from the French by Stuart Gilbert (Penguin Books, in association with Hamish Hamilton, 1966).
2. The consideration of *The Plague* is continued in Chapter 4.
3. John 5:24; Colossians 1:13.
4. Genesis 2:17.
5. It is intriguing that the "new" Heidegger, as he changed his position, tried to get a historic Fall into his new system. He says there was a Golden Age (before this Fall) at the time of the pre-Socratic Greeks; and then Aristotle, and those who followed him, fell. He says that their fall was that they began to think rationally. So Heidegger is saying that man is abnormal. There is no historic evidence for such a Golden Age, and certainly it is not correct that before Aristotle people did not think rationally, but it does indicate that the usual rationalistic answer to man's dilemma, which says man is as he has always been, is insufficient. In Heidegger's desperate theory, Aristotle takes the place of Adam, as the one who fell, and it does appear as if Heidegger sees himself as the one who will save. But notice that this concept of the Fall and salvation does not touch moral issues. Man's abnormality is not moral; in Heidegger's new system it is rather epistemological and methodological abnormality. Aristotle was not morally wrong in what he did, according to Heidegger; he was just introducing the faulty methodology of antithesis and rationality. There is no answer here for man's dilemma, but Heidegger has clearly shown that philosophy has no answer to man's dilemma on the basis of man and history now being normal. It would seem that Heidegger would like Christianity's answer, but without bowing to God — either morally or in acknowledging the need of knowledge from Him.

Chapter 4: God's Answer to Man's Dilemma

1. Cf. Chapter 3, Section III.
2. Simone de Beauvoir deals with the same problem in a slightly different setting in her book *A Very Easy Death* (New York: Putnam, 1966).
3. See B. B. Warfield, *Biblical and Theological Studies* (New York: Scribners' Sons, 1912), "On the Emotional Life of Our Lord," pp. 35-90.

Chapter 5: How Do We Know It Is True?

1. As the arch-revolutionary Einstein says: "The historical development has shown that among the imaginable theoretical constructions there is invariably one that proves to be unquestionably superior to all others. Nobody who really goes into the matter will deny that the world of perceptions determines the theoretical system in a virtually unambiguous manner." A man engaged in solving a well designed word-puzzle may, it is true, propose any word as the solution, but there is only one word which really solves the puzzle in all its forms. It is an outcome of faith that nature takes the character of such a well-formulated puzzle. The successes reaped up to now by science do, it is true, give a certain encouragement for this faith.
   (H. R. Post, "Scientific Theories," *The Listener*, February 10, 1966)
2. Romans 1:18-20, R.V.
3. In an article in *The Christian Century* of May 12, 1965, entitled "The Modernity of

Fundamentalism," John Opie, Jr. makes two main mistakes. He says correctly that historic Christianity (which he calls fundamentalism) is primarily separated from the new theology not in theological detail, but in epistemology and methodology, because it insists on rationality. However, he then goes on to say that historic Christianity is interested *exclusively* in rationality. This is not so. The other mistake he makes, a foolish one, is his saying that the kind of thinking upon which Christianity is based — that is, rational thinking — began with the Enlightenment. This view has no more support than Heidegger's when he says that it began with Aristotle, and is even more impossible to support. Other men in the new theology have made this same mistake. For example, Ernest R. Sandeen in his article "The Princeton Theology" in *Church History*, September 1962.

4. See Appendix A under "Rationalism."
5. 1 John 4:1-3.

SECTION IV

Chapter 1: Finding the Point of Tension
1. Acts 17:26.
2. Psalm 139:8.
3. Romans 1:32 – 2:3.

Chapter 2: From the Point of Tension to the Gospel
1. See Chapter 1, Section I.
2. The basic concepts presented here were put forth first in my article entitled "A Review of a Review" in *The Bible Today*, Vol. 42, No. I, October 1948.

    Romans 1:18 reads: "For the wrath of God is revealed from heaven against all ungodliness and unrighteousness of men, who hold the truth in unrighteousness." The context shows that this "holding the truth in unrighteousness" is related to the "general revelation" of the "mannishness" of man and the external universe in verses 19 and 20. The concept involved in the phrase "who hold the truth in unrighteousness" has two possibilities: in many of the newer translations it is translated as *hinder, hold down, stifle, restrain* or *suppress* the truth — which men have from the general revelation of the external creation and man's "mannishness." Probably a more accurate meaning, from the Greek word used, is that they *hold* that portion of the truth of the real world that they must hold (in spite of their non-Christian presuppositions); but because of their unrighteousness, their rebellion, they do not carry the logic of the general revelation to its natural and proper conclusion. Thus they are in the strict sense without excuse.

Chapter 3: Applying the Gospel
1. Hebrews 11:6.
2. Acts 16:30-32.
3. Bunyan's note at this place is: "Come unto me, all ye that labour and are heavy laden, and I will give you rest" (Matthew 11:28).
4. The ninth stage of *Pilgrim's Progress*.
5. The following references in the Bible will help anyone who wants to read more about becoming a Christian: John 3:15-18; Romans 3:9-26; Romans 4:1-3; Galatians 2:16; Galatians 3:24; John 8:24; John 14:6; Acts 4:12. Romans chapters 1 – 8 is a good section in which to see the unity of becoming a Christian and what follows after one is a Christian.

Escape from Reason

Chapter 1
1. *Leonardo da Vinci* (New York: Raynal & Company, 1913), pp. 163-174, "Leonardo's Thought."

Chapter 3
1. "On Science and Culture," *Encounter*, October 1962.
2. In *The God Who Is There* I have shown in detail the development under the line of despair in these areas (philosophy, art, music, general culture, and theology), from the time when they went below the line of despair until the present.

Chapter 4
1. (London: Allen and Unwin, 1961).
2. (London: Collins; New York: Harper and Row, 1959).
3. *The Listener*, 13 October 1966.

Chapter 5
1. (London: Vision Press, 1958).
2. (London: Secker and Warburg, 1954).
3. (London: Faber, 1952).
4. "Whatever Happened to the Great Simplicities?," *Saturday Review*, 18 February 1967.
5. *Kaddish Symphony*, 1963 (Columbia KL 6005 or KS 6005).
6. (New York: Berkeley Publishing Company, 1963).
7. *The Theatre of the Absurd* (New York: Anchor Books, 1961).

Chapter 6
1. (New York: Pantheon, 1966).

2. *Science and Hebrew Tradition*, Vol. 4 of Huxley's *Collected Essays* (London: Macmillan, 1902).

Chapter 7
1. Deuteronomy 5:23, 24.

He Is There and He Is Not Silent

Chapter 1: The Metaphysical Necessity

1. Some might say there is another possibility – some form of dualism – that is, two opposites existing simultaneously as co-equal and co-eternal. For example, mind (or ideals or ideas) and matter; or in morals, good and evil. However, if in morals one holds this position, then there is no ultimate reason to call one good and one evil – the words and choice are purely subjective if there is not something above them. And if there is something above them, it is no longer a true dualism. In metaphysics, the dilemma is that no one finally rests with dualism. Back of Yin and Yang there is placed a shadowy Tao; back of Zoroastrianism there is placed an intangible thing or figure. The fact is that in any form of dualism we are left with some form of imbalance or tension, and there is a motion back to a monism.

   Either men try to find a unity over the two; or, in the case of the concept of a parallelism (for example, ideals or ideas and material), there is a need to find a relationship, a correlation or contact between the two, or we are left with a concept of the two keeping step with no unity to cause them to do so. Thus in an attempted parallelism there has been a constant tendency for one side to be subordinated to the other, or for one side to become an illusion.

   Further, if the elements of the dualism are impersonal, we are left with the same problem in both being and morals as in the case of a more simple form of a final impersonal. Thus, for me, dualism is not the same kind of basic answer as the three I deal with in this book.

   Perhaps it would be well to point out that in both existence and morals, Christianity gives a unique and sufficient answer in regard to the present dualism, yet original monism. In existence, God is spirit – this is as true of the Father as of the Holy Spirit, and equally true of the Son, prior to the incarnation. Thus, we begin with a monism; but with a creation by the infinite God of the material universe out of nothing, a dualism now exists. It should be noted that while God thus created something which did not exist before, it is not a beginning out of nothing nothing, because He was there to will.

Chapter 2: The Moral Necessity

1. Note that in Christianity there is in this area of morals, as in existence, a sufficient answer concerning an original monism but present dualism. This rests on God being good, and creating everything good, but the nonprogrammed creature revolted and thus brought into existence the present dualism of good and evil, Yet these are not equal, for the evil is contrary to the character of God, which was the original moral monism. Thus, in morals as in existence, there is an answer both for the present dualism yet needed monism.

Chapter 3:The Epistemological Necessity: The Problem

1. *Escape from Reason* and *The God Who Is There*.

Chapter 4: The Epistemological Necessity: The Answer
1. For a more extended consideration of verbalized, propositional revelation, see Appendix I: "Is Propositional Revelation Nonsense?"
2. I have developed this thought in *The Church at the End of the Twentieth Century*.
3. See *The Church at the End of the Twentieth Century*.

Acknowledgments

THE GOD WHO IS THERE

Thanks are due to the following for permission to quote from copyright works:

Madame Marguerite Arp for the poem "Für Theo van Doesburg" by Hans Arp;

Dylan Thomas, *Collected Poems* © 1957 by New Directions Publishing Corporation. Reprinted by permission of New Directions Publishing Corporation;

The author and *The New Yorker* for an extract from "Figure in an Imaginary Landscape" by Calvin Tompkins, © 1964 The New Yorker Magazine Inc.;

Agence Hoffman for an extract from the Preface "A Sense of Wonder" by Henry Miller to *The History of Art* by Elie Favre (in the translation which appeared in *Vogue*, December 1964);

Dr. John Macquarrie for an extract from an article which appeared in *The Listener*, April 12, 1962.

Index